Praise for
Bombarded

"Cyrus Krohn is the best possible tour guide for how we got to where we are in terms of crossing the dual trip-wires of politics and digital. I worked with Cyrus. I have never disagreed with him more than I do on some key aspects of this book—and that is exciting! When two longtime friends and business partners come to a fork in the code to see our country saved, that's going to lead to a great read. I will guarantee this: You will know your digital/ political past after you read this, and you will be better able to control your future. If Cyrus is right, you may, in fact, be able to help save the world."
—**Todd Herman**, Conservative Talk Radio, Guest Host, *The Rush Limbaugh Show*

"In *Bombarded*, tech and politics veteran Cyrus Krohn makes a number of innovative proposals for restoring democracy at a time when it is uniquely under threat from digital disinformation. Developed by a leader in the field who has traveled through many of the institutions at the heart of the crisis, Bombarded should win praise on both sides of the aisle for its creative and pragmatic approach to the pressing problems that threaten the 21st century."
—**Daniel Kreiss**, Hussman School of Journalism and Media, University of North Carolina at Chapel Hill

"If you're hunkered down in your basement, trying to shield yourself from disinformation, data harvesting, deep fakes and micro-targeting, read this book. Digital political strategist Cyrus Krohn will scare you with his inside look at all the digital mayhem bombarding us and our democracy, but he says citizens can fight back—and he offers a "five-step program" to do just that. In a world of lies and fake news this book rings true."
—**Jill Dougherty**, former CNN Moscow Bureau Chief

"Cyrus Krohn is a clear-eyed warrior from the generation that built the internet and the shiny objects in the digital infospace that changed the way we consume media, make buying decisions and learn about politicians. This lively history of good intentions, blinder-vision, capitalists and tribal thinking is a warning and call to action even more relevant in this age of COVID-19 for elected officials, students of history, fans of science fiction, journalists, and anyone who wants to be a citizen activist to help fight the chaos in the digital infosphere."

—**Karen Jagoda,** Co-Founder, E-Voter Institute
and host of DigitalPoliticsPodcast.com

"Cyrus Krohn's journey from the White House to pioneering Internet strategy for Microsoft equips him with an arresting view on the future of digital political strategy."

—**Chris Widener,** *New York Times* bestselling author

"A source you can trust is like a four-leaf clover, hard to find, lucky to have. In an age when toxic messaging comes disguised as friends and family, Cyrus Krohn is a man you can trust. He has spent decades in the digital trenches, and has written a bracing intellectual guidebook that explains the unexplainable. He pulls back a complex, disturbing shroud, revealing how technology has vitally connected humanity, but has concurrently created opportunities to provoke hate, mistrust, gas lighting and political ill-gain; and has surreptitiously dissolved the aspiration to critically think. The insights and common truths herein have never been more relevant, and in sharing what he knows, Cyrus moves our national discussion forward, back towards an honest equilibrium."

—**Richard Bangs,** Internet pioneer, American author
and television personality focusing on international travel

"The Internet has a history and a future. Like its forerunner, the printed word, it can be used for good or ill—and has been used for both, with astonishing consequences. It can be enlightening, scary, addictive, troubling, fun, useful, powerful, and harmful. It has certainly changed the way we live and think. Cyrus Krohn is both a scholar of the Internet and a longtime inside player. His experience and insight offer a roadmap for understanding, interpreting, and going forward with perhaps the most influential factor of the last 125 years."

—**Margo Howard,** author, journalist and former Dear Prudence
advice columnist at Slate.com

9/10/22

BOMBARDED

HOW TO **FIGHT BACK** AGAINST THE **ONLINE** ASSAULT **ON DEMOCRACY**

CYRUS KROHN

Former Publisher, *Slate.com*

WITH **TOM FARMER**

Karen!
2032!
Cyrus

Made for Success
PUBLISHING

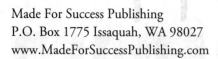

Made For Success Publishing
P.O. Box 1775 Issaquah, WA 98027
www.MadeForSuccessPublishing.com

Distributed by Made For Success Publishing

Library of Congress Cataloging-in-Publication data
Cyrus Krohn
      Bombarded (How to Fight Back Against the Online Assault on Democracy)
      p. cm.

      ISBN: 978-1-64146-532-8 (Hardback)
      ISBN: 978-1-64146-498-7 (Paperback)
      ISBN: 978-1-64146-518-2 (Audiobook)
      ISBN: 978-1-64146-531-1 (eBook)
      LCCN: 2020940774

Printed in the United States of America

For further information contact Made for Success Publishing, +1 425 526 6480 or email at service@madeforsuccess.net

To Charles and Jeannie Krohn,

After all the bombardments you've dealt with in life,
you remain steadfast parents.

TTFN.

TABLE OF CONTENTS

INTRODUCTION

My name is Cyrus Krohn and I do digital media. For 25 years I've invented it, promoted it, and used it to affect politics in the United States and internationally. But digital media disgusts you. It exhorts people who fear coronavirus to drink bleach and set fire to cellphone towers.[1] It douses you with rancid political propaganda. Between pandemics, it convinces your sainted grandmother to wire her retirement fund to some wily kid in Kazakhstan. It barks at you from every nook and cranny of your hectic life, and it's getting worse.

I'm going to map out what went wrong with a digital infosphere that in a single generation has grown to be both utterly indispensable and truly threatening—and propose fixes.

If you are flipping through this book standing in Hudson News at the airport, you may ask: Why trust this guy? Trust is in short supply these days.

My answer: Trust me because I started on the inside, as an enthusiastic digital innovator. I wasn't always an armchair critic of digital tech and its effect on our politics, which today is something like the effect of a school of piranha on a plucked chicken. I learned and built things within digital culture; I founded companies; I evolved. I've spent a quarter century steering clear of armchairs, on my feet at the five-way crossroads where media, elections, tech culture, marketing, and human behavior crash together. There are no lights governing the traffic at this intersection—no traffic cops writing tickets for reckless driving—and standing here gets more dangerous all the time.

As a digital foot soldier *en route* to becoming a strategist of modest influence, my teams and I thought computer technology might offer a marginally more efficient way to track voter behavior. Or advertise. Or distribute credible, respectable journalism. We did *not* foresee a seething stew of deepfakes, cults, and 24/7 cruelty. Trust me.

But today it's piranhas all the way down. The unique mechanisms of digital media have splintered us into a nation of theys. Conservative thinker David Brooks said, "There is Donald Trump's culture-war Theyism: The coastal cultural elites hate genuine Americans, undermining our values and opening our borders. And there is Bernie Sanders's class-war Theyism: The billionaires have rigged the economy to benefit themselves and impoverish everyone else."[2] In the real, physical world most citizens are measured, equivocal thinkers. In the parallel digital universe, shades of gray are for wusses.

Massive digital forces are corroding the fundamental pillars that support American social and political life. The damage seems illimitable. The endgame toward which we hurtle is terrifying. In early 2020, before COVID-19 hit, Joel Kotkin, the liberal demographer and urban futurist, wondered out loud: "Is America about to suffer its Weimar moment, culminating in the collapse of its republican institutions? Our democracy may be far more rooted than that of Germany's first republic, which fell in 1933 to

Adolf Hitler, but there are disturbing similarities . . . as happened in Germany, we are seeing the collapse of any set of common beliefs among Americans."[3] Within weeks of Kotkin publishing these words, the pandemic data wars that split the country made him look positively clairvoyant.

Already in these first pages, I've cited a conservative and a liberal. Get used to it; this is not a partisan book. I was raised in a Republican household by a conservative, deeply patriotic military man. I worked for the Republican National Committee, and have advised Republican candidates for office in Washington, D.C., at the state level, and elsewhere. Still, if you're looking for help owning the libs, close this book now and go browse the "Polemics" section. In these pages, we appraise not just political and marketing tactics in a hopefully evenhanded way, but the very fate of the republic, alongside which partisan mud fights look positively dinky. Suffice it to say that hardly any player has achieved glory here.

Our infosphere is paneled with funhouse mirrors, and as you'll see, crucial navigator-arbiters who once provided guidance have been sidelined, diminished, or outright vaporized. The onetime Google ethicist Tristan Harris calls the result "human downgrading." He says digital technology is helping to create social ills as threatening in their way as climate change: addiction, polarization, radicalization.[4] Digital technology may not be the sole culprit, but it binds the trends together.

Big Tech platforms now dominate information distribution. But they remain notoriously vulnerable to abuse and resistant to oversight. The tech elite have not exactly rallied to insulate the U.S. political system from Russian (and other-sourced) deception campaigns, which are as robust as ever. Nor, as I write, do they intend to—not in meaningful ways.

The challenge of coping with coronavirus sharpened public concern about new forms of data surveillance. Geolocation, internet-assisted contact tracing, facial recognition, and aggregated personal health information are all possible COVID-19 fighters, but problematic ones. The new privacy concerns sit alongside long-running ones, from spooky predictive analytics to secret algorithms that power microtargeted marketing. In a generation, political campaigns have journeyed from primitive targeting, via TV buys and mailing lists organized by ZIP code, to digital microtargeting: the capability to tell each individual voter what they want to hear, in any format, on any device. It's a near-perfect recipe for invasiveness and radicalization. But through it all Big Tech has taken a consistently cavalier view of citizen privacy.

And digital citizens themselves—that's us—have been asked to contribute precious little in the way of responsible civic behavior. You have to get certified to be a teacher or accountant, but online you can lie, cyberbully, inflame mobs, or gin up cancel-culture crusades, doing arguably more damage than the worst accountant ever, without a license and with virtual impunity. Presidential campaigns and your old Aunt Edna who forwards all those loony political diatribes? They do the same kinds of damage at different levels. (And the former may be manipulating the latter.) We deserve better from each other, and I see ways to get it without denting First Amendment rights. It's time we broached the responsibilities of digital citizenship alongside the privileges.

Even before COVID-19, the United States was in the throes of a debilitating trust crisis. A 2019 University of Nebraska study found nearly two out of five Americans were stressed out by politics; one quarter said politics had caused them to hate people, and 10% blamed politics for

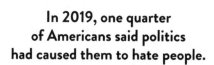

In 2019, one quarter of Americans said politics had caused them to hate people.

adverse physical effects.[5] The pandemic seemed to push us closer to meltdown mode, the day when nobody trusts anybody and nobody believes anything. Look at how quickly bizarre virus conspiracy theories got traction; look at how many Americans rejected official death tolls. When the metaphorical public square is this befogged, yesterday's truth is today's says-you assertion. Everything is disputable, opposable, and dismissible. We have arrived at a post-data world.

Some political forces see opportunity in the fog. I see disaster. The more citizens exit the process, the bigger the crisis. We're in danger of politics and democracy degrading into a weird sideshow for hardcore, eccentric enthusiasts only, in which a weary or irritated majority opt out with pillows over their heads, leaving the arena to the most cynical, angry, and shameless. Whatever you would call that, it would not be participatory democracy.

"For reasons I don't understand," mourned David Brooks in 2019, "we've had an epistemic explosion over the past few decades. Different American regions and subcultures now see reality through nonoverlapping lenses. They make meaning in radically different ways. Psycho-social categories have hardened."[6]

The reasons are actually not so hard to understand, and as we unpack them in this book, I hope you and Brooks will understand them better as well.

Steadfast squeamishness on the part of technology leaders about managing, editing, or regulating their platforms is one big reason we "now see reality through overlapping lenses." Fake news is not a new thing, or even an internet thing. Newspapers were taking sides and sowing division before shots were fired at Lexington in 1775. But only now, thanks mainly to digital tech, have we come to a point where outrageous lies readily outcompete sober truth for headspace, and performative social media behavior sprays flammable, acid rage around the field of play while indulgent platform providers gaze absently down from bulletproof skyboxes.

The sheer ubiquity of digital media is another culprit. At the turn of this century, the average American sat down at a big, boxy, almond-colored personal computer to surf the internet, usually commandeering the sole home landline. It was a compartmentalized, focused occasion, the way our forebears used to watch television. Today you're web-connected in numberless ways: computers, apps, phones, cars, kitchen appliances, doorbells and thermostats, Fitbits and blood glucose monitors and thermometers . . . you can even buy smart, connected yoga pants.[7] The so-called Internet of Things is on track to give the world 75 billion connected devices worldwide by 2025.[8] In recent years it has been an article of faith that smartifying any dumb object, be they yoga pants or thermometers, cannot help but improve your quality of life. Isn't everything better with an app attached? But every web connection is one more, usually woefully insecure, data pipeline—an exploitable, hackable path in and out of someone's life. The resulting environment taxes human coping capabilities and puts people at more risk. It is not hyperbole to suggest an inspired thief might find a path to your IRA balance through your smart dishwasher. It's enough to make you pine for the old

14.4 baud modem handshake noise that formally demarked the start of an internet session.

And then consider the format and character of incoming information. Edited digests are displaced by personalized feeds; algorithms shovel more of what they think you want onto your screens, omitting things you might appreciate if only you knew of them. The average Twitter feed is not only an insular, self-reinforcing info-bubble, but structured to pose a severe cognitive challenge. "When Twitter arrived in 2006," observed social psychologist Jonathan Haidt and technology ethicist Tobias Rose-Stockwell, "its primary innovation was the timeline: a constant stream of 140-character updates that users could view on their phones. The timeline was a new way of consuming information—an unending stream of content that, to many, felt like drinking from a fire hose."[9] Worse, the syntax of social media is deliberately designed to addict you. "The brain fires off tiny bursts of dopamine as a user posts a message and it receives reactions from others, trapping the brain in a cycle of posts, 'likes,' retweets, and 'shares,'" write P.W. Singer and Emerson T. Brooking in their seminal *Like Wars: The Weaponization of Social Media*.[10] If that doesn't sound too different from how opioids, vodka, potato chips, or video blackjack get to some people, well, that's the point.

Addiction is stressful, and people respond to stress in predictable ways. They go into defensive crouches, eliminating all but the familiar and reassuring. Or they unleash rage in a hopped-up, uncivil "voice" they'd probably never use in an eye-contact conversation. Our fragmented, siloed digital infosphere reduces empathy.

Internet political discourse makes it easy to dehumanize those beyond your personal info-bubble. A major cause of our political paralysis is the shredding of the social compact the United States used to have, the waning of *e pluribus unum* and the waxing of every-man-for-himself ethics. Dwelling in digital isolation makes things worse. As Robin Koerner, founder of WatchingAmerica.com, which collates global opinions about the U.S., says: "Your paradigm is your world." And digital media lends itself to small and impregnable paradigms.[11]

We're on a fatal path and we must change course.

I have a past. I spent years working to make digital media and marketing work more effectively, generating greater results for their sponsors. I now believe events in the past—in some cases, innovations I helped breathe life into and legitimize—explain much present trouble. I will discuss all that and propose steps I believe we must take to yank our teetering political system back from the brink.

I will propose steps to yank our teetering democracy back from the brink.

Amid the chaos, I see opportunity, even now. More citizens may be traumatized by politics, numb from pandemic terror and soaring deaths, and sick of being spammed and misled and repulsed. Yet most still crave trustworthy leadership. When political institutions, leaders, and Big Tech fail to answer that call, it opens up opportunities for other players. Today we see more private companies stepping gingerly into leadership roles and zones of politics and policy. They do it partly because customers, particularly younger ones, expect it; partly because it can be good business, lifting brands and eventually rewarding shareholders; and partly because companies are not all villainous and some—more than some—are capable of good, broadly beneficial works. This was never clearer than in the first phase of the coronavirus crisis. Yes, there was corporate villainy or stupidity, but many smart organizations flipped their mission toward societal service. How might such a company fill the trust void vacated by technologists, politicians, and media? I have some ideas.

America is in trouble. We are not yet a failed state, as commentator George Packer argued in sorrow at the height of COVID-19 panic, but predicting systemic failure is no longer absurd.[12] We imagined the digital infosphere would tie us together, but with its flaws and fissures, it has had largely the opposite effect. Yet some of my current work with polit-

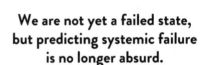

We are not yet a failed state, but predicting systemic failure is no longer absurd.

ical systems elsewhere convinces me de-escalation is absolutely possible. We can achieve a world less defined by rage, fear, and mayhem. I am as optimistic about what may lie ahead as I am dismayed by the dysfunctional here and now.

But before we address the present, let's first drop in on a plausible version of the near future. For the next few pages, let's imagine an election a few years—and presidents—from now. It's election night in a United States where hackable digital tech, unmanaged media, and microtargeted marketing have rampaged forward without brakes or scruples.

I promise we'll click back to present day shortly. But when you turn this page, it's Tuesday, November 2, 2032.

CHAPTER ONE

TUESDAY, NOVEMBER 2, 2032

"Janey, we've all been so worried about you. I'm glad you're home."

Him again.

His familiar voice rumbled from the kitchen as Janey Reynolds entered her apartment, tired from work and dance class and longing for the single can of hard seltzer she knew remained in her refrigerator. She rolled her eyes. As hard as she'd worked to avoid the toxic typhoon that was the 2032 election, she recognized President Kevin McCarthy.

The lights and climate system activated automatically as Janey crossed the few short steps into her small kitchen.

"Because it appears you've recently suffered a loss, I want the Reynolds family to know: My prayers are with you and yours," intoned the president. He sounded soothing enough—almost solicitous.

Yes, there he was. A nine-inch President McCarthy perched on Janey's quartz countertop—a hologram, projected by Rupert, her smart-home manager. Rupert was polite, knew Janey like a brother, and lived in a plastic case the size of a jam jar. The holo-president wore a blue suit and stood with hands clasped. His eyes followed Janey around the space.

"Rupert . . ." Janey began through clenched teeth. She unclipped her CoviCop sensor and tossed it on the counter with her antibody passport. The CoviCop blinked a steady green. She shrugged her work bag off her shoulder and let it flop to the floor.

"As you know, Janey, it's election day," said the president, seeming not to hear her. "So, I want to remind you of my administration's view on the punitive and unfair estate tax your family may face. Re-elect Vice President Stefanik and me, and we'll be working for you every day on this and other issues that matter to you."

Janey was at the fridge, rummaging for that cranberry hibiscus seltzer.

"And as you haven't voted yet, Janie," appealed the president, taking a step across the counter toward her, "do it now. Or any time before 9 p.m. Use your nearest convenient smart device to vote for McCarthy-Stefanik and our slate of great Republican candidates in . . ."

McCarthy paused for a fraction of a second, the only really overt flaw in his delivery, as the algorithm powering the digital display nailed down Janey's location.

" . . . Highland Park, Denver, Colorado."

Behind the refrigerator door, Janey popped the can open and gulped.

"I'm personally counting on you, Janey, to help me secure America, and keep us all safe from foreign health threats. Thank you. And, again, the Reynolds family has my personal sympathies."

"Rupert!" snapped Janey. "Enough!" President McCarthy flickered out, and Rupert launched some music in his place. It was dark outside now.

"Hello, Janey." Rupert's low, slightly playful baritone filled the room. There were tiny wireless speaker-camera combos everywhere. "There's nothing on your schedule for tonight. Are the lights OK? Would you like suggestions for dinner?"

Janey sank onto the sofa, fingering impatiently through the custom data feed on her Starbucks infoslate. She was a little irritated with Rupert, to be honest. She thought she had made it crystal clear that he was to block all that election stuff. She had finally succeeded in keeping most of it off the infoslates, meaning some acid squib of propaganda made it past the goalkeeper and into her field of vision only three or four times per day. But Janey also knew she was pitted against numberless smarter assailants, and her upgraded smart apartment bristled with vulnerable, hackable data channels. She resented the president tracking her movements; she guessed her stop at St. Patrick's just now, to light a candle for Mom, had inspired McCarthy's sorry-for-your-loss stuff. But so far as she knew, there was no way to make him stop.

In earlier days Janey had tried, gamely, to function as her own editor, as early internet theorists had urged. But winnowing truth out of the political precincts of social media was futile. Everybody, real or bot, seemed to think everybody else was a fascist or a moron or a snowflake or something, and Janey was pretty sure she was none of those things. Chiseling away to get at lucid reality was not exactly impossible, in the same way that flying to Singapore for breakfast was not truly impossible. But it required so much time and concentration that the effort had ceased to seem rational.

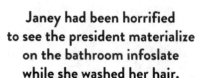

Janey had been horrified to see the president materialize on the bathroom infoslate while she washed her hair.

She felt abused. She had been horrified to see President McCarthy materialize unbidden and call her name from the bathroom wall infoslate while she washed her hair. (Now she draped a towel over the thing.) The former vice president, Alexandria Ocasio-Cortez, had briefly taken over her Honda's smart speedometer, promoting border liberalization and asking for a donation as Janey hummed out to the airport, late for a flight. She had been in the middle of a presentation at work, standing before a roomful of execs she wanted to impress, when a profane, unbidden anti-Duckworth spam video hijacked her smart MojoLens, practically blinding her before she could pluck the thing off her head. Mark Cuban, Mike Pence, and Hillary Clinton, the latter well into her 80s but still arch, lucid, and opinionated, had all commandeered her refrigerator screen. Hillary had somehow deleted her grocery list and all the week's e-discount coupons, too.

If it was really Hillary, because bad-news malware had done the same thing to Janey before. It could have been a coordinated cyber-campaign to make her *hate* Democrats. Janey knew it had become virtually impossible for the casual consumer to tell which messages were authentic. It had been this way since 2025 at least, though the confusion had begun in the 2010s, when she was growing up. Eventually, she figured it was easier to assume everyone was lying than to evaluate, one by one, a raging fountain of charges, assertions, and entreaties.

In principle, Janey was not opposed to politics. It was not that she did not care; it was that caring took up far too much headspace, and the rewards for such immense effort were far too hypothetical and puny. A decade ago, she had made a firm decision to cut it all out of her life, for two good reasons.

The first reason was the maddening ubiquity of suspect, often vicious content in this era of the Internet of Things. (Janey had complained to her friends that she suffered from an overdose of POT, or Politicians on Things.) The general tone was bad enough: Janey recoiled from social media's gutter sensibilities.

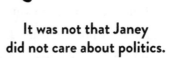

It was not that Janey did not care about politics. It was that caring took up far too much headspace.

It was worse that this stuff spurted from every data conduit in her life. It rolled in via the infoslates, home security systems and appliances, smart plumbing and electric systems, Janey's chipped and connected smartcoats and the anklet she wore in dance class, her car's system health monitors, the screens on ATMs and gas pumps and fast-food ordering kiosks that identified her and called out whenever she drew near . . . there was just no end to it. In 2032 the old, airy, facile advice from media and tech elites to be your own editor had curdled into absurdity. It was like telling food shoppers to treat all ingredient lists and nutrition labels as fiction and perform their own independent enzymatic analysis on every item in the store.

As far as Janey was concerned, politics in 2032 was a big bouquet of ruptured sewer pipes, flooding her apartment and car and nearly every public setting with bullshit. She could not turn every tap off—nobody could—but she had sworn to do her damnedest to try.

Her second reason for boycotting politics was more personal. She knew there was no link, *zero* link, between the politicians' promises of security and prosperity and what happened in real life, and she had a dead father to prove it.

Back when the coronavirus reached the United States in early 2020, Dad was a ruddy, tireless, beloved supermarket manager in central Texas. A pillar of his small city. The number of confirmed cases grew. Reporters on TV and online were alarmed, Janey in her college dorm in Boston even more so. But not Dad. On FaceTime, he pointed out calmly that the government said things were under control—and everyone who wanted a test could get a test. This was no bigger than flu season, he said. Texas was a long way from New York or Seattle, he said. Relax, Dad said. He flew off to a company recognition thing in Orlando.

Janey tried to relax. But that FaceTime would be the last time she saw Dad. A week later, in the second week of March, her campus suddenly closed. Frantic university admins bundled Janey aboard a charter bus to Logan Airport as the world caved in around her. The bulletins piled up. The NBA ended its season, March Madness was canceled, Wall Street was crashing, Tom Hanks had the virus, and then Mom called.

Mom was frantic. Out of nowhere, Dad had developed major COVID-19 symptoms. Fighting for air, wracked with chills, no sense of taste or smell. He was in the ER, but the hospital had no test kits. Soon he needed a ventilator, but the hospital had only two ventilators for eight candidates. An aghast Janey flew back to Texas, willing the plane forward as she listened on her iPhone to government briefers saying everything was under control and the hospitals didn't actually need the ventilators they were begging for.

Dad died gasping in a hospital corridor, whereupon Janey resolved to believe nothing else she heard from politicians about

COVID-19. Or much of anything else. She took elaborate mask-and-glove precautions for herself and her shattered Mom, avoided online conspiracy theories and misinformation, and finished college from her kitchen table in Texas. The university shipped her stuff home at the end of spring semester. Her commencement was a videoconference. She'd flipped her tassel alone in the kitchen, staring dully into Dad's laptop. When a vaccine became available a year later, she and Mom were first in line in the CVS parking lot.

So Janey never voted, and in her circle of friends, only a couple felt different. At some vague, abstract level she understood not voting made her derelict in her duty as an American citizen. Then again, Janey thought: A lot of people don't vote, and the country's still here. Sorry, not sorry. I have bills to pay.

"Rupert," said Janey, "Call Anita, will you?"

When President Donald Trump was impeached by the House of Representatives in December 2019, the *Washington Post* called modern-day America "a country riven by political tribalism whose leaders cannot even agree on a common set of facts."[1]

At the start of the 2020s, a collective hope hung in the air that the Trump impeachment and acquittal would be our low point. We had paid the political and social cost of dueling worldviews. The nation had been to the brink, many thought at the time. We had all been wounded in battle and now would step back from the precipice. All of us—politicians, their managers and hustlers and fixers, the opinion-making Twitterati, what little remained of establishment media, pollsters and old-school pundits, and particularly the voters—wanted better. We could do better than political tribalism. It would be in everyone's interest to stipulate a common set of facts, then forge policy from there, and we had it in us to make it happen.

But then came the pandemic, and Americans fought over every fact with genuine rage: the lockdowns, the death toll, the efficacy of masks and gloves, the unemployed and hungry and how—whether—to feed them. Impeachment the low point? How wrong we had been—not just in the throes of the crisis, but in the whole dispiriting decade that led to 2032.

"Hey, Janey, what's up?"

"I had the day from hell. You want to hit the Royal Horse later?"

"Nah, I brought my work home tonight. Got my head down all evening. Did you vote?"

"Why start now?" Both women laughed. What a pointless exercise. "I came home to another pity-gram from my little robot president," said Janey. "If it's really him and not the Russians. Somehow, he knows I lost Mom last month. He mentioned it again tonight."

"Honey, you know about geolocation. You leave a bright yellow trail all over town. Did you stop at St. Patrick's on your way home and light another candle?"

Janey said yes.

"Yeah, that's it. The A.I. in the sky sees you go to church at random times, outside service hours, and decides you're in crisis. Minutes later, McCarthy's working the point into his pitch. You've seen it happen lots of times."

"I know it. Doing my best to tune it out. And I keep meaning to turn off the tracking function on my smartcoats."

"Wouldn't fix anything," Anita said brightly. "Leave it on, turn it off, they still know. Are you going to at least see who wins the election?"

"It won't affect me," said Janey, idly poking through her data feed again. "I'll probably hear something tomorrow. Why don't you buzz me in the morning? I trust *you*, anyway."

"Back to work, babe. Bye."

"See ya." Janey was drifting. She'd found Instagram brag-pics from a friend vacationing in Portugal, and a pang of material envy swamped any enthusiasm she might have mustered for electoral politics. I'm in Colorado in November, she thought, surrounded by lying politicians I can't delete. I should be in Portugal myself.

One of the most influential analyses of human behavior in the back half of the 20th century was *Exit, Voice, and Loyalty*. Albert O. Hirschman, a Harvard economist, argued that people dissatisfied with an organization or institution—a carmaker, airline, restaurant, or political framework—choose one of three possible responses: speak up, walk out, or shut up and take it.[2] As the 2010s ended, American voters had seemed to be speaking up, convinced that mass complacency had permitted elites and minority interests to hijack the government and it was time to fight back.

Hirschman published in 1970. He'd figured out a lot about economic behavior and applied it wisely to political systems. But he did not foresee digital media, nor its principal attribute: malignant untrustworthiness. In Hirschman's mid-century world, most voters got their facts from CBS News, *The New York Times*, and their ruling establishment kin, including healthy city dailies across the country. They based voting choices on data they trusted. The *Exit, Voice, and Loyalty* analysis was predicated on decision makers being able to tell what was going on. If your state legislates a gun ban, reasoned Hirschman in 1970, you'll know it and understand the implications, thanks to trusted information brokers. If you don't like what you see you can move to another state, join a political countermovement, or stay where you are and grouse.

But what happened when those establishment journalists—often resented, but usually trusted—were superseded by digital platforms that disclaimed, even disdained, the kind of editorial judgments and scrutiny that made their predecessors important? What if those living with a new gun ban can't discern for certain what the new law says, or how it affects them? What if you don't recognize most sources, and don't trust any of them? Worst of all, what happens when ubiquitous, cynical campaigners make things up to convince the public of things that aren't true?

In 2032, peoples' digital devices routinely piped lies: professionally crafted, highly polished, often convincing lies, relayed placidly by unregulated platform owners, who saw the labor associated with elevating truth as an unwanted cost center. Most Americans were profoundly dissatisfied with their political systems and choices. But it turned out there was a fourth valid action option for the disaffected, one Albert Hirschman hadn't thought of, because in his time it would not have been rational. It was in 2032, though. Beyond exit, voice, and loyalty lay denial. Earplugs. Pretending important things simply aren't happening—or aren't important enough to justify combing through daunting, taunting heaps of disinformation.

In Ernest Hemingway's *The Sun Also Rises*, Mike Campbell is asked how he went bankrupt. He replies, famously: "Two ways. Gradually and then suddenly." The collapse of the information environment in the United States in the 2020s proceeded along similar lines.

Janey finished her cranberry hibiscus hard seltzer and heated up some chicken noodle soup. Triumphantly she stumbled upon a bonus, overlooked second seltzer in the fridge behind an acorn squash and drank that, too. She seethed quietly over her Instagram friend's Portugal pics and trolled through her own photo files, looking for something she might pass off as a counter-brag. Her infoslate feed presented scattered posts from her few friends interested in the election, relaying results as they trickled in—McCarthy takes North Carolina! Duckworth takes Massachusetts!—but Janey swiped past them quickly. She didn't know if they were true. In any event, all she knew for sure about Democratic nominee Senator Tammy Duckworth, after more than 18 months of nonstop campaigning and frantic barrages of messaging, was that she had prosthetic legs. It was about the only Duckworth data point people agreed on, Janey thought.

In truth, she thought as she crumpled her second seltzer can, American national politics in 2032 was just another small, peculiar, sealed subculture, with its own star system, obscure codes and rituals, and a hyper fan base of eccentrics. Like pro golf, she thought, or a *Star Trek* convention. Nothing that required—or rewarded—normal peoples' involvement.

Pundits had framed 2024 as another "change election." The public seemed at the end of its tether. The coronavirus recovery had been erratic, marred by fractious interstate fighting. Flareups and spot lockdowns continued through 2022. Over and over, promises of progress or victory were trumpeted, then broken and forgotten. Retail and travel never surged back; the Dow languished. The financial markets had suffered not only from COVID-19 but cyber-attacks from opportunistic offshore adversaries. The government had mostly not been up to the task of shielding private systems from Russian and Iranian hackers. Although unemployment remained stuck between 9% and 12%, interest rates and inflation were rising. At big-city piers, cruise ships seized from bankrupt lines rode at permanent anchor, repurposed as homeless hostels.

The exhausted, splintered Republican party nominated Trump's vice president, Mike Pence of Indiana. Pence beat out Nikki Haley, former South Carolina governor and United Nations ambassador, for the 2024 nomination, then invited her onto the ticket. The Democratic party countered by nominating a rebranded, more experienced Sen. Kamala Harris of California. After the 2020 race, Harris had returned to Capitol Hill and compiled a productive, honorable record.

Harris, no favorite of Democratic progressives, shocked what was left of the political world by adding to the ticket one Rep. Alexandria Ocasio-Cortez of New York, who turned 35 in October 2024; she was just barely eligible to hold the office. The hard-core liberal wing of the party was transitorily mollified, but establish-ment pundits assumed Harris-AOC was dead on arrival. The ticket would carry the liberal coasts, they predicted, but had no prayer in

Texas, Arizona, or the northern swing states. And that was before the waves of poisonous, fraudulent digital media attacks crashed in.

As so often happens, the pundits were almost right. What turned the election in the final weeks was Harris' decision to pound home two issues, and only two: health security and automation. A four-year health crisis had exposed the terrible weaknesses and inequities in American medicine, and artificial intelligence was subsuming millions more jobs than COVID-19.

It was a double-barreled security pitch, and it worked. Turnout was lower than 2020, but Harris-AOC carried Pennsylvania, Michigan, and Florida and eked out a narrow win, in both the Electoral College and popular vote.

Immediate doubts flared across digital channels about the legitimacy of the result. Republicans in close-run states leveled charges of liberal-engineered vote fraud and demanded recounts. Electronic voting machines were impounded. False vote totals were circulated on Facebook and Twitter to obscure the truth, whatever it was.

For those who saw advantage in discord—including Russia and China, not to mention legions of freelance or mercenary activists in the United States and abroad—the insight to bear in mind was that with the American media sphere so atomized, it was no longer necessary to debate the data. Inventing alternate data worked just as well. A national Pew survey conducted in January 2025, 10 days before Harris was inaugurated, found 34% of Americans doubted she had "really won," and 29% agreed that "Harris will never be my president." 41% erroneously believed Vice President-Elect Ocasio-Cortez was being installed illegally, as she was born outside the United States. Inauguration Day was marred by violent skirmishes on the National Mall. When roaming protesters moved north to Pennsylvania Avenue, the usual celebratory parade was cancelled for the new president's own protection.

Under President Harris, the United States rejoined the Paris Climate Accord and reversed some environmental moves by prior administrations regarding light bulb standards, auto fuel economy standards, and so on. But while the House was firmly Democratic, the Senate remained fiercely Republican. Expansion of Medicare, though favored by a strong majority of Americans, looked as if it would take many years. Improving employment security was costly and Congress was scared; the coronavirus deficits were already virtually insurmountable. The Ocasio-Cortez Green New Deal never got a hearing. The new chief executive was relentlessly attacked by liberal activists for not doing enough, and by legacy Trumpists and traditional conservatives for attempting entirely too much. Facebook and Reddit were choked with anti-Harris memes and fake news, many verging on hate crimes.

Then in 2026, six months before the midterms, COVID-26 erupted in Asia. A new strain, spreading four years after COVID-19 was declared under control. There were renewed lockdowns and travel bans. Wall Street swooned further. Consumer confidence sank and factory layoffs soared. There was sporadic violence in states where significant numbers considered the new virus to be another New World Order plot to control the population.

In the '26 midterms, the House returned to Republican control, and under Speaker Kevin McCarthy the new leadership began impeachment proceedings against Harris, contending that her failure to defend the nation from COVID-26 constituted a probable "high crime."

To constitutional scholars and a commanding majority of the public, impeaching Harris was partisan nonsense; Trump had not been re-impeached for his response to COVID-19. Gallup found 67% believed the Republican case was "baseless." But it did not really matter. There was a ready, rooting cohort online, reveling in alternative facts. Harris did not dignify what she regarded as an absurdity by providing witnesses or evidence in her own defense, and she was impeached along partisan lines in October 2027. The Senate voted 55-45 to remove her from office in January 2028—12 votes short of the majority needed, handing Harris a backhanded acquittal just weeks before the Iowa caucus kicked off the 2028 election.

President Harris was finished. In 2028 she limped to re-nomination but was soundly defeated in November by House Speaker McCarthy, who ran with upstate New York U.S. Rep. Elise Stefanik, a partisan hero since the Trump era. One month after taking office, President McCarthy re-withdrew the United States from the Paris Climate Accords, whereupon House Democrats launched a fundraising campaign to flip the House in the 2030 midterms so they could impeach him. Impeachment, or the imminent threat thereof, became a constant motif of government. Every president with an opposing party in command of the House could count on getting impeached, probably over and over.

Was it the character of government in the 2020s that drove Americans away—or the erosion of down-the-middle journalism offering an undistorted view of government? It was a chicken-egg story, really. One fueled the other. But in passive-aggressive fashion, the public made its disgust clear. After upticks between 2012 and 2020, election turnout trends reversed in 2024 and would, in years to follow, tumble into steady, forlorn decline. 55.7% of eligible voters cast ballots in the 2016 presidential election;

eight years later, in 2024, turnout slid to 51.4%. McCarthy's resounding win in 2028 was tempered by a doleful side note: For the first time, turnout for an American presidential election fell below the 50% mark. In each cycle, more Americans spurned partisan pleadings that their vote mattered like never before. With each cycle, get-out-the-vote drives found less traction.

With each new cycle, also, fewer voters identified as Democrats or Republicans. In 2020, Gallup reported that only 31% of Americans still called themselves Democrats, 30% Republicans. By 2032 the appeal of the two so-called major parties had shrunk further: Only 20% of voters said they were Democrats, 18% Republicans.[3] Most Americans found themselves politically stateless.

Some of the decline was down to demographic changes; in the 16 years from 2016 to 2032, a fair slice of the GOP's aging white male core died—many of coronavirus—and went unreplaced. But a lot of it was down to public confusion, irritation, and exhaustion. The ranks of hardcore true believers on both sides thinned, and the ranks of the stateless swelled. They may not all have fled to the middle—many simply put politics out of their minds—but they were sure fleeing virulent party dogma.

On Tuesday evening, November 2, 2032, as Janey Reynolds stirred her soup and glowered at pictures of Portugal in her Denver living room, cable news channels, at least, still offered live coverage of the election results. But viewership had been shriveling for years. With each election, fewer people hung on the outcome, and of those who still did, most got their fix by refreshing their phone browsers or tapping like woodpeckers at their infoslates. The old-school broadcast news divisions, vestigial compared to their heyday, quit covering the national political conventions in 2028. In 2032, for the first time since 1948, presidential election returns would not appear on broadcast TV. NBC was airing a *Saturday Night Live* political clip show pulled from

In 2032, for the first time since 1948, presidential election returns would not appear on broadcast TV.

the archives, CBS was going with a 3-D NFL game, and ABC programmed a bank of sitcoms. Those who still cared who the next president of the United States would be could find the news elsewhere. There were plenty of sources, even if not all were above reproach.

Nonetheless, 73-year-old Brian Williams, the last of the old-school anchors, was holding court on NBCNewsStream, the online channel.

Pinched and graying, Williams was almost certainly working his last big election. A tad melancholy at his shrunken circumstances, but marshaling his patented chipper on-camera persona, he arranged himself on a modest low-budget studio set. He remembered the glory days when American elections were national moments and the major networks went all out for a combined, rapt audience of 75 or 100 million. Jaw-dropping graphics, remotes by the dozen, maps projected up the side of 30 Rock. Tonight, he had been told privately, the business side of the company was hoping for, maybe, two million viewers. His set and graphics were small and without detail, designed to look good on a minuscule phone screen, or an infoslate. The lighting, he noted, was local-news flat, and most of his field correspondents would file radio-style, via iPhone. The Cecil B. DeMille era of election broadcasts as a fixture of American life was over.

Williams bit his lip as he waited for his cue and the red light on camera one. It was like seeing the World Series plummet from top-tier network fare to MeTV. Most of the country, he knew grimly, was now cynical, no longer sentimental, over what Dan Rather used to call the election night "dance of democracy." Many—make that most—were no longer convinced they were watching democracy in action, and journalists could not do much to prove otherwise.

He and his production team were worried for other reasons, too. Like all legit news outlets, print and video, the network had been bombarded for months by death threats, sortable into complainants who would attack if NBCNewsStream reported the Republican, McCarthy, reelected, and those who would storm 30 Rock if Williams projected victory for the Democrat, Tammy Duckworth. Williams knew—but would not say on air unless events forced his hand—that in some major cities, National Guard riot-control units had been discreetly placed on standby for election night.

Which was the worse fate for an aging journalist? he thought. To see a big slice of the country erupt because people no longer believe the truth? Or to see it ignore a leadership contest because people no longer believe in the system?

The red light came on and Williams quickly called New York, Vermont, and the District of Columbia for Duckworth.

Janey Reynolds was unaware of what Brian Williams was up to. If you mentioned his name, chances are she could not have placed it. Instead, she was scanning her Starbucks infoslate for Starbucks news.

Because she liked the company's policies on fair trade and packaging waste reduction, Janey had joined her local Starbucks cadre in 2030. Her best friend Anita was diehard Apple, for the Apple privacy and cybersecurity platform. Others on her feed aligned themselves with Abbott Labs, for the company's pandemic leadership, or Impossible Foods, to help push beef consumption further to the margins of American culture.

As a Starbucks person, Janey did more than follow and share news of Starbucks sustainability initiatives and lobbying work. She shared news of Starbucks product rollouts and quarterly profits on her feed with guileless enthusiasm, not because she felt obligated, but because she genuinely felt Starbucks was on her side.

Janey trusted Starbucks. Starbucks did not try to fool her with fake news. It seemed to respect her intelligence. The company did not make things up, so far as she knew, and unlike politicians did not hurl cruel, stupid public insults at other coffee brands. In the 2020s, when Starbucks gave up paper and plastic in favor of newly invented sustainable containers derived from quick-degrading cotton fiber, Janey, who had given up traditional politics, found something to follow in Starbucks. She gave her friends Starbucks gift codes for Christmas and made contributions in their names to the Starbucks Climate Progress Coalition, or STACPOC. Because she felt Starbucks was doing so much for her, she wanted to do more for Starbucks all the time. And when Janey had an idea for an environmental policy, she reached out to STACPOC on social media. She wrote notes to Starbucks an average of twice per week, sometimes about topics that had nothing to do with climate issues. And Starbucks listened! STACPOC wrote back—at least, a semi-convincing A.I. engine wrote back—and thanked her every time. She noticed her lattes now cost less than Anita's, too.

Surveys in the late 2020s showed STACPOC drew more public approval, and was considered a more potent policy force, than either of the old political parties.

When Starbucks began offering banking and brokerage services in 2029, Janey happily migrated. She had Starbucks health insurance and took a Starbucks package vacation to Costa Rica as soon as COVID-26 was controlled and flights resumed. If it was a health risk, she told herself, Starbucks wouldn't let her go.

Janey dared to dream of working for Starbucks someday. The company shared her priorities and made tangible changes in the world—changes she, Janey, thought she would make herself were she ever president of something. She did not know the name of the congressman representing Colorado's 1st District, where she lived, and since COVID-19 Janey had asked for nothing from any public servant beyond a driver's license. But Starbucks, she thought, could do anything.

In the 2020 primary election, a mini-banner ad for Elizabeth Warren showed a soaring airliner, as if it were pushing cut-rate package vacations, with the copy: "We're flying ONE LUCKY WINNER and their guest to meet me! Enter now!" Pete Buttigieg constantly dangled a slim chance to "grab pizza with Pete" in return for small donations. Campaigns sold branded swag by the boatload—not just yard signs and bumper stickers but beer cozies, hoodies, mugs, you name it. It was a little bit Vegas, a little bit Sea World gift shop, but all business.

By 2032 the script was flipped. A lot of businesses found they could mimic political parties. They could focus public pressure to drive policy change—even lead. The leadership opportunity was clarified by four factors.

First was lack of progress in Washington on issues a majority of the public viewed as priorities, from health security to climate change to immigration to income inequality. Second was elected representatives' explicit disinterest, in many cases, in accountability to constituents. Some members of Congress went years without holding office hours or town halls. It could take some weeks to answer email. Some didn't bother.

Third: As time passed, more younger voters expected companies in their orbit to display some ethical code. People who didn't ever vote could nonetheless camp on social media and tap out indictments all day long of companies they thought palsied by moral turpitude. There was certainly a business cost to ignoring that kind of reputational slam, whether it was grounded in reality or not.

The fourth clarifying factor, of course, was the speed, ease, and impact of digital media itself as an omnidirectional communicator as well as all-around rabble-rouser—although sometimes companies got mired in unwinnable, checkmate-style dilemmas.

When it yanked the National Rifle Association's discount code after the 2018 Parkland mass shooting in Florida, Delta Air Lines got a brief round of attaboys from left-leaning media. A few days later the Republican-majority General Assembly in Georgia, where Delta is headquartered, did some counter-yanking, spiking a big tax break for Delta. Georgia's lieutenant governor, Casey Cagle, promised to "kill any tax legislation that benefits Delta . . . Corporations cannot attack conservatives and expect us not to fight back."[4]

In late 2019 the Hallmark Channel, a conservative TV network airing mostly romantic movies, pulled a commercial for a wedding-planning service called Zola that showed two women at the center of a marital ceremony. Hallmark sought to appease a pressure group called One Million Moms. 24 hours later, facing greater pressure still from the LGBTQ online community, Hallmark executives reversed themselves and offered to restore the Zola spots, suddenly giving One Million Moms the back of their basic-cable hand. By then, they had succeeded only in making literally everybody mad. The only remaining step was for LGBTQ advocates and One Million Moms to assault each other online, which they did with gusto.

Navigating the new digital media world of instant pressure campaigns, rapid-fire judgments, and cancel culture proved a wild ride, especially for old companies learning new tricks. A reputation-threatening Twitterstorm could blow up in the time it took a traditional crisis-communications team to book its meeting room. But in the 2020s, corporate interests got better at providing leadership as government got worse. Companies learned to pick their issues with more care and less reactive emotion, aligning themselves primarily with causes relating to their brand. They learned to communicate with speed, agility, and authenticity, three qualities not so common throughout government. They found ways to make customers, even complainers, feel valued for more than their purchasing power. They made significant investments in cybersecurity and knocking down false stories fast. This made them look good compared to political discourse, which was top-heavy with false stories.

There were still bad corporate decisions made owing to fear, arrogance, or myopia. But by election night 2032, the country's most admired, trustworthy companies were being rated in surveys as more positive forces than politicians; more believable and virtuous; less likely to try to exploit Americans; and more likely to affect meaningful social change, mostly because they learned to play digital media instead of playing victim.

At any rate, Janey Reynolds loved the recognition she got for belonging to the Starbucks cadre, and not just the discount lattes.

"Janey." It was Rupert, softening the volume of her Lizzo playlist and turning up the apartment lighting grid. "I have Anita for you on a voice call."

"Put her through, Rupert, thank you." Janey had done enough Starbucking for one night. She sat up on the sofa and laid her infoslate to one side.

"Hey, babe," called Anita. "I aced my work and I'm at the Royal Horse after all. Clip your passport back on and rock down here."

"Aaargh, I don't know." Janey stretched. "Now it's, like, eleven, and I have to work tomorrow. And anyway, isn't the election on? I don't want to be around a bunch of people counting votes and doing victory dances." She swiveled to give Rupert a private stink-eye. "I get enough of that crap at home."

"No, that's what's great!" enthused Anita. "Nobody at the bar *cares*! We're watching an Avalanche game and doing Aperol shots. I promise you, no election stuff." She giggled. "One guy here wanted to turn it on, but we threw him out. And it turns out it's not even anywhere on the TV menu! We looked! You're safe!"

"Well. . ." Janey stole a look at her infoslate. A misspelled headline had broken through her junk-blocking defensive line.

DUCKWURTH FRAUD! It read. She rolled her eyes and turned the thing screen-side down.

"OK, one quick one. I'm on my way."

At about 1 a.m. Eastern time, early compared to some other election nights, the Associated Press called the 2032 presidential race without Janey noticing for Republican incumbents Kevin McCarthy and Elise Stefanik. Once again, the GOP had pieced together an Electoral College broken-field run, holding the southern tier, most of the west between Illinois and the coast, plus Minnesota, Ohio, and Pennsylvania. Duckworth won the expected New England and mid-Atlantic bloc, the west coast, Nevada, and New Mexico. She took Wisconsin by a razor-thin margin, coming as she did from neighboring Illinois, and Kentucky thanks to her running mate, the still-popular former governor there, Andy Beshear. McCarthy won everywhere else, taking 332 Electoral College votes to Duckworth's 206.

As Brian Williams relayed the AP call to his modest online audience, he kept one worried eye on his own infoslate, perched out of camera range. Banner headlines already proclaimed Duckworth the real winner, the victim of voter suppression and Iranian cyberattacks, or the target of voting machine tampering. Progressive activists urged real-time street protests. Some advocated violence. Apparently small crowds were gathering in Times Square and outside 30 Rock, but not big enough to justify live shots. Later, Williams noted on air that there were reports of unrest, mostly in deep blue states where the outcome was never in doubt. He downplayed the turmoil angle, but social media was swept by frightening livestreams of civil disorder.

☗

In an oddity, the Democratic Party flipped the House, picking up 10 seats to finish with a slim three-seat majority. Republican opponents instantly contested the totals, demanded recounts, and flooded social media with bots insisting the House had been stolen by liberals who hated America. But at her Queens victory party the jubilant minority leader, former vice president and reinstalled House member Alexandria Ocasio-Cortez, announced impeachment proceedings against President McCarthy would begin the week of his inauguration.

National voter turnout hit a new low in 2032 at 44%. Elderly Americans voted in the most robust numbers, as had long been typical. But as they died, overall turnout kept declining. It was like watching sinking sales figures for rear-wheel-drive V-8 cars. The worst-performing demographic was women 18-34, who turned out at a 21% rate.

Because ten states now allowed e-voting via infoslate or other digital device, and there were no paper backup records, numerous vote counts were corrupted or delayed; some precincts in Indiana, Tennessee, and West Virginia mysteriously never reported at all. These factors assured that a true, final popular vote total would never be certified. The Federal Election Commission said it believed—*estimated!*—Tammy Duckworth beat Kevin McCarthy in the popular tally by 3.6 to 3.8 million votes. It was a significantly wider margin than Hillary Clinton had achieved over Donald Trump in 2016.

The NBCLiveStream election night special attracted 850,000 viewers at its peak. The NFL on CBS drew an audience of 21.4 million. The *Saturday Night Live* compilation of antique political sketches NBC aired on its flagship network, programmed against its own political coverage, drew 6.7 million.

No matter whose side you were on, the post-election surveys were depressing. When the Pew Center asked non-participants why they had not voted, 27% said they had been confused by digital messages about the candidates. 32% said they had blocked some or all campaign coverage.

23% said they had not believed the election was real.

On election night Janey returned to her apartment well after midnight with a head full of Aperol. Rupert turned on the lights but knew to keep them dimmed when she came home at this hour. She had mercifully forgotten about the election, and nobody at the Royal Horse had reminded her.

So things would have stayed until morning had Janey not shuffled to the refrigerator for a glass of water. As she grasped the door handle the integrated screen lit up. Replacing her shopping list was the tanned, stern face of President McCarthy.

During the campaign, the avatar had looked almost fatherly. Now, not so much.

"Janey, I'm glad I caught you," intoned the president-bot. "We've won a great victory tonight, as I'm sure you know. I'm very sorry to know you did not cast a vote."

Janey stiffened.

"I hope you enjoyed time with your friend Anita at"—there was that fraction-of-a-second hesitation again, as the algorithm consulted Janey's geo-record—"the Royal Horse Tavern, on Navajo Street."

Did the president sound angry? Judgmental? Merely disappointed in her? Was she imagining things?

"How is your family doing . . . Janey?" asked the president. "You know, our vision—"

"RUPERT!"

CHAPTER TWO

PORTRAIT OF THE DIGITAL STRATEGIST AS A YOUNG MAN

Away with 2032 and disenfranchised, disengaged Janey—for now, anyway. We're safely back to present day. In coronavirus times, however, I am not sure how reassuring that is.

When I helped coax the internet to maturity as a political force, I did not predict it would prompt a zero hour of reckoning for our health, belief systems, politics, and democracy itself. Yet the COVID-19 pandemic was a fateful inflection point on each front, with our shared but massively flawed digital infosphere at the epicenter.

At least the sun rose as usual on a spring morning in 2020 in the Pacific Northwest. Not much else was normal. I got up early and made tea. My wife and children were still asleep upstairs. Our family lives on a quiet and leafy street on the outskirts of Seattle. It's a bucolic, friendly setting with close-set houses. The rambling Krohn place is strewn with books and toys. We have brewpubs and a neighborhood grocery within walking distance. Before the pandemic, I got the kids rousted from bed and ready for school, and they played with friends in the street in the afternoons.

All of that was on hold in 2020 while we learned and lived social distancing. No clasping hands with neighbors and no going out for a beer. No Purell in the stores and no school for the kids. It's a prosperous education district, and during the home-schooling period they gave out free laptops to children in need. In most of the rest of the United States, I knew, kids on the far short end of the inequality stick were on their own, and at least 22% of American homes still lacked an internet hookup.[1] Our digital revolution left millions on the outside looking in. When digital life is the only life left, as it was in the lockdown period, that means trouble.

I stirred my tea and headed for my cluttered home office, listening for birdsong in the treetops—our typical soundtrack to sunup on a fair day. It was eerily quiet outside. No traffic hum from the freeway in the distance. Nobody was driving to work.

My father served with distinction as a lieutenant colonel in the United States Army. He saw combat in Vietnam and later wrote a celebrated history of the 1968 Tet Offensive. After Tet, a political disaster for the Lyndon Johnson administration that fired antiwar sentiment at home, Washington policymakers previously bullish on the Vietnam campaign began using the term "agonizing reap-praisal"—meaning it was time to concede their current strategy was unlikely to lead to victory.

While my computer booted, I considered the state of digital politics, and how in the coronavirus moment the internet was both a lifeline and, tragically, making everything worse. We were undergoing digital bombardment—we had been for some time— but the crisis put exclamation points on everything. Our pervasive, but invasive and untrustworthy, technology accommodated so many misinformed, sabotage-minded, or hateful actors. I thought how the COVID-19 pandemic brought so many problems with the internet to a frenzied head. And I thought: We, too, are due for an agonizing reappraisal. Our digital world isn't working. The eventual wane of the coronavirus crisis wouldn't change that.

I had COVIDTracking.com bookmarked. It was my habit to check the rising casualty numbers. The COVID Tracking Project was a good-faith, grassroots stat-compilation effort by independent journalists and "volunteer data-grabbers."[2] They were trying their best to update positive diagnoses and deaths. But other efforts produced different tallies. Early in the pandemic, the positive diagnosis count from the Centers for Disease Control and Prevention were oddly, dramatically lower—about 40% lower.[3] (Later the once-authoritative CDC seemed to go AWOL, its health recommendations spiked by the White House or awkwardly retracted.) Johns Hopkins University death data came out different still. News organizations compiled their own numbers. It was the central conundrum of the digital infosphere modeled in miniature: tons of data, but no clarity. No authority. No definitive, consensus story. That's where 25 years of internet information culture got us. You pick a source you like or trust none at all. *You* figure it out.

So many competing estimates had the curious effect of reducing trust in *all* of them. Two-thirds of Americans in May 2020 disbelieved COVID-19 death tolls. Democrats insisted they were too low; President Trump encouraged the view that they were too high, inflated by cynical hospitals to score more Medicare funding, and many Republicans concurred.[4] Your view depended on your belief system, and in the digital infosphere, comprised of millions of sealed-off, self-reinforcing echo chambers, you could believe whatever you wanted.

Until 2020 many, including me, believed it would take a genuine, clock-stopping cataclysm to reunify the American public. Such a crisis came only once per generation or so, but when one arrived, it worked. It worked in 1941, after Pearl Harbor; in 1963, when JFK was shot; and, briefly, in 2001, after 9/11. In those turning-point years our routine squabbles receded, suddenly looking puny and trivial next to current events.

In the pandemic, though, we saw an unprecedented collapse of authority, and we had never seen media and belief systems in such disarray. For JFK and 9/11, Walter Cronkite and Peter Jennings soothed the nation. For COVID-19, internet trolls raked our skin raw.

Prior catastrophes unified the country. This one was tearing it apart. Nick Bilton at *Vanity Fair* called COVID-19 "the first true epidemic of a polarized, plugged-in era."[5]

Support for (or opposition to) mass-scale testing, proven a key ingredient for success in other countries fighting the virus, became a political litmus test in the U.S. Even basic health precautions became political statements. Wearing masks and gloves? Avoiding close contact with strangers to slow the spread? Businesses closed? Gestures of solidarity, perhaps; of empathy for your community— or signs of contemptible, sheep-like servility and violations of constitutional freedoms. "Dropped by a department store to buy a toaster oven," tweeted a conservative media figure named Todd Starnes. "Mandatory hand sanitizer squirt and mask. One-way aisles . . . The country as we know it has been destroyed. And I still don't have a toaster."[6] Liberals made "I still don't have a toaster" an instant meme. But liberals online also seemed to take nasty, triumphal, I-told-you-so pleasure in sharing obituaries of those who mocked the virus, then died of it.

People enraged by lockdowns hooked up online with people who think vaccines cause autism, and people who like assault weapons and fly Confederate flags, and people incensed by face masks. They let loose a consolidated pastiche of grievances in protests coast to coast. "Don't believe this #scamdemic!" read a sign in Harrisburg, Pennsylvania. "No tests, no vaccine, no masks!" said one in Tennessee. Emergency physician and Brown University professor Dr. Megan Ranney told *The New York Times*: "This group has moved the reopening debate from a conversation about health and science to a conversation about liberty. They've redefined the debate so it's no longer about weighing risks and benefits and instead it's this politicized narrative. It's like taking a nuanced conversation about gun injury and turning it into an argument about gun rights . . . the small minority dominates the conversation."[7] There was also evidence that certain chapters of the reopen-America-now movement were artificially manipulated into being by unknown political forces—Astroturfed, as the pros say. Facebook groups like Operation Gridlock Los Angeles and Operation Gridlock Tennessee bore nearly identical descriptions.

Three times as many Republicans as Democrats said they would refuse a COVID-19 vaccine, 20% versus 7%, according to a May 2020 Morning Consult poll.[8]

"Rather than a coming together, the crisis has demonstrated how for decades Americans have conducted a political version of social distancing: the herd-like clustering of conservatives and liberals into like-minded communities caused by the allergic reaction to compatriots holding opposing political views. Once again, we have seen the familiar two Americas divide, the usual knee-jerk tribalism," reflected Nick Bryant, New York correspondent for the BBC.[9] But a divide this deep, so animated by rage and delusion, had no familiar historical antecedent, and relatively recent internet conventions, I knew, bore blame.

When authority retreats, monsters advance. Egged on by YouTube, Facebook, and Twitter posts, self-styled coronavirus truthers in Europe and Quebec burned down dozens of 5G cell towers in the lunatic conviction that 5G wireless networks abetted the pandemic.[10] There was evidence state-sponsored bot accounts were moving people to arson: "We've definitely seen plenty of organized disinfo around 5G-coronavirus," said the Global Disinformation Index.[11] Simultaneously, an anti-vaccine activist with dubious scientific credentials named Judy Mikovits swept the internet promoting a sinister conspiracy linking COVID-19 to Big Pharma and Bill Gates; millions on social media seemed to buy her baseless "Plandemic" video.[12]

You could even believe the virus itself was fake news. Other, camera-equipped truthers stalked U.S. emergency rooms and posted videos with the hashtag #FilmYourHospital, citing any empty space they found as proof COVID-19 was made up.[13]

An Arizona man died consuming chloroquine phosphate to cure the virus, a therapy President Trump had touted as a possible "game changer."[14] A Florida county commissioner went viral when he announced that aiming a blow dryer up your nose could kill coronavirus.[15] Televangelist Jim Bakker was sued for hustling fake $80 coronavirus cures online.[16] Shopify closed down thousands of fresh-sprouted scam websites with the terms "corona" or "covid" in their URLs.[17] WhatsApp, operated by Facebook, circulated numberless fake cures, hoax stories, and sinister, often racist fables about COVID-19's origins; encryption features meant to protect privacy made moderating WhatsApp content nearly impossible.[18]

Yonder, another disinformation-tracking concern, reported that while junk conspiracy stories normally took six to eight months to jump from fringe internet platforms to the mainstream, coronavirus junk was making the leap in three to fourteen days.[19] There was no way to stay ahead of all the derangement, scams, conspiracies, and general stupidity blooming online like digital kudzu.

The federal emergency response was glacial, but social media was a hot battlefield. The bombardment was constant, and elected leaders were among the most ardent bombardiers. At the head of an unprepared, wheel-spinning Washington, President Trump and his loyalists used Twitter to savage their critics on a near-hourly basis. When Trump berated governors for being unprepared, some counterattacked online with increasing who-gives-a-shit-anymore public asperity: "You should be leading a national response instead of throwing tantrums from the back seat . . . Get off Twitter and do your job," tweeted J.B. Pritzker of Illinois.[20] At the height of the emergency, the secretary of the Treasury of the United States, Steven Mnuchin, found time to mix it up on Twitter with rocker Axl Rose after Rose called him an asshole.[21] Essential American support systems were faltering all over the place, and this was what we got. Imagine how the Cuban missile crisis could have played out if JFK and Gen. Curtis LeMay had traded insulting tweets for all to see about the wisdom of nuking Havana.

Journalist Garrett Graff, whom I think is right about a lot of things, wrote that our collective COVID-19 response "should stand as one of the most beautiful moments in our country's long history—a moment of shared, galvanizing national spirit . . .

In the absence of meaningful national leadership, Americans across the country are making their own decisions for our collective well-being."[22] It was often true. In many corners of social media, noble civic instincts glowed. There were legions of home seamstresses answering the #WeNeedPPE call, compensating for their country's primitive failure to come up with basic things like face masks. There were teachers reading through screen doors to lonely grade-school kids stuck at home. There were shattered ICU nurses pouring their hearts out on Instagram after double shifts. So many stories of individual and institutional heroism, you could surf the web with a lump in your throat all day.

As I sat at my desk in a morning sunbeam, the chirping birds outside seemed to echo Graff's optimism. But in truth, to rip off Charles Dickens, it was the best of times and the worst of times online. The digital infosphere turbocharged and rewarded people's darkest impulses. So many Americans used the internet to spray misinformation, malevolence, and cruelty across a panicked land.

During the lockdown, as the death toll soared, CNN media correspondent Brian Stelter once missed filing his nightly e-newsletter on deadline. The next day he admitted on Twitter to having had a brief, modest breakdown, crawling into bed, and crying. "Now is not a time for faux-invincibility," he tweeted. His humanity attracted shocking, repulsive waves of social-media scorn: "Cry me a river." "This is absolute BS." "This is pandering and likely scripted." "Snowflake." "Toughen up, buttercup."[23]

For Instagram notoriety, idiot teenagers in the Virginia suburbs of Washington, D.C. posted videos of themselves coughing on supermarket produce. Copycats were inspired: "We have learned that this appears to be a disturbing trend on social media across the country," said police in Purcellville, Virginia.[24] A Pennsylvania cougher-terrorist forced a store to trash $35,000 worth of fruit and vegetables.[25] And kids answering a cretinous online #CoronaVirusChallenge licked toilet seats and subway handrails to earn likes, some reportedly contracting the disease.

When they went viral, of course, they were shamed. Shaming campaigns rolled across the web in supersonic waves. It had not crossed my mind, in my early digital days, that among the things the internet would be best at would be convening revenge mobs to draw and quarter people. But social media made a great virtual kangaroo court. The hashtag #Covidiots helped the masses shame in shorthand. Two would-be profiteers in Tennessee bought up 17,000 bottles of hand sanitizer, planning to resell it online at huge markups, but when profiled by *The New York Times* they were showered with online death threats, ejected from Amazon, forced to donate everything, and shamed into oblivion.[26] In Florida a pugnacious, flush-cheeked spring breaker sneered at the virus on TV: "If I get corona, I get corona! I'm not going to let that stop me from partying!" When his sound bite went, um, viral, he was internet famous in the worst way. Identified by hometown reporters back in Ohio, he posted an Instagram apology, suddenly chastened and pious ("I will continue to reflect and learn from this and continue to pray for our well-being"). An unmoved Reddit jury debated whether society should ostracize the kid for life, or just several years.[27]

I scrolled through my Twitter feed. The tea was cooling now. Here came a thread by a despairing science authority, a biology professor at the University of Washington not far from where I sat, Carl T. Bergstrom. "We're fighting a battle against the biggest crisis in decades," he tweeted,

"But we are also fighting on a second front that we did not anticipate, fighting a battle against misinformation and disinformation in a hyper-partisan environment where our predictions and recommendations about the pandemic are deeply politicized . . .

"Every day there are new scicomm [science communication] crises blowing up, and the thing that kills me is that they are almost without exception MANUFACTURED with political intent . . .

"For me, this is the heartbreaking part. It turns out we're not all in this together."[28]

It broke my heart, too. Internet culture had long helped attenuate respect for expertise. It elevated the random, anonymous shouter. It sustained counterfeit data, because the impulse to share overwhelms the impulse to investigate or verify. Look where we were now. Americans held irreconcilably different ideas about what was actually happening, programmed in large part by the way our digital infosphere isolates and reinforces ideologues. Worse, they were now conditioned to attack and destroy those who differed.

So while some countries mustered popular solidarity and consensus and flattened their curves, the United States fought with itself, sometimes literally and fatally. A store guard in Michigan and McDonald's employees in Oklahoma were shot by customers opposed to face masks.[29] In Alabama, a cop body-slammed a Walmart customer for *not* wearing one.[30] Protesters opposed to stay-at-home measures compared themselves to victims of Nazi oppressors, but one tried to burn down a Jewish nursing home in the belief COVID-19 was unleashed by a Jewish cabal.[31] Vigilantes beat up innocent Asians in American streets to exact revenge for what the White House called the "Chinese virus." All inspired at least in part by internet media.

The world watched in horror. UNESCO reckoned we were in the grip of a spreading "misinfodemic." "The world must unite against this disease, too," said U.N. Secretary General António Guterrres.[32] France is romantically fond of U.S. ideals and values, especially in a crisis, but Dominique Moisi, political scientist at the Institut Montaigne in Paris, said, "America has not done badly, it has done exceptionally badly."[33] Fintan O'Toole, Ireland's top political columnist, wrote that the U.S. was exciting a new emotion among its overseas allies: pity. "Will American prestige ever recover from this shameful episode?"[34] A transborder poll in spring 2020 found only 33% of Canadian citizens still trusted Americans; the prior November it was 58%. (The same survey found Americans trusted Canadians more than other Americans, too.[35]) By most estimates the U.S. response to the pandemic was indubitably the worst in the developed world—and the costliest in terms of human life.

It seemed certain that on the other side of the crisis, we survivors would be reassessing everything. Not just our health care and emergency response systems, which buckled early, like wicker bridge abutments. Global supply chains, voting and elections, concerts and ballgames, food processing, airlines and cruise ships, office life, federal versus state authority, bars and restaurants, the 40-year neoliberal consensus: every pillar of our political and economic lives.

I hoped we would reassess the internet, too.

On lockdown the country seemed to be not only obsessively taking its temperature but taking stock. It was agonizing reappraisal time. I was certainly appraising my career in online politics, election strategy, publishing, and marketing, and my role in events that led me—all of us—to a rare and sobering crossroads, but with a chance, in the face of COVID-19, to engineer a better political future online and off. To quell the bombardment.

"Hey, Cyrus." It was Rob Goodling talking. Rob was a staffer in the Old Executive Office Building next door to the White House, and a good guy. I was an intern sworn to do whatever Rob asked, or for that matter anyone else in the office of Vice President Dan Quayle.

"We're going to connect all the computers on this hall. I want you to run cable under all this carpet, from one end of the building to the other."

Goodling wanted me to string up the OEOB's first computer network.

Wasn't GSA supposed to take charge of projects like this? We were entering the '92 election cycle, came the brusque answer. GSA would take too long to get this done.

I had picked up a little about ISDN lines in college—very little. But enough, it seemed, to qualify me for dropping to hands and knees in the storied, ornate second-floor corridor outside Quayle's ceremonial office, running cable past Bill Kristol's quarters, and those of David Beckwith, the Quayle communications director, and saying excuse me to Jack Kemp, who was trotting around working on the Bush administration's Competitiveness Council.

If I'm honest, I did a real hack job. They showed me where to plug the lines into the computers, but to get them from one end of the building to the other I had to yank at ornamental carpet and tape cable to venerable walls and woodwork. A few years ago, I saw news of a fire in the OEOB and wondered if my handiwork had finally shorted out. But back then, it worked. I jury-rigged a crude LAN so administration officials with computers could transition away from photocopies, carbon paper, and running up and down the corridor and start sending e-messages. It had never been done in there.

It was young me's first brush with digital connectivity, technology, and politics. 1991.

I was installed as the lowest of the low on the Quayle org chart because while writing speeches in the Pentagon, my Army father had grown friendly with some of the vice president's men. One in particular stood out: Les Novitsky, a sincerely demonstrative patriot who never showed up to work without the Stars and Stripes on his person, usually in necktie form. One summer day at home, I lost a coin toss with my brother Josh and had to drive to pick up our younger twin brothers from Hebrew school in the Virginia suburbs of D.C. Cooling my heels in the synagogue parking lot, a certain deputy assistant to the vice president recognized me—Dad and I look alike—and strolled over. It was Les. Would I be interested in coming in for a couple of days, doing some filing, and helping get the office together? The place was a mess. Would I, I said. If I'd won that coin toss and stayed home, who knows if you'd be reading this.

In days I was flitting between OEOB and the West Wing in my best suit, flashing my newly laminated orange badge, seeing how things worked and taking it all in. Getting that view was more important to me, frankly, than advancing the interests of one Dan Quayle—though he turned out to be a perfectly gracious man. I grew up in a Republican household, but not an ideologue; I had few strong political leanings. I acquired a rep as a hard worker ready for any mission, even if it meant wrecking that good suit laying cable under Bill Kristol's puzzled gaze, and my tour of duty was extended.

My family had virtually programmed me to gravitate to public affairs. Dad had fought for American values in Vietnam. When the war ended, we lived on or near military installations, moving to a new address every two years or so: Fort Monroe, which I found the most interesting because the *Monitor* fought the *Merrimack* in 1862 in the waters just beyond its walls; Fort Stewart, Fort Brucker, and stints over in Mannheim and Bad Kreuznach; and finally Fort Myer, across the Potomac from Washington, D.C.

Wherever we camped, I watched my father rise every morning and put on fatigues or his dress uniform, the base paused for taps every afternoon at five, and every night the family gathered around the network TV news. And then my father would moderate a discussion of what Tom Brokaw had just said—leading with his own views but demanding ours as well. I learned to read a lot of newspapers for added self-defense. I attended Pentagon ceremonies that caught my interest. I was also dispatched at a tender age to international camp in Canada, the Taylor Statten Camps, which count Prime Ministers Pierre and Justin Trudeau among their alums. All this, long before most Americans knew what a connected computer was, sharpened my interest in geopolitics and current events.

One of my Team Quayle missions involved accompanying the vice president to the CNN Washington bureau, north of Capitol Hill near Union Station, for an appearance. I liked the bureau's go-go atmosphere and can-do people, and after the electorate had its way with the Bush-Quayle ticket in November 1992 I went in search of something new to do. I landed an unpaid internship at CNN, with *Larry King Live*. *LKL* had worked the '92 election hard, booking candidates for long interactive sessions and requiring them to field live viewer phone calls. Even President Bush acceded and took calls on Larry's air. I admired that. For candidates to mix things up on TV with random Americans was a minor revolution in campaign coverage. It was egalitarian. It broke barriers between remote elites and regular joes. It seemed to promote civility and mutual respect, and I wanted to be part of efforts like that.

Eventually I got an actual paying job at CNN helping to produce *Crossfire*, the infamous left-versus-right debate program launched a decade earlier by Tom Braden and Pat Buchanan. By the time I joined the franchise, Buchanan was alternating in the right-wing chair with Bob Novak. Braden was gone, replaced by the soft-spoken, deliberate, liberal editor of *The New Republic*, Michael Kinsley. Novak versus Kinsley could be a decibel mismatch, but never an intellectual one.

One day in 1994, Kinsley ambled into the producer's bullpen in the *Crossfire* office, cleared his throat, and pronounced:

"Um, the internet is going to be huge one day."

Kinsley ambled into the producer's bullpen. "Um, the internet is going to be huge one day."

There were some discreet eye-rolls, as often occur when the talent brings the producers a brilliant show idea they picked up from talking to God knew who. The internet? An obscure playground for hobbyists and weirdos haunting Usenet boards. By now CNN had set up web connections for us, it even had a fledgling website, but the network still seemed to think it was background noise, a fad bound to subside. Like Rubik's Cube, or the California Raisins.

Michael pressed: "We should do a show on internet pornography. Because there's a lot of it now, and if pornography is moving to the internet, everyone else is going to. Everything follows sex."

It was hard to resist sex-based logic. We launched our primitive Netscape browsers and spent the next hours dutifully performing research. Yes, there was porn aplenty in cyberspace.

We booked the show and it worked. A light bulb went off for me. Michael was dead right, and not only about web porn. (Coming events would prove the adult entertainment industry a web pioneer. From e-commerce to streaming video and subscription models, porn blazed a lot of virtual trails.) The internet was going to be important, probably more important than TV executives cared to admit. I flashed back on my caveman-grade LAN marring the OEOB's wainscoting. Connected computing could become a new nexus of technology, media, and politics. I wanted to be part of it.

Little did I know Kinsley was ahead of me there, too. On his weekends he was sneaking out of Washington and flying around the country, talking to investors, shopping an idea for a legitimate online magazine.

Prodigy, CompuServe, AOL: those were the World Wide Web's big dogs in 1994. They were portals but functioned like walled-off theme parks. How you'd distribute an editorial product outside park confines, or even attract attention to it, were giant questions. But Microsoft was trying to launch a theme park-slash-portal of its own: the Microsoft Network, soon shorthanded as MSN. Kinsley was acquainted with Steve Ballmer, then Microsoft's executive vice president of sales (and later CEO). Michael and Steve had Harvard in common. Ballmer and MSN's general manager, Russ Siegelman, thought it might be a neat coup to sign Kinsley and get him producing original content of . . . some kind. Bill Gates signed off and *Slate* was going to be a thing.

When news broke that Michael Kinsley, *establishment pundit Michael Kinsley*, was giving up a position of influence in *Washington* to move out to *Seattle*, leaving *television* to have a go at this eccentric *internet* thing that only geeks and pervs got, the phones in the *Crossfire* production office jangled off their hooks. The fax machine melted. Was the CNN star out of his mind? What had possessed this noble mind to forfeit his status and standing—no sane soul abandons a job in *television*—to go tinker with computers in the distant, drizzly Pacific Northwest? Seattle was a punch line in Neil Simon plays for New Yorkers, a synonym for Siberia. Beltway boulevardiers muttered about Michael's judgment.

I wanted to go too.

I marched into Michael's cramped CNN office festooned with yellow Post-It Notes to himself.

"Michael, it seems like everybody under the sun wants to come and join you on this new endeavor," I began. I didn't know how true that was, but it seemed like a positive thing to say. "I'd be remiss if I didn't throw my name in the ring."

Kinsley looked up at me. He seemed genuinely surprised, maybe even touched. "Really?"

Really, I said. Let's go.

"Well, let me get out there. Get my bearings. I'll call you as soon as I can."

I thought he was letting me down gently. I couldn't blame him. Think of all the hot hires he must be fending off. Who was I? A few days later, I helped him pack up his house and he moved to Seattle on Christmas Day. That, I thought, was that. But a few weeks later my phone rang. Kinsley calling. Whether I was the ideal lieutenant, or he simply couldn't find a better-qualified taker, I got the gig—*Slate*'s number-two hire.

I drove cross-country with a friend in February. On the way, as a crash course in Microsoft culture, I read *Microserfs* by Doug Coupland and Fred Moody's *I Sing the Body Electronic*. There were throngs of technoids who idolized Bill Gates and Microsoft and would have crawled through broken glass for a job offer. I had one, I was headed for Redmond, and I didn't even know that much about the place.

I learned fast. On day one I showed up on the perpetually rain-damp Microsoft campus, a sprawl of nondescript low-slung black-glass buildings tucked into stands of fir trees, wearing my Washington uniform: suit and pressed shirt. The Microserf working across the hall from the new *Slate* office eyed the new guy with either disdain or pity and crossed to my door.

"Um, let me just explain a couple of things. That's not how it works." The uniform here was polos or T-shirts and slacks.

Kinsley and I were assigned a couple of experienced Microsoft executives for handholding. One, Betsy Davis, told me I was permitted three verbal, face-to-face questions per day. Communication was supposed to occur electronically. Betsy forced me to figure out the in-house messaging system and the Microsoft intranet. But she would also help us build a team and find the right designers and developers.

A few days in, Michael appeared clutching a two-page handwritten memo. Handwritten! Here at Microsoft! But anyway.

"This is my vision for an online magazine," he murmured. "I don't entirely know how we're gonna do it, but, um, your job is to turn this document into a website." Today we have WordPress and Wix and many such templates to launch a website in mere hours. In 1996 it took months, and a lot of custom coding.

I moved into a houseboat on Lake Union at Gasworks Park Marina, one dock over from the place Tom Hanks' character occupied in *Sleepless in Seattle*, and the long days began.

Michael was *Slate*'s editor; I was doing a little bit of everything else but was specifically responsible for figuring out a bulletin-board feature for the new magazine. Michael wanted some kind of community forum where *Slate* readers could post comments—an animated letters-to-the-editor zone. At *Crossfire* we put opposing views on TV, but unlike *Larry King Live* we took no viewer calls. We wanted to merge those two approaches at Slate, introducing an audience-participation element into political debate, facilitating banter. The dominant free-standing online bulletin boards at the time were Echo and The Well. They could be dark, intimidating and snarky, as could tech culture itself. Ours was going to be bright, welcoming, and erudite.

We called *Slate*'s forum The Fray.

The site came together in five pell-mell months. Before we launched, Michael made the cover of *Newsweek* in a yellow rain slicker with a salmon, fronting a long takeout exploring Seattle's sudden national allure. "Swimming to Seattle—Everybody Else is Moving There. Should You?" asked the cover. It was nice kickoff publicity for us, even if the piece maintained a bemused East Coast distance.

Slate launched in June 1996. The forces stirring to life would, two decades later, lead to the end of *Newsweek*. At the time, though, we felt like anything but giant killers. We were just trying to hit our marks and publish.

We ran a daily feature called Today's Papers, a compact digest of wisdom from the big establishment papers, originated by a brilliant insomniac called Scott Shuger who stayed up all night compiling it. We had Mickey Kaus overseeing Chatterbox, a quick-take column of reactions to political events. Economist Herb Stein, Ben Stein's dad and chair of the Nixon-Ford era Council of Economic Advisers, moderated an organized dissent-in-text feature we called Committee of Correspondence. Herb also launched the Dear Prudence advice column, soon handed off to Margo Howard, who, as the daughter of Eppie Lederer, aka Ann Landers, was virtually genetically equipped to make the franchise the success it quickly became. And we had The Fray.

We were a lab for fascinating experiments. Michael wanted *Slate*'s text design to be easily read, not clunky HTML, so we experimented with the ClearType screen typography system from Bill Hill, one of the great innovators in screen-reading software. We plugged in Microsoft's embryonic text-to-speech software so people could listen to *Slate*, or at least try. We tried charging a subscription fee when nearly all other content on the web was free, except porn. (Even with signup bonuses like Microsoft Encarta CD-ROMs, that idea lasted less than a year.)

All were new ideas. Many presented *Slate* management with trouble of some kind. In some cases, we sowed seeds that would grow to trouble the digital infosphere.

We sought to import traditional, journalistic editing standards from the analog world to the internet. The technology experts at Microsoft saw that as a virtue, a value-add. At first, we had writers email us their drafts for review by the chain of command (then fax the work as follow-up—then phone us to make sure the file had arrived—such were the days).

But we found out delivering fresh material to *Slate*'s fans meant moving faster than traditional technique would allow. Scott's newspaper digest was ready in the middle of the night and needed to go live right then. Mickey wanted to post with nonstop speed, bypassing a deliberate chain of command.

It was a fateful moment when the team decided we were going to allow Kaus, and then other writers, to publish directly to the *Slate* content management system, bypassing our editorial filter.

Mickey's Chatterbox (soon rechristened Kausfiles) was, of course, a blog. Maybe one of the first. I don't recall the word "blog" in play then, I think we just called it expeditious publishing, but in retrospect sidelining the editorial filters was a huge and pivotal call. You can draw a line right from Kausfiles to the trust crisis we're in today. (That's not a shot at Mickey, who was great.) How could *Slate* verify the accuracy of what he or any writer posted under our banner? How could readers know what was true? The answer at the time was: We'll fix flaws afterward, once they're spotted. (And Kinsley was conscientious about running big, prominent corrections.) But that doesn't work in airline safety, and it didn't work here either.

As for The Fray, we expected courteous exchanges of ideas. (Remember, this was years before today's big social media platforms existed.) What we watched happen, which surprised us, was users with political biases gravitating toward enclaves within The Fray where they felt most comfortable—seeking out reinforcement. The politesse we imagined was rare in practice; in the office we called the rudest users The Fraygrants (rhymes with vagrants, as in, we kind of wanted to send them on their way) and wondered how and whether to rein them in.

The problem wasn't just tone of voice. It was the fragmentation. If cable TV news exacerbated fragmentation—and around this time, Fox and MSNBC were stirring to life to finally challenge CNN—the internet was only taking it further.

Even so, we did not see trolling and other negative behavior as threats to the whole information culture. On the contrary, I at first thought they'd be beneficial, especially to the political process. The internet was going to allow any political candidate or organization to connect with voters directly—and go so deep and rich, you could find yourself saturated in information that catered to your value system. We were all frustrated with the hurry-up formats of political debates on TV and superficial 30-second political ads, so at the time we actually thought richly stocked, biased enclaves were a fine idea.

But even as we were trying to build credibility for the *Slate* brand, rendered in Kinsley-karma Harvard crimson, we were using it to advance an editorial mechanism that could not verify the accuracy or veracity of entirely unfiltered content, some user-provided. Kinsley certainly didn't feel we had created a

Frankenstein's monster, or protocols that defined internet discourse downward. But that was the ball we put in play.

Microsoft wanted to understand the economics of online publishing, starting from the premise that print economics were flawed—they were right about that—and digital media could be a remedy. (*Slate* became profitable with me as publisher, although credit really belongs to my predecessor in the slot, Scott Moore, who went on to be president of MSNBC.com.) But Kinsley never set out to put *Time* and *Newsweek* out of business. He thought *Slate* would simply become a nifty complement to establishment media.

As *Slate* got traction, the next thing our patrons wanted was to introduce political debate and advertising online. In 1996, GOP New York Gov. George Pataki and his Democratic challenger, Peter Vallone, had experimented with internet advertising—they were among the first if not the first—and Microsoft saw both civic virtue and potential profit in going bigger in 2000.

It was a tantalizing prospect that raised a new plethora of questions, if not for the technologists, certainly for me. How does an internet operator provide candidates with equal time? How do we calculate the lowest fair unit rate for banner space? What if a campaign wants to pay a premium to pin advertisements to certain hot keywords—is that fair? What if Candidate Smith wants to buy out your site's home page for the week before election day—what can you do for Candidate Jones? If the answer is nothing, how would Microsoft, or any company in Microsoft's position, avoid seeming to be in the tank for Smith?

How should ad designers handle disclaimers giving viewers an idea of the ad's source and funding authority? In the late 1990s, there was no Federal Election Commission guidance for online political activity. We did our best to cobble together our own, cribbing from FEC rules for other media. Trevor Potter at the FEC was a helpful point of contact. But in truth, more than 20 years later, there are still no straight-up answers to most of these questions.

Uncertainty loves company. MSN joined up with the Markle Foundation and some other portals to create an online vehicle for political candidates and ideas called Web White and Blue 2000. Also involved was Doug Bailey, who had consulted on the 1976 Ford campaign and had founded the *Hotline*, ancestor to *Politico*, way back in 1987, in the internet's genesis days. We had a lot of company and expertise if not a roadmap of the new world.

Web White and Blue 2000 was aspirational, high-minded, public-square stuff. It allowed campaigns to come upload position papers and videos (though at circa-2000 connection speeds, some viewers saw more buffering than content) and talk more about their issues.

For many, it was new ground. I made a deal to put former democratic Sen. Bill Bradley on the site, and he recorded some content into a small video camera. "I'm Bill Bradley," the senator intoned solemnly, "and if you're watching this, that means you're on the internet." Bradley talked about his issues for a couple minutes with the stentorian gravity of a 1930s BBC broadcaster. John McCain's campaign saw the internet as its own bubble, divorced from the bigger political sphere; all it wanted to do was run banner ads about stopping internet taxation.

It was an education for all of us, one the Markle Foundation declared a net success—perhaps more successful than the 2000 Bush-Gore election itself, which ended in confusion and disarray—and from then on, online political strategy was a legitimate field, even if the guidelines were still pretty much carved in Jell-O.

By mid-decade I think Microsoft realized how difficult and thankless the internet content business really was. *Slate* still fought to resolve core content management dilemmas but was thriving financially at last. Nevertheless, in 2004, Microsoft sold it to *The Washington Post*, and the *Post* wanted to move production back to D.C. Kinsley, who'd been in charge since launch day eight years ago, departed rather than return east. While pedaling away at *Slate*, I had married a Pacific Northwest native and did not necessarily want to go back either. I was relieved when my Microsoft handler asked if I'd stay on and develop video content for MSN.

Online video was more viable now—faster "broadband" DSL connections were proliferating—and YouTube would not launch until 2005, so we saw an opportunity. We did a few interesting things. MSN was the first to live-stream New Year's Eve from Times Square, and we produced a sort of political talk-back feature with Judy Woodruff at *PBS Newshour*, where viewers could post a written question for a political figure and *Newshour* would plant that figure in front of a camera, record an answer, and upload it.

As a content producer I was still growing market share, attracting more internet ad revenue, making money for Microsoft, and now watching in horror as friends back east in traditional media began losing jobs, thanks in part to the shift in media consumption habits I was working on. (CNN, my old shop, was hurting. Soon after I departed, Ted Turner sold the network to Time Warner, and now it might as well have been called CNL: Constant News of Layoffs.) We definitely saw the landscape shifting.

But we were essentially producing TV on the internet—still trying to apply old-school editorial controls to linear content. Looking back, some of it was hard to justify. Anybody who wanted to see the ball drop in Times Square was surely watching Dick Clark on ABC, and the *PBS Newshour* thing was really a slow-motion, unwieldy version of talk radio.

What could MSN do that was truly internet-centric and revolutionary? A smart innovator named Todd Herman proposed a YouTube-style format where any user could upload content. But *Slate* had probably satisfied Microsoft's interest in presenting unedited, unmoderated content, and in any event the company had just wrapped a years-long defense against antitrust action and might have been skittish about more controversy.

YouTube debuted, Yahoo called, and I moved my family south to Santa Monica in 2005.

It was invigorating. Lloyd Braun and Terry Semel, from ABC and Warner Brothers respectively, were newly in charge at Yahoo and planned to run it like the media giants they exemplified. These were not technology kings struggling to figure out content; these were content people who would leverage digital tech in exciting, risk-taking ways. Braun was famous for green-lighting *Lost,* the prime-time ABC drama so risky and weird half its fans didn't understand it.

Yahoo Media Group would create shows, like a television network, but with intrinsic internet sensibility. Traditional models would be reinvented for an interactive environment, where the audience played a role. Vehicles like Yahoo Answers could be mated, somehow, with interactive video. Somewhere in there would be political programming.

I was happy to play. I would get to work with Neeraj Khemlani, a genius former *60 Minutes* producer who functioned as a creative engine for Braun and Semel, and Richard Bangs, the renowned travel-adventure author and host; Bangs had founded Mungo Park, an early Microsoft travel publishing imprint, and helped birth Expedia. Yahoo in 2005 looked to me like the 1927 Yankees. I was happy to get in the lineup and swing.

Yahoo in 2005 looked to me like the 1927 Yankees. I was happy to get in the lineup.

Amid the 2006 midterms, Semel noticed candidates popping up on all the big web publishers, even YouTube, but not us. I, with a little mileage in digital politics, was asked to even the score.

We did our best. We booked Hillary Clinton for Yahoo Answers. We got Mitt Romney to participate via a video application called Jumpcut, where the campaign made raw B-roll publicly available and Yahoo users edited their own 30-second Romney spots. My big challenges were figuring out the analytics end—understanding user behavior and traffic flow—and the legal headaches. For example, the 2008 Romney campaign would later choose one of those Jumpcut mashups to air on New Hampshire TV during primary season. Was that an in-kind contribution? From whom? From Yahoo, which provided the toolset? What do FEC guidelines have to say about *that*?

And I was learning a hard truth about internet content, as were Lloyd and Terry. Blending broadcast and interactive sensibilities was in practice no easy trick. Steer too hard toward traditional, linear, highly controlled content, and you might as well be TV. Correct too far in the other direction and there could be legal problems, or the unmoderated online chaos could make you flash on Dr. Hunter S. Thompson's description of his post-binge Vegas hotel room: "Like the site of some disastrous zoological experiment involving whiskey and gorillas."[36] Pretty much describes the tone of any YouTube comment thread today.

I began to doubt I, or any content producer on the web, could really achieve a sublime balance between responsible editing and user freedom.

But the internet did offer another unique, ripe dimension: user data. By the truckload.

The Republican National Committee was calling from Washington. It was looking for someone to run the digital side of the 2008 campaign. The RNC caught me at the right moment, a lot of us thought Clinton would edge Obama for the Democratic nomination, and I flew back to D.C. to interview. The hiring manager was a woman I knew slightly from my OEOB cable-laying days, Anne Hathaway (not the actress). I accepted an offer to direct the committee's e-campaign division and flew back to California, pondering how to tell my family, whom I had promised upon leaving *Slate* that we'd never have to move back to Washington, that we were moving back to Washington.

They took the news with uncommon good grace and I laid plans. We hauled our stuff across the country and moved into a comfy old townhome in Old Town Alexandria, where the neighbor I bumped into as we both took out our trash at midnight turned out to be Sen. Mark Warner. I was back in the swamp, for sure.

Everything went great, until it didn't.

I am moderate politically, historically a center-right guy, and I had what I thought were honorable goals for the gig. I thought that if we could open up communication mechanisms online, we could reverse the polarity of power flow within the GOP from top-down to bottom-up, and voters would have more influence. As head of digital I could introduce input into the Republican thought process from anyone who cared to pipe up. (Call me an idealist. Considering what happened in the 2010s you might want to call me more than that. I guess I can take it.)

To sharpen internet message delivery, I also wanted to do what the Obama campaign was doing successfully with static voter files: marry them to dynamic data showing us where those voters spent their time online and what they liked. We'd look at their social media habits and utterances, create deeper profiles of voters likely to be on our side, and build outreach models that embraced them and spoke their language. Here, I thought, were the keys to the digital kingdom.

The Republican voter-data effort lagged the DNC's in those days (although the tables would turn later in the decade with tools like Data Trust, a GOP data ecosystem that collects and enhances voter files and puts them to work in campaigns). But I saw a golden opportunity to draw even. Then, five months in, came the morning when a certain colleague entered my office to play hatchet man.

He closed the door, sat down, and leveled a hard gaze across my desk. Shut it down, he said. Your vision isn't going anywhere. It's dead in its tracks. Step away from the keyboard.

We were not going to dynamize static voter data. I had dragged my family to Washington for too little.

Looking back, I suspect the decision saved me from myself. I have always taken risks, but this initiative represented risks I didn't fully appreciate at the time. Cybersecurity was not as big a preoccupation as it later became, but our systems were surely vulnerable to hackers. Data in motion is data at risk. We probably didn't have as much in-house software acumen as necessary. And think of the bad press in the event of a breach.

I would have a long time to ponder the privacy and security implications of manipulating data with such innovative abandon. But the day the hammer dropped, I was devastated. The entrance to the Washington Metro's Capital South station is across from RNC headquarters on the Hill. I remember standing at the head of the escalator, staring dully up at the clouds. With his key insight vetoed, his breakthrough spiked, what was a digital director going to do for the whole coming campaign?

It was a long Metro ride home to Alexandria.

Eventually I found other ways to help the McCain campaign. We built an online ad database that pushed our voter files to a secure location where a third party correlated the data with registered users on Yahoo, MSN, AOL, and elsewhere. (It was 2008, remember.) We identified a pool of around 40 million likely supporters and served up online ads that addressed their interests.

Cautiously, like a Broadway-bound show previewing in Baltimore, we tested our system in a small pond—the Louisiana gubernatorial race, where the Republican horse was Bobby Jindal. The RNC chairman at the time, Mike Duncan of Kentucky, signed off on the experiment, and Karl Rove helped oversee it. It was a lesson in the power of data-driven microtargeting, both thrilling and sobering.

We zeroed in on parts of Louisiana where we wanted to boost voter registration and served banner ads inviting people in those target zones to register to vote. We could tell who was clicking through and tracked them all the way to election day. The big LSU-Auburn football game happened to fall on the same day, so turnout was a challenge all around and there was some early voting—but when the dust settled, we could prove the efficacy of the campaign. 76% of the Louisianans who clicked on the ad and registered to vote actually followed through and cast ballots.

The RNC was pleased. We hustled our digital campaign report over to McCain campaign headquarters like eager small boys. The Obama campaign was outspending us, and we wanted the McCain brain trust to allocate several million dollars to digital efforts like this. We *knew* they worked. Here was the PowerPoint.

It will gladden the hearts of Democrats to know we were unceremoniously dismissed. Despite us brandishing proof of success, the McCain campaign wasn't going to join the RNC digital program—it would stick mostly to traditional, time-tested media and ground-level outreach. We never got funded, and the rest was history. (Eight years later, in 2016, a reverse story unfolded: Donald Trump's campaign went digital on all cylinders, the reticent Clinton camp preferred tried-and-true media strategies, and . . . you know the rest.) I pitched some other ideas to Team McCain that were a little bit out there, like projecting hologrammatic McCains at multiple campaign events around the country so he could seem to be in more places at once. Again, no sale. In the 2020 race, though, Andrew Yang played the hologram card, and during the pandemic lockdown Israeli President Reuven

Rivlin addressed his people as an augmented reality hologram beamed to mobile phones.[37] It'll be fascinating to see where this technology stands by, let's say, 2032.

Between Team Obama's digital proficiency and the stock market crash shortly before the election, it became brutally obvious that McCain-Palin was going to lose. Winners get White House jobs; losers limp off and start consulting firms. After 2008, I only licked my wounds for a short while. I left the RNC, consulted, and worked for a series of startups where my experience mattered. With my old MSN friend Todd Herman, I co-founded Crowdverb, an advocacy company that used crowdsourced, aggregated data to mobilize political activists and promote products. I helped run Cheezburger, the giant online bank of memes and sticky shareables. I traveled abroad at the behest of pro-democracy nonprofits, trying to export digital-political expertise to places like Costa Rica, where the Russians are every inch the assiduous saboteurs they are in the United States, and Malaysia.

I kept tabs on national politics as digital weapons finally proved indispensable. I watched the quality of internet discourse continue to crater, becoming life-or-death terrifying as the COVID-19 pandemic hit. And I had a lot of time to think.

I flirted with supporting third-party presidential candidacies in 2008 and 2012, and in 2016 joined the steering committee for Republicans for Johnson-Weld, the ill-fated Libertarian Party candidate. (Don't tell my father.) I believe internet polarization has helped weaken our two major parties and at some point—I was clearly premature—the internet could facilitate a viable third-party movement, which will attract a core cohort of patriots tired of being bombarded.

The online debate we helped pilot at *Slate* with The Fray, all those years ago, is no longer remotely wholesome or edifying. It's uncivil and increasingly harmful; the platforms where it plays out, vulnerable to abuse or hijack. It has been a long, strange journey from The Fray to Twitter shame campaigns, #FilmYourHospital virus-denier videos, and fake coronavirus cures on WhatsApp that not even WhatsApp can decrypt. The instability is only going to get worse.

My mindset has shifted. I entered digital life believing in the internet's great potential as an equalizer—an accelerant of community and civility. I have learned harsh lessons. Earlier, I harvested user data without pause; now I have misgivings. I now believe the internet is one of the most disconcerting, damaging elements in our democratic process. The dominant form of connectivity today, to my horror, heartens fringe actors—cranks, eccentrics, and extremists. It connects them to like-minded allies and convinces them of false potency. That is not at all what we set out to create, but it's what we've got on our hands now and we have to try to restrain the beast.

I'm raising teenagers. Kids born digital, as they say, who have never known a culture where media was not brakeless, hopelessly splintered, intolerant of thoughtful analysis, even routinely and shockingly abusive. Yet they pay no attention to TV and newspapers; the version of the world they see over the internet is all they know. I want them to reach adulthood in a world that welcomes thoughtful moderation and shades-of-gray reason, not sets fire to it. I'm writing these words, and making the recommendations in the following pages, for them.

We will have to try a lot harder, in the coronavirus era and its aftermath, to counter instability.

We will have to try a lot harder, in the coronavirus era and its aftermath, to counter instability. That is what the rest of this book is about. I believe we've embarked on a new era of technological advancement that will have profound effects on the way our government and politics evolve—or devolve. This is our zero hour. It is time to go to work.

CHAPTER THREE

CODING ISSUES

The Democrats' critical election tech was a "shitshow," allowed the tech CEO. A "tangled morass" compared to the GOP's coolly humming get-out-the-vote juggernaut. "These systems, they're not designed super intentionally from day one, which frankly nothing in the political ecosystem has been."

The CEO vowed his new startup would fix what ailed the Democratic Party. Its digital problems, anyway.

His name was Gerard Niemira, and when he offered up those sound bites to *Wired* in 2019, he was trying to rev up something revolutionary for his party. I understood his perspective, though I was not on his side of the ideological tracks. Niemira's upward path had been similar to mine. He had worked on the 2016 Hillary Clinton campaign as "director of product." There he'd grappled with a legacy data system called Vertica that in Niemira's estimation was kneecapping the whole shebang. "Our data ecosystem is so crazy and overcomplicated and requires so much expertise to run even the simplest parts of these tools," he told the *Wired* reporter, Issie Lapowsky. "It took me four months of being on the [Clinton] campaign to finally understand exactly what was going on."[1]

From what I saw of 2016 as an outsider, I didn't disagree. In the wake of Clinton's loss, a blame-Ivan narrative took hold on the Left. Conventional wisdom gelled fast in anti-Trump quarters: Russian meddling on behalf of Donald Trump had thrown the election. The Democratic operation had been screwed by Kremlin-backed hackers and canny online disinformation campaigns.

That was only half the story—perhaps not even half. Offshore chaos agents sure played a role, pumping the digital infosphere full of fake news. And I'm in no way overlooking scandalous tactics on the part of—among others—Cambridge Analytica, which leveraged Facebook user profiles in scary ways. But to blame trolls alone for Trump's win is to overlook something else: The 2016 Trump digital media team, directed by Brad Parscale, outscored the Democrats on a regulation playing field.

Parscale appalled the old-school political media fixers because he wasn't one of them. He was a small-time hustler from San Antonio who'd come up building cheapo websites for plumbers and gun shops, bid low on a gig of similar scope for Trump International Realty, and found himself embedded in the Trump campaign.[2] His political inexperience meant he was uninhibited about experimenting with digital media. The upshot was the most impressive, effective internet work ever done in a presidential campaign.

Facebook executive Andrew Bosworth agreed. "[Trump] didn't get elected because of Russia or misinformation or Cambridge

Analytica," Bosworth wrote in an inside-the-company post in late 2019. 'He got elected because he ran the single best digital ad campaign I've ever seen from any advertiser. Period . . . they just used the tools we had to show the right creative to each person."[3]

And for reasons I don't claim to fully understand, the Republicans maintained their edge in 2020. There's no brain-power barrier to the Democrats achieving technological parity. None of this is sorcery. But "Republicans have a big advantage this time," conceded Democratic media consultant Ben Nuckels before the coronavirus hit. "They not only have all the data from 2016 but they have been building this operation into a nonstop juggernaut."[4]

The Democrats wobbled into 2020 juggling natural disadvantages both structural (a hard-to-thread Electoral College) and ideological (the long-running, acidic schism between progressives and moderates). They regarded Trump's reelection like the incoming asteroid in *Deep Impact*, an extinction-level event to be thwarted at any cost. Yet they diverted extraordinary energy to knifing or trying to excommunicate each other. (Rep. Alexandria Ocasio-Cortez told *Politico*, bizarrely, "In any other country, Joe Biden and I would not be in the same party."[5]) Democrats struggled to articulate a unified brand or broadly appealing alternative agenda. Yet adroit message design and digital platforms can compensate for a lot of those problems. Surely the Democrats' digital game, at least, could be made to draw even with the GOP's, or even surpass it given the top-quality IQs on the case.

Or not.

Vulnerabilities: we've got a few. In truth, American elections are vulnerable to four distinct types of nonpartisan, equal-opportunity digital threats.

The first, of course, is disinformation from all kinds of trolls, cranks, and mayhem-makers known and unknown. Then come technical attacks from exterior troublemakers out to play havoc with digital resources—scramble them, shut them down, deny service, or make them unusable—and sap confidence in election systems, at both public and expert levels. Those are the two factors that get most of the jittery press. But I think two other threats are just as important: complacency on our own part, which leads to inadequate defenses, and incompetently designed or intrinsically flawed home team technology. When any or all of these threats have an impact, they can make people question the reliability of the process and wonder whether democracy, the way we do it today, is truly giving people results they want.

American elections are vulnerable to four distinct types of equal-opportunity digital threats.

The knives are out right now for targeted digital marketing. But targeted marketing is just an efficiency engine, albeit one sometimes used in this era in unnerving, creepy ways. The microtargeting techniques used on the internet today, which drive custom messages inspired by user profiles, geolocation, and other data? They're the spiritual descendants of telemarketers hustling prepaid burial plots in Florida ZIP codes they know are thick with oldsters. You take your pitch to where you know receptive customers are.

Advertisers have been targeting buyers this way since forever. There's a reason you don't find tampon ads in *Popular Mechanics* or motor oil commercials on *Days of Our Lives*. Market segmentation as an abstract concept is not sinister, just smart and cost-effective. Paying to deliver a message to an unreceptive person who will never respond to your offer is called a "blown impression," and a dumb use of money. But until the internet, market segmentation was comparatively clumsy. Blown impressions in analog days were commonplace and unavoidable. (19th century department store magnate John Wanamaker used to say, "Half the money I spend on advertising is wasted. The trouble is I don't know which half."[6]) In *Mad Men* days, the ad agency had a blurry but fair idea that the primary viewers of *Days of Our Lives* were stay-at-home moms and older women who ran households; hence, spots for floor wax aired there. But Don Draper never received real-time readouts of every soap opera fan in America who watched the show, drove to the store right after the credits rolled, and bought floor wax, and also hamburger and Hawaiian Punch, using a Visa card. That kind of impact report is commonplace in digital media today. Don could infer that his targeted ads had worked, or hadn't, only when the floor wax sales figures rolled in weeks or months later.

Gradually, predictive marketing technologies shrank the gut-hunch elements of the game. The more the message-makers knew about you, the more surgical their targeting became. Predictive marketing determined what mail-order catalogs, credit-card pitches, and charitable appeals you received—as it does today. (You help, too, when you check those boxes on forms or screens and agree to receive "offers of interest to you.")

With internet media and individual data profiles plus unlimited computing power, we can figure out far more. A data analytics start-up where I worked in the 2010s catalogued unique attributes for almost every adult consumer in America. Give us that *Days of Our Lives* fan, and we could tell you her favorite brand of mustard. And how often she buys sneakers, and whether she's ever flown first class. Almost anything. If you wanted to reach female heads of household who bought Grey Poupon and wore Reeboks into Delta Air Lines SkyClubs, we were your guys.

But when it came to improving targeting dexterity, political campaign consultants always trailed the advertising world. In the 1980s, before the consumer internet was a thing, "Most voter lists were barely an improvement over the phone book," wrote political consultant Hal Malchow. "These lists could tell you who was registered to vote and sometimes whether the voter was registered as a Republican, Democrat, or Independent. Usually, that was it. Even this information was difficult to acquire . . . Today, a very different situation exists." Malchow wrote this in 2003. "Almost all counties have computerized their voter lists. [B]oth parties provide precinct targeting data, which measures strength of the party vote in the voter's district and whether or not the precinct is a 'swing precinct'. . . Finally, all of the data used for commercial direct marketing also are available for political professionals.

"Unfortunately, few campaigns tap this treasure trove of information. Even where the information is available, it is seldom examined."[7]

That was the state of the art I helped improve at the RNC, and the Trump campaign went next-level in 2016. (The Center for Digital Democracy found just 8% of the Clinton campaign media budget went for digital, compared to 50% of the Trump campaign budget. Clinton spent $75 million more than Trump on media, but perhaps suffered for hewing mostly to old-school channels with cruder targeting capabilities.[8]) Hal Malchow did brave pioneer work bringing mature statistical modeling and scientific measurement to political campaigns. He's in the American Association of Political Consultants Hall of Fame. But in 2003, Facebook and Twitter were still in the future. Today, digital platforms and better-developed microtargeting make those pesky blown impressions ever-rarer.

"If you have to buy TV in a place like Los Angeles, you're committing to a really expensive move, and it's less targeted because it's such a huge, diverse city," said Kenneth Pennington of Middle Seat, the Democratic digital strategy group. "On Facebook, you're hitting people that you know are in your persuasion or 'Get Out the Vote' audience, and you're not having to pay for it being a big city."[9] Modern targeting tactics can work so well and so subtly, almost literally by osmosis, they make the deployer look psychic.

Here's where the qualms come in. In the abstract sense, optimizing standard marketing tools to advance a political outcome is fair play and smart strategy. Partitioning voters in the digital infosphere via microtargeting techniques, and administering persuasive messages one recipient at a time, can be disorienting and disruptive, but it's still fair play; campaign advertising is not journalism. It's under no obligation to present both sides of the story. But identifying credulous ideologues or low-information voters? Gorging them on fake news, and manipulating their known terrors and biases, so they end up not knowing which way is up, believing falsehoods, or embracing a parallel reality? Over the line.

Dirty tricks work. Politicians and campaigns have always had them in their kitbags. In 1988, Vice President George H. W. Bush ran the Willie Horton TV spot, attacking Michael Dukakis for furloughing a convicted murderer who promptly committed rape. That was effective negative advertising, distasteful but ultimately admissible. When his son George W. Bush ran for the GOP nomination in 2000, though, and his "architect" Karl Rove ran a fake phone poll in South Carolina asking voters how they'd feel about John McCain "if you knew he had fathered an illegitimate black child," that was a dirty trick—grist for a whispering campaign based on a lie—and damnable.[10] It sank McCain in the South Carolina primary and perhaps changed the course of history.

There's a red line in there somewhere. Is it persuasion or propaganda? Negative advertising or character assassination? Truth-bending or reality-smashing? What is new in the digital era is how easy it's become to commit despicable acts of political discourse, how uncheckable and potent they can be, and how negligible the penalties are for building virtual alternate reality domes. 2016 proved the efficacy of lies and disinformation. *LikeWar: The Weaponization of Social Media*, by national defense experts P.W. Singer and Emerson T. Brooking, says fake news received more engagement on Facebook than the top stories from all the major traditional news outlets combined.[11] Which means we'll continue seeing more of it.

Sometimes it's campaigns that cross the line, and sometimes it's freelance hustlers exploiting the digital infosphere for profit. Sometimes it's both at once. Parscale's 2016 Trump campaign team not only copped to online voter suppression, it bared its modus operandi to *Bloomberg News* in loving detail: "We have three major voter suppression operations under way," boasted a Parscale lieutenant, aimed at depressing turnout among white liberals, young women, and African Americans—that is, key Hillary

Clinton cohorts. (Team Trump told black voters in Florida, "Hillary Thinks African Americans are Super Predators," and Clinton lost Florida.[12]) The Parscale operation would wrap a kernel of truth in a welter of slant, decontextualization, and fearmongering and aim the package at surgically chosen cohorts predisposed to believe it. It was the old Willie Horton gambit on digital steroids.

The Trump campaign retained Cambridge Analytica, which applied psychographic modeling techniques to 50 million Facebook user profiles to identify and target American voters prone to influence by pro-Trump propaganda. (The Facebook data was obtained by murky means; most profile owners never gave permission for it to be used this way. After the election, Parscale dismissed psychographic-driven microtargeting as ineffectual; Cambridge Analytica claimed its work had proved integral to Trump's victory.[13])

While Parscale and his team were coloring within the lines— just barely—the Trump bandwagon gained extra velocity from outright lies generated elsewhere. The Kremlin's Internet Research Agency, a merry band of expert propagandists, flooded Twitter and Facebook with bots, trolls, pro-Trump agitprop, and fake content designed to shake faith in the system. From a bang-for-buck standpoint, it might have been the best $1.25 million per month the Kremlin ever spent.[14] And *LikeWar* presents a vivid snapshot of a colony of youthful, nihilistic fake-news jocks in Veles, North Macedonia in 2016, the best of whom made tens of thousands of dollars per month pushing pay-per-click nonsense content to American Facebook users:

> "The Macedonians were awed by Americans' insatiable thirst for political stories. Even a sloppy, clearly plagiarized jumble

of texts and ads could rack up hundreds of thousands of 'shares'. . .

"The viral news stories pumped out by these young, hustling Macedonians weren't just exaggerations or products of political spin; they were flat-out lies. Sometimes, the topic was the long sought 'proof' that Obama had been born in Kenya or revelations that he was planning a military coup. Another report warned that Oprah Winfrey had told her audience that 'some white people have to die.' In retrospect, such articles seem unbelievable, but they were read on a scale that soared past results of the truth . . .

"Of the top twenty best-performing fake stories spread during the election, seventeen were unrepentantly pro-Trump. Indeed, the single most popular news story of the entire election—'Pope Francis Shocks World, Endorses Donald Trump for President'—was a lie fabricated in Macedonia before blasting across American social networks."

It was, concluded *LikeWar* authors Singer and Brooking, an almost comically cheap and effective route to information control—over certain susceptible voter cohorts, anyway. "At the same time that governments in Turkey, China and Russia sought to obscure the truth as a matter of policy, the monetization of clicks and 'shares'—known as the 'attention economy'—was accomplishing much the same thing."[15] Fake news was also good for the economy of hardscrabble Veles, which had perhaps never seen so many new BMWs.

Our political system has roots in an old, expired era of anointed institutions and consensus belief. On our way to today, we passed through a professionalized mass media era—think

Don Draper—but now have landed in a new, third era of technology-intensive campaigning. (Hat tip to Daniel Kreiss at the University of North Carolina for coming up with that three-step framework.) These days, voters steeped in digital media have shorter, more scattered attention spans. They're conditioned to expect personalized appeals, even if they're unaware of, or uncomfortable with, the data profiling behind them. Campaign staffs may or may not be highly professionalized; college interns running Twitter accounts can short-circuit a campaign's managerial pecking order and speak for the whole operation in real time. The quality of a campaign's technological infrastructure can vary dramatically, too, depending on funding and in-house competence.[16] But compared to making TV ads and buying time on broadcast and cable, pitching a candidate via targeted media online is cheap, efficient, and effective, and the message-masters can observe results in real time. Used right, profile data harvested from digital platforms can make fundraising drives more potent, boost rally crowds, and support better-targeted TV ad buys back in the analog world. It can give shoestring campaigns a shot against far fatter bankrolls. A great leveler, amirite?

"The ability to see exactly where campaigns are spending their money online, and with what messages they're driving to which voters, gives us an unprecedented window into a campaign strategy. We can see exactly what voters campaigns are prioritizing, and where they see their path to victory."[17] The utterer was a confident Democratic digital strategist, speaking to *The New York Times* in early 2020. Her name was Tara McGowan, a former CBS News journalist and Obama campaign veteran. She had just founded a nonprofit called Acronym. Acronym's mission was to catalyze next-level digital success on the progressive side of the divide with targeted ads, voter registration drives, and investments in select for-profit technology ventures. Old-school political consultants competing with McGowan for campaign gigs were suspicious. But Ozy.com, the hip online magazine, called McGowan "the Democrats' most dangerous digital strategist . . . a weapon of a woman."[18] Like Gerard Niemira, the scornful tech CEO, McGowan and Acronym were out to boost Democrats into the online major leagues. To get them to parity, at least, with the GOP.

There was much ground to gain. Even after the lessons of 2016, the Republicans were way ahead, especially on the money front.

The disinformation blitz aside, in 2016 Russian hackers punched numerous holes in U.S. election technology, too. They stole Democratic and Clinton campaign emails, weaponized them, and probed the defenses of election websites in every state in the union, with occasional apparent success. Many known hacking cases at the state and local levels, like a reported election-eve breach of Florida election software provider VR Systems that froze laptops and corrupted voter lists at North Carolina polling sites, have been glossed over or forgotten.[19]

Did Russia's hack-and-leak operation really tip the election to Trump? Kathleen Hall Jamieson, a communications professor at the University of Pennsylvania, argues in her book *Cyberwar* that Russia helped Trump win, but the debate is unresolved. What's not in doubt, however, is how unprepared and vulnerable the U.S. was—or how much Vladimir Putin benefits from promoting chaos in Western political discourse. The willfully unedited digital media sphere presents an ideal operating theater.

There was no evidence in 2020—none—that offshore attacks on U.S. politics were lessening in intensity. Peter Pomerantsev, a propaganda expert and former Russian TV producer, told Congress years ago how committed Putin's Kremlin was to this form of asymmetric warfare. Can't compete on military or economic terms? Wage an information war on Western democracies. "We always ask, 'What does Putin want?'" Pomerantsev testified. "He sees the 21st century that is going to be like this—endless subversion, disinformation, economic manipulation—and he might be right." He went on, "This is permanent war."[20]

In January 2020 a California cybersecurity firm, Area 1 Security, said it had detected Russian efforts to infiltrate computers belonging to Burisma Holdings, the Ukrainian gas company implicated in the impeachment case against President Trump. "The timing of the GRU's campaign in relation to the 2020 U.S. elections raises the specter that this is an early warning of what we have anticipated since the successful cyberattacks undertaken during the 2016 U.S. elections," said Area 1 CEO Oren Falkowitz.[21]

And as 2020 rumbled into a higher, noisier gear, it was crazy to worry only about Russia. China, Iran, North Korea, and Saudi Arabia were all thought capable of testing U.S. election defenses, not to mention motivated to do so. The pandemic distracted the country and made it more vulnerable; it was a good time to try something. And foreign tactics were replicable by stateside malefactors. "The most important piece that I tell everybody," said Anthony Ferrante, an Obama-era NSC cyber expert, "is now that it's been done once, everybody can do it."[22]

Experts studying election systems in the U.S. say many flaws remain. Some counties and states still use outdated voting equipment and insecure election software: At the 2018 DEFCON hacker conference, an 11-year-old needed less than 10 minutes to penetrate a sandbox copy of Florida's state election website and change vote totals. Only three states conduct mandatory, scientifically rigorous post-election audits to ensure the final vote count is accurate. "We're still in a situation going into 2020 where there are significant gaps left in the security of election infrastructure," said J. Alex Halderman, a University of Michigan computer science professor who studies voting equipment. "Until we ensure that all of the doors are locked, there will be ample opportunity for foreign adversaries to disrupt or, in the worst-case scenario, change the outcome of close elections."[23]

The federal government seemed in no particular hurry to secure those doors. As Halderman likes to say, there are more federal requirements for whiskey and plastic bottles than for voting equipment, and Trump administration officials stoutly denied Russian interference occurred in 2016, well after everyone else in a position to know affirmed it did. Congress authorized nearly $900 million for better election security in 2018 and 2019, but let states spend the money however they pleased. "Money without some requisites means states could print bigger 'I Voted' stickers instead of actually improving their systems. That's a huge error,"

There are more federal requirements for whiskey and plastic bottles than for voting equipment.

Sen. Mark Warner, top Democrat on the Intelligence Committee, told *Rolling Stone*.[24] National cyberdefenses in 2020 were said to have improved compared to 2016, but still be pockmarked with the digital equivalent of unlocked doors and windows. What about political campaigns themselves, which are some of the primary victims of online disinformation? On the whole, they were oddly quiescent in the face of possible existential doom. "Most political campaigns are unwilling to spend what it takes to set up effective cyberdefenses," said *The New York Times* in early 2020.[25]

Trump began his re-election drive far ahead on digital spending, strategy, and data analytics. Brad Parscale was not merely Trump's digital director this time, he was running the whole thing, which suggested digital media would be at the center of everything. There was talk of the Trump campaign spending $1 billion—an incredible number considering that just eight years earlier, in 2012, Barack Obama and Mitt Romney combined spent $1.12 billion.[26] There would be relentless attacks on Joe Biden's health and character, China for COVID-19, and the establishment press—the campaign was said to have doxxed dozens of influential journalists, stockpiling records of ancient missteps, ready to execute timely takedowns at opportune moments. And Trump benefited from a smoothly synchronized and obedient media support system including Fox News, Sinclair Broadcasting, conservative websites, Facebook foot soldiers, right-wing radio hosts, YouTube influencers, retweeters, and bots, all ready to relay and amplify whatever the campaign said. (*Breitbart* editor Matthew Boyle has said the real, ultimate goal is "the full destruction and elimination of the entire mainstream media. We envision a day when CNN is no longer in business. We envision a day when *The New York Times* closes its doors," he said in a 2017 speech.[27] Until then, Doyle will have to settle for convincing a certain cohort that there's no such thing as truth, which he has done.)

And how would the Democratic Party respond? The Democrats did not have the GOP's eagerly compliant multimedia ecosystem; Democrats online could usually be found fighting among themselves. But they had equal access to most of the same digital bats Republicans were using to hit home runs. Microtargeting custom audiences, and gaming online advertising systems to connect with known sympathizers, was eminently possible. There were no bars on Democratic creativity, speed, or inventiveness. For both parties, the political pros agreed, Facebook, Google, and Twitter would be at the center of the media universe, and critical to victory.

Maybe fake influencers would be, too. According to the *Los Angeles Times*, in early 2020 the short-lived Mike Bloomberg presidential campaign planned to pay "deputy field operatives" $2,500 a month to, well, *pretend* they liked Bloomberg on social media networks.[28] The Bloomberg camp also reportedly retained Tribe, a "branded content marketplace" that connects influencers-for-rent with products and services that want to appear popular online.[29]

And if digital Astroturfing didn't give the Democrats an edge in the digital infosphere, there was always lying. Lying was known to work.

As the 2020 campaign began, Washington journalist McKay Coppins of *The Atlantic* conducted a thought experiment in the pro-Trump infosphere. Using an alias on Facebook he liked Trump campaign pages, followed Trump allies, and joined private MAGA groups. The tsunami of microtargeted propaganda that came his way changed how he apprised *all* Facebook "news," not just Trump agitprop shared by true believers. After a few weeks, Coppins—a shrewd and grounded reporter, generally admired for having his wits about him—no longer knew what was true and what wasn't. Coppins called the forces working on him "a strategy that has been deployed by illiberal political leaders around the world."

"Rather than shutting down dissenting voices, these leaders have learned to harness the democratizing power of social media for their own purposes—jamming the signals, sowing confusion. They no longer need to silence the dissident shouting in the streets; they can use a megaphone to drown him out."[30]

With no moderating influences in the digital infosphere, Coppins imagined the worst-case scenario:

> "On Election Day, anonymous text messages direct voters to the wrong polling locations, or maybe even circulate rumors of security threats . . . As news outlets scramble to correct the inaccuracies, hordes of Twitter bots respond by smearing and threatening reporters. Meanwhile, the Trump campaign has spent the final days of the race pumping out Facebook ads at such a high rate that no one can keep track of what they're injecting into the bloodstream.
>
> "After the first round of exit polls is released, a mysteriously sourced video surfaces purporting to show undocumented immigrants at the ballot box. Trump begins retweeting rumors of voter fraud and suggests that Immigration and Customs Enforcement officers should be dispatched to polling stations. 'Are Illegals Stealing the Election?' reads

the Fox News chyron. 'Are Russians Behind False Videos?' demands MSNBC.

"The votes haven't even been counted yet, and much of the country is ready to throw out the result."[31]

Many months before election day it was easy, and perfectly rational, to lack confidence in the system.

As public concern rose about election integrity, tech innovators toyed throughout the 2010s with the promise of e-voting. Casting ballots via the internet seemed like the answer to a host of problems plaguing elections. Conventional polling places are cumbersome to run, equipment- and labor-intensive, and often depend on unskilled, minimally trained volunteer support. Voting by mail has not been shown to result in serious fraud but brings its own problems, from a shortage of specialist ballot printers to the precariousness of the Postal Service. A system revolving around a secure app might attract more young voters, notorious for low turnouts, and even appeal to shut-ins or people with mobility issues. E-votes could be tabulated instantly at low or no cost. The COVID-19 crisis amped up talk of alternatives to physical polling sites in public places, particularly when the April 2020 Wisconsin primary forced voters to venture out to those sites while the infection rate was spiking.

But e-voting would not be a national silver bullet in 2020. It presents a bigger encryption challenge than tapping your phone to order a Subway footlong. A system has to both anonymize your vote, making sure nobody can tell it was you, and authenticate it, making sure you are you. Most smartphone users don't maintain rigorous cyberdefenses, so hackproofing is an issue. Electoral integrity depends not only on layers of public infrastructure, but on public trust. High-profile failures on the firing line would erode confidence, maybe discourage participation, and generate backlash from voters, journalists, and campaigns. Yet I knew more than one cybersecurity CEO in the 2010s who talked glibly of an imminent e-voting revolution, as if the algorithmic, usability, and obvious security issues were all as good as squared away.

Broad certitude about Russian meddling in 2016 cooled the cheerleaders' jets a little. But quick, simple, broadly accessible e-voting remained a long-term goal. People just had to see the advantages proven—perhaps in some high-profile situation. Besides, whatever the American consumer wanted or needed in the last years of the decade, the breezily confident response was: There's an app for that. We reached for apps reflexively around the clock. Apps replaced hoary old methods for booking flights, finding lovers, making restaurant reservations, and transferring money. We lived on Planet App now. Why not make apps intrinsic to election support, too? How hard could it be?

After work on February 3, 2020, Iowans flocked to 1,678 caucus sites, plus 99 satellite sites outside state lines, to do their thing. The Democratic primary season to this point had been crowded and frenetic, with more than 20 announced candidates vying for the presidential nomination. Yet no clarity had emerged about front-runners or voter priorities. The Iowa caucus would be the scene of the first real, officially recorded votes of the 2020 election. The party was desperate for a little lucidity—an authoritative result to slice through the partisan cacophony in online stories, ads and social media.

In truth, the caucus process had become pretty hard to defend. A rural state more than 90% white was a funny place for an increasingly diverse, urban Democratic Party to kick off presidential balloting. The requirement that caucusgoers actually show up was a discouragement to shift workers, the elderly, and those without cars. Proceedings could be tedious and plod on for hours, alienating the young or half-interested. And Iowa in 2012 and 2016 had delivered unclear results anyway. The 2012 GOP caucus put Rick Santorum and Mitt Romney in a virtual tie, and at the 2016 Democratic event, the same frustration befell Bernie Sanders and Hillary Clinton. You could make an argument to stick a fork in Iowa. But Iowans deftly lobbied the major parties to protect their high-visibility we-go-first position, and the establishment press wasn't too irked. It liked the quirky, countrified, idiosyncratic caucus ritual. The caucus looked like fun on TV; it was a Manhattan editor's idea of storybook heartland participatory democracy.

The night of February 3 offered everything those editors expected from Iowa: high school gyms clumped with civil-tongued, flannel-clad partisans, cable TV live shots from dark and icebound small-town streets, campaign victory events in the biggest "ballrooms" modest three-star hotels could offer . . . everything but results. Any results.

First dispatches from the Iowa Democratic Party alluded to needed "quality checks" on incoming results. This was plausible. New rules for 2020 meant precincts had to report three sets of numbers: raw totals reflecting caucusgoers' initial preferences, revised totals once people initially aligned with low-popularity candidates were allowed to switch to more popular ones, and totals that translated those "final alignment" figures into state delegate awards. It was fiendishly complicated. But as hours dragged by, journalists began hearing that the problem was more than layers of procedural complexity. It was the app tasked with reporting the numbers.

It was called IowaReporterApp. It didn't work.

Precinct captains and other field operatives had been wrestling with IowaReporterApp all day. Sometimes it wouldn't download; sometimes it froze on their phones. (Yes, the crucial task of reporting timely results was dependent on people's personal devices, with goodness knows what security precautions.) Installing the app called for two-factor authentication and PIN passcodes, a lot to ask of often elderly, non-tech-savvy field volunteers. Sometimes, when they tried to load in three tiers of caucus results, the app dumped all the data.

The press quickly learned the Iowa Democratic Party had little or no Plan B in case of app failure. There was a thinly staffed phone center, but precinct officers remained on hold for hours or got hung up on. Pro-Trump trolls on 4chan, the fringy online bulletin board, got hold of the call-in number and posted it, urging others to "clog the lines," which they duly did.

Party leaders at first denied any technology problem existed, but would not say when they'd produce numbers. They disconnected on frantic campaign operatives demanding answers. The Bernie Sanders campaign released its own independently compiled totals and claimed victory. Pete Buttigieg staked the same claim and left the state fast.

People didn't know who to believe. Iowa was in meltdown. The whole point of campaigns investing an aggregate hundreds of millions of dollars in Iowa, over the course of a year or more, was for two or three to claim breakout momentum *on the spot* and fly on to the New Hampshire primary that very night looking like winners. It's not the handful of Iowa delegates who matter. It's the chance for a few top-performing candidates to spin a credible the-people-have-spoken narrative their way, right now, for a press machine starving to inject clarity into a topsy-turvy race. On that front, all the Democratic candidates' investment in Iowa looked utterly wasted.

Finally, Iowa Democratic Party chair Troy Price copped to "coding issues" with the app. But the party refused to say who was responsible, or even disclose who supplied the technology that had wrecked Iowa's brief quadrennial national moment.

The stonewalling worked—for two or three hours. But a little after midnight on caucus night, *HuffPost* outed the architects of the disaster. The app had come from a low-profile tech firm called Shadow. The CEO of Shadow was Gerard Niemira, the guy who'd vowed to end the Democrats' technology "shitshow." Shadow had backing from Acronym, the progressive digital services nonprofit run by Tara McGowan, the Democrats' "most dangerous digital strategist."

Obama campaign manager David Plouffe was on the board of Acronym. He was doing on-air punditry on MSNBC on caucus night, vamping with the "Precincts Reporting" tally stubbornly stuck at 0%, when Shadow and Acronym were outed. He looked like he wanted the 16-ton weight from Monty Python to drop on him from the studio ceiling. "I have no knowledge of Shadow," said Plouffe. "It was news to me."[32]

But back when Shadow opened for business in 2019, McGowan, on behalf of Acronym, took credit for "launching" the company. Both Acronym and Shadow described their relationship as an acquisition.[33] "With Shadow, we're building a new model," she'd crowed, and told a podcast Acronym was Shadow's "sole investor."[34] Now Shadow was blamed for doing for Iowa what electrostatic discharge did for the *Hindenburg*. Sources told *The New York Times* the app had been rushed out in just two months, riddled with flaws, and never properly tested at scale.[35] There were reports that the Department of Homeland Security had offered to evaluate IowaReporterApp, but been told no thanks. And Tara McGowan, it turned out, was married to Buttigieg senior strategist Michael Halle, and the Buttigieg campaign had contracted for other digital services from Shadow.[36] For internet conspiracy-mongers, *that* was the cherry on the shrapnel sundae. It was all they needed to claim the Acronym-backed Shadow app was a secret plot to move votes from Sanders's column to Mayor Pete's. (There was no evidence of this, but on the internet you don't need evidence to fire up a virtual mob, just a holy-moly-would-you-read-*this* kind of word grenade.)

Suddenly Acronym could not put enough real estate between itself and Shadow. McGowan now insisted Shadow had *lots* of investors, not just Acronym, and was merely one small potato among Acronym's *many* ventures. Overnight, Acronym scrubbed references to Shadow off its website.[37] We *launched* Shadow? *Acquired* them? Are you kidding? We barely *know* those guys.

But everybody with an opinion was pouncing at once, all with more or less the same brutal take. Because of the digital screwup, establishment media mavens who'd cherished the Iowa caucus pageant suddenly wanted it beaten to death with pool cues. It was a catastrophe, a disaster, a fiasco, a "perfect storm of incompetence"[38]; it had to be stopped. "The Iowa caucus debacle represents one of the most stunning failures of information security ever," pronounced a CNBC op-ed the day after. "Voters will be paying close attention to how party leaders ensure that votes going forward have clear contingency plans in place, not just to protect against hackers, but from all types of technology failures, including applications that might not work."[39]

The Iowa Democratic Party had paid Shadow about $60,000 to develop IowaReporterApp. In the world of tech development, that's not much money. The Iowa party leadership may have imagined they were getting a cool, reliable app like those they knew as consumers—the United Airlines app, say, or the Charles Schwab app—but $60,000 wouldn't cover the coffee for United's IT team. Perhaps the Iowans didn't know how to ask for or assess scalability and security. Perhaps Shadow had made a rookie error I saw in my days at the dawn of the consumer internet: The gig-hungry development agency agrees to whatever budget the client can afford, not one that covers the actual cost. Train wreck to follow.

It would take nearly a week for Iowa's tabulators to cautiously venture that Buttigieg and Sanders had played to a tie, probably. The putative caucus results delivered the same agonizing paucity of clarity as in 2012 and 2016, with Buttigieg assigned a tiny 0.09% edge along with a ton of caveats. The Associated Press and other news organizations said the final numbers were too suspect for them to call a winner,[40] and a *New York Times* postmortem indicated as many as 10% of precincts had misallocated their delegates anyway.[41] The best that could be said for Shadow's work in Iowa was that it provoked overdue skepticism and scrutiny of an electoral tradition that might have been dangerously haphazard for a long, long time.

It was the most notorious U.S. electoral meltdown for 20 years. Not since the hanging-chad drama in Florida that tainted the 2000 Bush-Gore election had American electoral integrity looked so full of holes. Surveying Iowa reminded me of screenwriter William Goldman's famous summing-up of Hollywood: "Nobody knows anything." And here the uncertainty had been sparked not by badly designed paper ballots and illegible pen marks but by digital tech.

Coding issues! Iowa's app from hell reverberated in deep ways that disturbed politics watchers no matter where they stood on the left-right spectrum. The drama was, to borrow a phrase from spy literature, the sum of all fears. Here came self-described digital revolutionaries casting shade on the sleepy status quo and promising to improve everything with gee-whiz tech. For a pivotal event, they convinced party bosses to toss out reliable low-tech reporting protocols in favor of a new, never-tried high-tech replacement. But the disrupters didn't seem to know as much as they intimated. Their bright ideas did not simply make things worse; they broke the whole process, draining it of value and credibility. They poured fresh kerosene on a master narrative already burning strong, a narrative both sinister and alienating: With digital tech, you just can't tell what's true and trustworthy. And unmasked amid the morning-after rubble of the caucus, the hotshots went silent, passed the buck, or scrubbed their websites.

Iowa blew up at a moment when everyone wanted—needed—some sign that the political system rewards trust. If some new, mewling popular regime in Latin America or southeast Asia had held an election like the Iowa caucus, American democracy watchdogs would call a press conference to deplore it. (At least there was a time when American watchdogs occupied the moral high ground it takes to issue judgments like that. Perhaps in this era of domestic chaos they had best pipe down about other countries' faults.) Ahead lay the lumbering, expensive, and no doubt caustic balance of the 2020 contest. It was hard to imagine the American people placing their confidence in a system whose results were disputed and debated for days or weeks after the voting was over. What Iowa portended for the future of e-voting was anyone's guess.

There was no evidence that nefarious Russians had hacked IowaReporterApp, though analysis suggested it was chillingly, ridiculously vulnerable. (Veracode, a security firm, reviewed the app at *ProPublica*'s request and concluded it "was so insecure that vote totals, passwords and other sensitive information could have been intercepted or even changed . . . Because of a lack of safeguards, transmissions to and from the phone were left largely unprotected."[42])

The terrible lesson of Iowa 2020 was that we didn't need the Russians to wreck an election.

But the terrible lesson of Iowa 2020 was that we didn't need the Russians to wreck an election. While a new passel of rapacious Macedonian disinformation edgelords was counting on the 2020 election to keep them in Cristal and BMWs, we didn't need them to blow up public faith in the process. With enough home-grown hubris and bad decisions, enough resistance to sober, methodical, peer-tested, oven-tempered investments in trustworthy technology, we could blow things up ourselves just fine.

CHAPTER FOUR

TECHLASH

Contact tracing via cellphone networks was key to getting coronavirus-paralyzed America over the crisis, said many health experts, but most Americans didn't trust Big Tech to oversee any such project.

In fairness, only about half this privacy-sensitive nation said it would tolerate phone-based contact tracing under *any* circumstance. 51% were OK with the CDC taking charge, according to an Axios-Ipsos poll. But just 33% trusted the major tech companies. The only prospective honcho the public liked less was the federal government; a mere 31% said, sure, put Washington in control.[1]

The major technology concerns brought a big pandemic-fighting toolkit to the crisis-management table. From the first weeks, the White House sought to tap expertise at Apple, Amazon, Facebook, Google, IBM, and other firms. Smartphone location data in aggregated form might be useful in tracking infection transmission trends; it might help predict COVID-19 hotspots or direct medical resources.[2] A startup called Unacast already used phone GPS data, supplied by games, shopping, and utility apps, to power a "social distancing scoreboard," grading U.S. counties on an A-to-F scale.[3]

But taking things further posed a non-technological problem: deep public suspicion about tracking and monitoring. Countries like South Korea and Israel had gained ground against the pandemic using Big Tech resources like these. But authorities there faced a lot less public cynicism about tech titans' motives. The American presumption seemed to be that any surveillance initiative, even to curb mass death, would somehow be used against the living.

Fear of how a technology platform running a contact-tracing program might actually exploit your personal data, with or without consent, was hardly a paranoid outlook. Tech powers had for years given users ample basis not to trust them. Since way before the coronavirus.

In normal, uninfected times, the swarming white-lit floor of the annual Consumer Electronics Show in the Las Vegas Convention Center smells like any trade show: scorched popcorn, fumes from acres of cheap just-laid carpet, and human fatigue. For decades, I achieved moderate success in the digital world while never forced to make a pilgrimage to CES. But in January 2020 fate caught up with me. Owing to professional commitments, I found myself trudging, footsore, among 170,000 eager tech worshipers from 160 countries.[4] There were 4,400 exhibitors to see and miles of aisles to hike. But like everyone else I kept my eyes peeled for the two most coveted prizes at CES: a digital gadget with intrinsic world-changing potential, and a place to sit down.

Even before COVID-19, there was existential dread abroad about Big Technology in 2020. I expected . . . if not *introspection*, exactly—the digital world hardly ever opts for introspection—at least some nod to current complexities. In the months preceding the show, a former Facebook backer and cheerleader attacked the company as a "catastrophe," and Mark Zuckerberg was carved up in a Capitol Hill hearing. Elizabeth Warren was talking about breaking up Amazon, Google, Apple, and Facebook for the same reasons the feds got AT&T broken up in the 1980s: anti-competitive, monopolistic hegemony. Microsoft President Brad Smith published a book that seemed like a virtual invitation to Washington to negotiate better-regulated operating conditions. Surely these heavy questions would preoccupy the crowd.

But at CES such talk was virtually taboo. CES is the technology industry's safe space, a determinedly uncritical zone. Tech industry keynotes at CES—staged in huge, yawning venues at vast corporate expense—are mostly attaboy bromides calling for transformation without cost or sacrifice, rarely self-searching, never rueful. The establishment press plays along, mostly ignoring policy questions in favor of breezy glimpses of new gee-whiz consumer goods—especially those that can do some cool trick in a twenty-second demo on live TV. There was even an online reality-show competition called *Last Gadget Standing*. CNET this year was particularly enamored of a $449 robotic lap dog named Jennie that keeps company with needy seniors, a $125 Y-shaped toothbrush you stick in your mouth whole, and Pampers Lumi, a smart sensor on a diaper said to enhance babies' sleep quality.[5]

I did not check out Jennie the robot dog, but she had admirers aplenty. I had other stops to make. Whenever we attendees on the CES show floor paused at an exhibitor, a cheery booth staffer in a bold-hued corporate-logo polo asked to scan our badge. For downloading our contact details, we were usually rewarded with some small branded knick-knack. (More advanced strategists offered a few minutes of collapse in a comfy chair.) These casual microtransactions occurred by the million at CES: When the badge owner handed over personal data, they virtually assured themselves a future barrage of emailed demo invitations or sales meeting requests. For this, people plodded away with a pen or tote bag or squeezy rubber stress reliever. Each little trade like this was, of course, an ironic microcosm of the lopsided deals consumers strike online every second of the day, consciously or not. But if CES badge-wearers thought to protect their identity and data in these not-so-innocuous swaps, most suppressed the impulse. Those squeezy rubber things looked too good.

Outside the CES pleasure dome, Big Tech was of course in trouble—not yet with government regulators or prosecutors, maybe, but certainly with the average citizen. Surveys caught a gathering sense of frustration and irritation with technology providers, plus wisps of resignation. A November 2019 Pew Research Center report told a tale that might have sounded like Sanskrit on the peppy show floor in Vegas: 81% of Americans believed the potential risks of companies collecting data about them outweighed the benefits. Although billions had been invested in high-profile, power-branded cybersecurity efforts during the 2010s, 70% believed their personal data was less secure than five years ago.

Most Americans, according to Pew, lacked confidence that companies were good stewards of their data: 79% said they were "not too" or "not at all" confident that companies will admit mistakes and take responsibility if they misuse or compromise personal information; 69% doubted firms would use their personal information in ways they would be comfortable with; 81% believed they had little or no control over the data companies collect about them; and 59% said they understood "very little" or "nothing" about what those companies do with their information.[6]

Yikes. A normal industry suffering such a trust crisis might acknowledge the kernel, at least, of a serious threat. It is hard to succeed in the cornflake or shampoo rackets if 79% of your market doesn't trust you. Yet Big Tech seemed to think itself immune, and the vibe at CES said so. The Chinese concern Huawei, for example, is identified as a threat to U.S. national security; both Republican and Democratic leaders agree on it,[7] and the Trump administration has rallied allies to shut Huawei out of critical digital infrastructure. But the Huawei booth at CES was mobbed. They had cool stuff.

Politico correspondents Nancy Scola and Cristiano Lima reported the Huawei and similar tableaux at CES with telegraphed bemusement. "[T]hrough it all ran a carefree, even triumphalist streak—a display of spending and celebrity appearances in which tech's travails in the capital were barely a blip," they wrote.

"Of the [United States] national policy debate, there's still a feeling that it's kinda far away," said Zach Graves, the head of policy at the right-of-center tech advocacy group Lincoln Network, calling Washington too slow-moving and too ignorant of how tech works to merit much concern. "There's still a little bit of the attitude of 'Build it, disrupt, and deal with the regulation later.'"[8]

Ah, those poor, slow-moving representatives of the people . . . too old and jowly to appreciate Big Tech's special brand of disruptive transformation. CES did stage one solitary panel discussion on Elizabeth Warren's ideas regarding trust-busting Big Tech behemoths. It went off without fanfare in a quieter, faraway precinct of the Convention Center, a world away from the teeming mobs admiring Jennie the dogbot. The session was also notably uncontaminated by anybody taking Warren's side. "It would have been even more lively if a 'break 'em up' advocate was also on the panel," Robert Atkinson, president of the Information Technology and Innovation Foundation, told *Politico.*[9]

But a lively discussion depends not only on multiple points of view but mutual respect. And in 2020 the high church of Big Tech, the Consumer Electronics Show, was mainly modeling dismissal. Even before resistance to coronavirus contact tracing, a techlash was gathering in the world at large. A popular backlash, a broad and angry if slow-building rebuke of a rapacious, exploitative business sector configured to, in Mark Zuckerberg's immortal phrase, move fast and break things, leaving others to sweep up the pieces and bind the wounds. By 2020, Big Tech's traditionally careless innovation culture had scoped and scaled upward—from breaking incumbent business verticals like storefront travel agencies, local newspapers, and the landline phone business . . . to injecting toxins into the sinew of democracy itself.

The integrity of elections, authoritatively curated information, the quality of public discourse, sources you can believe: All these things are threatened by Big Tech, as surely as Netflix threatened Blockbuster. Surely this clear and pervasive danger merited front-and-center scrutiny at CES, under the tech industry's brightest spotlight. But no. Scan your badge, take a selfie with Jennie, move on. So much coolness still to see.

You can subdivide the players that have gotten us into this crisis into three rough groups.

First, the most pervasive and influential digital innovators and platform providers, whom I'm referring to collectively as Big Tech. Second, advertisers, marketers, and data analytics mavens, who bring us a long history of research-based, targeted messaging and today exploit Big Data with ever-increasing effectiveness. And Third, the principal forces that leverage Big Tech and Big Data together. Here I'm talking about politicians and campaign managers, advocacy groups, PACs, and information aggregators, companies, hacktivists and chaos agents, and even individuals—all of whom manipulate the information environment, reduce citizens' ability to make informed judgments, and advance their own objectives.

After a generation of mostly unobstructed progress, the terrain in 2020 was changing under Big Tech's feet. Digital media had advanced from a geek's hobby to society's spinal column. The concerns had scaled up from merely driving Borders out of business to shrouding politics and elections, and the essential business of understanding and choosing leaders, in a thick fog of lies, insults, and manipulation.

After a generation of mostly unobstructed progress, the terrain in 2020 was changing under Big Tech's feet.

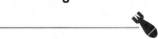

These were giant concerns compared to the old days, when technocrats hosting CES demos won standing ovations for making a stuttering streaming video sort of work. But Big Tech's cultural sensibilities had not evolved accordingly. Tech culture had become a perfect storm of technical mastery, ubiquity, a rebellious teenager's instinct for evading responsibility, and historic curatorial unconcern.

To understand where Big Tech acquired its collective insouciant attitude toward digital citizens, look west, to Seattle in the late 1970s—and the beginnings of Bill Gates' Microsoft.

When Gates first came to public attention, he was no icon—not yet—but the culture greeted him as an almost cuddly nerd archetype. Gangly and uncombed, he was just 21 when he co-founded Microsoft in 1976, and he looked 14. He came off like a less self-assured Anthony Michael Hall in a John Hughes movie, a folk hero to the socially abject. Way before Windows was a gleam in anybody's eye, when Microsoft was readying MultiPlan, a spreadsheet program and precursor to Excel, Gates resisted any direct contact with customers. Gates biographers Stephen Manes and Paul Andrews wrote:

> "Gates . . . succinctly summed up Microsoft's policy in an internal memo: 'We do not talk to any End Users.' End users—the people who actually ended up working with software—had never been Bill Gates's favorite people. End users tied up the phone with stupid questions. End users stole software. Microsoft's flat-fee OEM [original equipment manufacturer] deals minimized its exposure to piracy by those same questionable end users. Gates was far happier dealing with OEM customers and letting them handle the rabble."[10]

Gates had to have his arm twisted into selling software direct to individuals. Even then, he briefly isolated the venture as a separate unit, Microsoft Consumer Products. Pesky consumers.

Well into the consumer PC era, and then the rise of the civilian-friendly World Wide Web, tech's high priesthood remained derisive toward laypeople. It surfaced in sometimes casually brutal ways. (Tech support jocks working the phones traded knee-slappers about "stupid" users, like the senior citizen who thought the pop-open CD drive tray on his desktop computer was a coffee cup caddy. The device had no label nor instructions; an empathetic person might call this a tech usability shortcoming, not a customer idiocy tell. But that's not how the beloved anecdote passed into legend.) Even the odd customary term for a technology customer, "user," had a pejorative, dehumanizing ring. As a friend observed, only two industries call their customers "users," and the other one is based in Colombia.

It's hard to overestimate Gates' long-term cultural influence on tech sector attitudes and leadership style. Gates' behavioral notes remained totemic a generation later. Not only was Gates brilliant, not only was he opaque and elusive, intolerant of most other mortals, gruff, and the opposite of empathetic, but acting this way made him the richest man on Earth.

The Gatesian example was widely imitated in Big Tech, right down to his view of end users. When I moved to Seattle in the mid-1990s to help launch *Slate,* I was surrounded by tyros attempting to replicate the Gates success formula, though mostly without the "brilliant" part. Fast-talking internet hustlers spoke of "owning eyeballs" and making sites "sticky" to ensnare people. On consumer-facing websites, sneaky anti-customer conventions took hold, like negative opt-out boxes to fool the distracted, where instead of actively ticking a box to receive or join or buy something, you have to notice and *untick* a box to *avoid* receiving or joining or buying something. There were infuriating rashes of pop-ups that took over your browser, or customer support channels that were nearly impossible to find, or recurring, auto-billed subscriptions that were almost impossible to cancel. The breezy, who-cares attitude toward end user rights was maybe best exemplified by dense, tiny-type Terms of Service agreements designed to defy reading—although, to complete most any transaction, you have to certify you've done so. Big Tech makes it easy: You can click the "I Agree" box without summoning the TOS text itself. Goodness knows what you're agreeing to. It can be like signing car loan papers in pitch darkness.

But any user pique about the tedious aspects of the World Wide Web was of small concern to Big Tech. The orgy of eyeball-farming in pursuit of wealth drowned out everything else.

The storm drains in Seattle and Bellevue in the late 1990s seemed to geyser $100 bills. Everywhere I looked, the most demented, dead-end ideas for internet businesses got funded by venture capitalists panicked about missing the next big hit. For every Amazon there were dozens of duds in the first dot-com boom—from Kozmo and Webvan, the cash-flushing grocery delivery services, to the virtual currency Flooz nobody remembers, to Pets.com with its beloved but soon unemployed sock-puppet dog. But a lucky many attached themselves to other IPO-bound rockets at the right moments and became wealthy. After a year or two with an at least momentarily sexy startup, preferably in a cool exposed-brick open-plan office cluttered with blocky, whirring computers, dogs, and a foosball table, any random young punter might totter back into the Northwest drizzle having pocketed more than both their parents would earn in two whole working lifetimes, with their 30th birthday still years ahead.

The scale of the possible rewards warped some tech people at a molecular level. Paul Schell was mayor of Seattle 1998-2002, through the inevitable crash: "There were too many people getting too rich, too fast, and honestly believing they earned it. Our . . . daughter had a friend who started working as a secretary at Amazon, and she ended up being worth $4

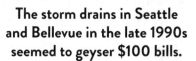

The storm drains in Seattle and Bellevue in the late 1990s seemed to geyser $100 bills.

or $5 million. And she was explaining to her dad, well, I worked really hard, Dad, for that $5 million."[11] It was like a crazy lottery that could be won without much experience, or an MBA or long-term durable business idea, or even profits. It could certainly be won without a high-touch customer service ethic.

Steve Jobs at Apple, the other tycoon, the alt-Gates, was ascribed far more mystic design and branding sense. Apple products were fashion icons, intuitive and sensual; they purred their way onto your lap and into your purse and pocket and made grown adults go gooey. (Microsoft's utilitarian, sometimes difficult-to-decipher Windows aesthetic, not so much.) Jobs had a far better idea than Gates of how to stroke and cultivate his fan base, who revered him as a beneficent deliverer of miracles, back when the iPod and iPad really did seem like miracles—*Star Trek* props made real. But Jobs was no avuncular father figure either. If anything, he was more abrasive and severe than Gates. Apple maintained a cool distance from customers. As time passed, the company made whim-like product changes that seemed more likely to please aesthetes than make life easier, deleting the headphone jack from the iPhone 7 and standard USB ports from Mac laptops. At the end of the day, while most Apple products were sexy, they were all expressions of what Apple in its unilateral, inscrutable wisdom wanted to do for—or to—customers.

Some technology titans seemed to look at users the way westward settlers regarded herds of buffalo on the Great Plains: as an inexhaustibly exploitable natural resource. Unless ideating a new labor-saving app for the upper-middle class, the tech elite tended not to empathize with end users' inner lives (let alone advocate for them in ginger areas like privacy), any more than a 19th-century buffalo hunter prayed for the souls of the beasts he shot. The business culture defined by Gates and Jobs gave this mindset a tacit blessing: Keep customers faceless, keep your distance; keep your eye on what they might be convinced to believe, do, or buy next.

This considered, chilly gulf between voracious digital innovators and a citizenry more or less at their mercy helped precipitate today's trust crisis. One wonders how Big Tech culture might have evolved in friendlier ways had its founders been more humanistic and embracing. Imagine Herb Kelleher running Microsoft while Bill Gates ran Southwest Airlines. Or John Bogle, inventor of index funds and champion of the little-guy investor, running Apple while Steve Jobs took charge of Vanguard. The mind reels.

For all the oracular powers they were said to possess, first-stage web innovators foresaw pretty much none of the internet's eventual transformative applications. In the same way Depression-era futurists could imagine larger, faster steam locomotives but not 747s, early-stage internet thinkers did not envision Amazon, eBay, Craigslist, YouTube, or Spotify; all those things were surprises. So were Facebook, Instagram, Twitter, and the other social media movers. (Not even Twitter imagined how Twitter would metastasize.) They didn't anticipate the clunky, boxy, wired-to-the wall PC would be lapped by hand-held mobile devices hooked into robust wireless networks—at least, not so quickly. (Microsoft, preoccupied with protecting its Windows franchise on desktops and laptops, famously missed the mobile phone and handheld tablet revolutions.) The business of search, and the awesome power that came with optimizing and monetizing search functionality? Another surprise, courtesy of a company not founded until 1998: Google.

And although cybersecurity software did exist in the 1990s, if any visionary of the time foresaw today's minefield of hacks, DDOS attacks, data breaches, identity theft, and ransomware, they seem to have kept it to themselves. They built vulnerable infrastructure riddled with attack vectors, and so inspired a whole new category of bad guys. In the early 1990s, there were only a few tens of thousands of known malware samples on the internet. By 2014, it was estimated that 500,000 unique malware samples were spotted *daily*.[12] Only in the 2010s did cybersecurity become a hot sector, with more than 1,000 startups chewing through VC capital, plotting IPOs, and dressing airport concourses with flashy brand campaigns bristling with rockets and stone fortresses and padlocks. RSA, born as a small and sleepy cybersecurity conference for a few unsung cryptographers, mushroomed into a giant annual CES-ish trade show in San Francisco for 45,000; it conveyed nonstop optimism while cyberattacks kept proliferating, and also smelled of charred popcorn and carpet glue.

At the dawn of the 2020 electoral cycle every critic of Big Tech had an alpha target in their crosshairs—Facebook—and a standard demand: accountability. Everyone knew Facebook had piped insane volumes of misinformation out to the 2016 electorate. Facebook practices raised elemental questions about whether people understood what they were voting for, or why. The company had been knocked back on its heels by plausible stories of Russian interference. Electoral integrity—faith in the infosphere people use to make decisions—hung in the balance.

Struggling to respond, Facebook managers were discovering what every ink-stained newsroom pro already knew: Editing is hard. They also found that in the shadow of 2016, their standard dodge—that because Facebook was a platform, not a media company, it bore no responsibility for third-party actions—was now getting laughed out of the public square. Facebook could no longer excuse itself as a passive pipeline, like a cable television provider, which you could hardly blame when your toddler overheard swear words on HBO. Facebook policies and algorithms actively shaped its users' individualized infospheres, ergo their ideas of reality.

In certain countries, including the U.S., Facebook in late 2016 rolled out partnerships with third-party, independent fact-checking organizations. Product managers promised to use technology to flag false stories; the fact-checkers would assign ratings and add reference articles. False-rated stories would be demoted by Facebook algorithms, getting less play in peoples' feeds. But demonstrably fake stuff would not be yanked, necessarily; nor would its originators be banned, so long as they were real people and not fake accounts. "If a Facebook Page or website repeatedly shares misinformation, we'll reduce the overall distribution of the Page or website, not just individual false articles," assured Facebook's Tessa Lyons, while also conceding, "We need solutions beyond fact-checkers."[13]

The measures looked like small beer. In 2019, tech sector venture capitalist and early Facebook investor Roger McNamee crucified his progeny in a 350-page takedown-slash-expiation, *Zucked: Waking Up to the Facebook Catastrophe,* wherein he decried Facebook's "invasive surveillance, careless sharing of private data, and behavior modification in pursuit of unprecedented scale and influence" and charged CEO Zuckerberg's idealism was "unbuffered by realism or empathy."[14] (McNamee testified that he approached Zuckerberg and Facebook COO Sheryl Sandberg in torment, days before the 2016 vote, sharing his gut apprehension that Facebook was warping the election and threatening U.S. democracy, only to be icily rebuffed.)

Facebook wasn't the only public target. Google's head of international relations, Ross Lajeunesse, quit over Google's refusal to compensate for development of custom-censored search products for the China market—a project code-named Dragonfly—with sincere human rights initiatives:

> "[E]ach time I recommended a Human Rights Program, senior executives came up with an excuse to say no. At first, they said human rights issues were better handled within the product teams, rather than starting a separate program. But the product teams weren't trained to address human rights as part of their work. When I went back to senior executives to again argue for a program, they then claimed to be worried about increasing the company's legal liability. We provided the opinion of outside experts who re-confirmed that these fears were unfounded. At this point, a colleague was suddenly re-assigned to lead the policy team discussions for Dragonfly . . . I then realized that the company

had never intended to incorporate human rights principles into its business and product decisions. Just when Google needed to double down on a commitment to human rights, it decided to instead chase bigger profits and an even higher stock price."[15]

So much for "Don't be evil," the Google motto still lingering in the public mind, though it actually vanished from the corporate code of conduct in spring 2018.[16]

Tools and Weapons: The Peril and Promise of the Digital Age was the book from Brad Smith of Microsoft, who cannily urged Big Tech to take more responsibility. "When your technology changes the world, you bear a responsibility to help address the world you helped create," he wrote.[17] Former Secretary of State Madeline Albright blurbed a rave: "Brad Smith understands that technology is a double-edged sword—unleashing incredible opportunity but raising profound questions about democracy, civil liberties, the future of work and international relations."[18] While the occasional Microsoft move still raised eyebrows, Smith seemed to have sensed the zeitgeist shifting and staked out smart, pragmatic ground.

But it was raining hostile op-eds. Roger McNamee booked endless hits on cable news. Conventional wisdom queen Peggy Noonan called Zuckerberg an "imperious twerp" and noted Big Tech's $55 million lobbying spend in Washington in 2018.[19] A June 2019 Pew Research survey showed the percentage of Americans who thought Big Tech was good for the United States collapsing a wild 21 percentage points in four years, from 71% to 50%.[20]

The techlash was brewing, out there on the Great Plains. Maybe the buffalo had finally had it up to here with their hunters.

In fall 2019, Zuckerberg was questioned at a House hearing on Capitol Hill and did not seem to grasp the import of the moment.

Mark Zuckerberg is our era's one-man embodiment of Big Tech, succeeding Bill Gates and Steve Jobs as the industry's main avatar and target. Gates in his time was rumpled and halting; Jobs, ascetic and wizardly. Zuck, on the other hand, manages to present as both hapless and sinister, no mean feat. His distance from regular mortals, his alien-ness, is part of the cultural narrative. Whatever benefit of the doubt Gates and Jobs once enjoyed is gone for Zuck. (Alex Moffat on *Saturday Night Live* plays Zuck as perplexed by—and terrified of—simple human contact.)

Say what you will about Rep. Alexandria Ocasio-Cortez, she knows how to frame a zinger in the committee room, and Zuck should have seen her coming. What, AOC asked, is the point of fact-checking stories on Facebook when prominent paid Facebook ads are allowed to parade fiction masquerading as fact?

> **AOC:** "Would I be able to run advertisements on Facebook targeting Republicans in primaries saying they voted for the Green New Deal? If you're not fact-checking political advertisements, I'm trying to understand the bounds here of what's fair game."
>
> **Zuckerberg:** "I don't know the answer to that off the top of my head."
>
> **AOC:** "Do you see a problem here with a complete lack of fact-checking on political advertisements?"

Zuckerberg: "Congresswoman, I think lying is bad. I think if you were to run an ad that had a lie, that would be bad. That's different from it being—in our position, the right thing to prevent your constituents, or people in an election, from seeing that you had lied."

AOC: "So you won't take down lies? Or you will take down lies? It's a pretty simple yes or no."

Zuckerberg: "Congresswoman, in most cases, in a democracy, I believe people should be able to see for themselves what politicians they may or may not vote for are saying and judge their character for themselves."[21]

"Yeah, right," sneered columnist Tom Friedman, recapping the exchange. "As if average citizens are able to discern the veracity of every political ad after years of being conditioned by responsible journalism to assume the claims aren't just made up."[22]

Zuck's ungainly equivocation united right and left in outrage. Republican Charlie Sykes, peeved, shot back: "[F]act checking is not inconsistent with free speech and is decidedly not hostile to democratic norms. Truth is not antagonistic to freedom; think of it as the oxygen of democracy.

"But, wrapped in his boundless self-regard, Zuckerberg avoids asking himself whether democracy can survive the asphyxiation of reality. So, he refuses to do what other media companies have done for years . . . Mark Zuckerberg won't save us. But he's wrong not to try."[23]

From across the aisle came Ocasio-Cortez's rejoinder: "The future, and our future, is in public systems, and it's in publicly owned systems, because we need to take power over our lives again. I don't know about you, but I don't want Mark Zuckerberg making decisions over my life."[24]

Things could hardly have gone worse for Zuck up there. He had played the usual Big Tech face cards: a show of solicitous concern, twinned with the old mantra, the unshakable commitment to moving fast and breaking things. It usually worked, or it wouldn't be the go-to play. But we had arrived at a new level, perhaps without Zuckerberg realizing it. What looked ripe for breakage here was not another Jurassic business vertical, like encyclopedias or cable television. Most industries crushed by internet forces and Big Tech were practically asking to be disrupted anyway. But this—*this* was democracy on the block.

Democracy was not asking to be disrupted. It was already under strain: Election turnout was slumping. The worst-performing demographic on election days was voters under 30; more voters identified as neither Democrat nor Republican but independent.[25] The whole system was afflicted with cynicism, misinformation, and corrosive sums of money. It needed stabilization, confidence-building strategies, and inducements to citizens to participate. Wouldn't fixing politics be an inspiring challenge for Big Tech? Not that any private interest had the power to remake things single-handedly, but now that tech platforms comprised people's dominant information channel—and they were so polluted, so suspect—surely they might wish to try?

No. On the key questions—will you take responsibility for stemming the lies that flow across your platform? Will you stop taking money for abetting disinformation campaigns?—the answers were no. There would be some modest gestures to demote fake stories when they were spotted, some fact-checkers deployed, but other than that, the American people were on their own.

The irony hit like an ISP outage on Cyber Monday: We've got an app for the most trivial of needs, like finding out if it's dark outside, but when it comes to election integrity, we got nothing. Hilariously, as Zuckerberg left the hearing room, Democratic Sen. Elizabeth Warren bought Facebook ads claiming Zuck had endorsed Donald Trump for reelection. Entirely false, troll move, but because Warren was a real person, the lie qualified to stay up.[26] Zuck's own employees took their dismay with their boss to the streets: "Misinformation affects us all," complained more than 250 in an open letter to Facebook management. "Our current policies on fact-checking people in political office, or those running for office, are a threat to what FB stands for. We strongly object to this policy as it stands. It doesn't protect voices, but instead allows politicians to weaponize or platform by targeting people who believe that content posted by political figures is trustworthy."[27]

Imagine you own the biggest supermarket in town. It is your policy to stock any food product from any provider that pays you to rent shelf space. In your frozen aisle are many varieties of Hot Pockets. One day an ersatz Hot Pocket supplier, nothing to do with the real deal, pays you to mix counterfeit products up with the legit ones. Among the authentic Ham & Cheese and Pepperoni Pizza Hot Pockets, your shoppers are suddenly puzzling over Peppermint Salami flavor and Clock Parts & Pencil Shavings flavor . . . they kind of *resemble* Hot Pockets, but there's no nutrition label or ingredients list, and the small print on the box is in Russian. Imagine further that your stony silence as consumers are hospitalized draws interest from Congress, and you land in a Capitol Hill hearing room:

AOC: "Do you see a problem here with your complete lack of verification that these fake Hot Pockets you sell, which make people really sick, are actually from the Nestle Corporation, supplier of authentic and tasty Hot Pockets?"

You: "Congresswoman, I think counterfeit, poison food is bad. I think if you were to sell a fake Hot Pocket stuffed with clock parts and pencil shavings, that would be bad. But it's not our job to prevent people in our store from buying food that will make them sick."

AOC: "So you won't pull those horrible, sick-making items from your store? Or you will? It's a pretty simple yes or no."

You: "I believe people should be able to see for themselves what food in our store they may or may not purchase and judge their character for themselves."

That'd be the end of your retail career, right there. You wouldn't get out of the hearing room and back to your Uber alive. Now imagine the stakes are bigger than merely clarifying the true nature of microwave snacks. The issue is helping a well-informed electorate choose a government—oh, but you don't have to imagine that.

In 2020, Facebook moderated the line Zuckerberg laid down in that congressional hearing room—a little. New rules proscribed "misleading manipulated media" if it met two criteria: It had to be "edited or synthesized" in a deliberately misleading way, *and* "It is the product of artificial intelligence or machine learning that merges, replaces or superimposes content onto a video, making it appear to be authentic."[28]

By "manipulated media," Facebook meant deepfakes: sophisticated computer-generated videos depicting events that never happened; or public figures saying things they never actually said. In the run-up to the December 2019 UK election, uncanny deepfakes made the online rounds showing Labour Party head Jeremy Corbyn endorsing his fierce rival Boris Johnson ("Back Boris Johnson to continue . . . A prime minister that works for the many, and not the few.") and Johnson throwing his support to Corbyn ("Only he, not I, can make Britain great again").

Such put-ons—the above were produced by a British think tank to draw attention to the deepfake problem—were now candidates for excision from Facebook. But critics instantly jumped on the narrow criteria. Not all altered videos were covered. Satire or parody were spared. A viral video of House Speaker Nancy Pelosi, edited so she appeared to be drunk, viewed millions of times in 2019? That was fine. "Facebook acknowledged that its fact-checkers had deemed the video 'false,' but Facebook declined to delete it because, as a spokeswoman said, 'We don't have a policy that stipulates that the information you post on Facebook must be true,'" reported *The Washington Post* with a straight face.[29] Nor did the revised Facebook policy appear to redline videos with mislabeled footage or out-of-context quotes, which could be just as misleading to the unwary as any deepfake.

The world didn't love it.

Facebook's obstinacy about fact-checking political content—never mind banning fabrications—created an opportunity for Twitter. When it came to political content, Twitter in 2019 had a still grimier reputation, if such a thing was possible. The platform was never meant for even frivolous political broadcasting. It was first deployed in 2006 as a kind of group-send SMS app when many smartphones lacked native text capability. The idea was for small circles of friends to stay in touch, not to change the course of nations. The 280-character format (up from 140) required users to fire off short bursts of words that, inexplicably, could not be edited once posted, only deleted. Reading an endless Twitter stream of up-yours-pal political invective was often as not an indulgent, vertiginous, guilty experience, like eating a whole sack of Chips Ahoy—the opposite of life-affirming.

And Twitter sure seemed to enforce house rules of decorum selectively. Nobodies earned time-outs for attacking and abusing people, but verified blue-check-rated public figures, newsmakers, were often cut some slack. That included President Trump, for whom berating foes on Twitter was second nature. Never-Trumpers were always demanding suspension of his personal account for terms violations. Whether Trump was good for business or Twitter just feared inflaming the president and his posse, it never happened—although a gadfly Twitter account, @SuspendThePres that did nothing but copy presidential tweets verbatim was promptly banned for "glorifying violence."[30] Twitter and its CEO, Jack Dorsey, had been thrust into a wholly unanticipated role in the nation's political wars, and had not always gone to the mat, exactly, in defense of truth, comity, and edifying discourse.

It was something of a surprise, then, when in May 2020 Twitter suddenly slapped fact-checking labels on two particularly dubious Trump tweets attacking mail-in voting. The action elicited howls of rage from Team Trump and, from the president himself, a grumpy executive order to see about going after Big Tech for suppressing free speech. (Trump wasn't the only blue-check Twitter player so sanctioned. A Chinese foreign ministry spokesman who claimed COVID-19 might have been imported into China by the U.S. military got the same treatment.[31]) Earlier, and more consequentially, Twitter outright banned all paid political advertising, globally. "We believe political message reach should be earned, not bought," tweeted Dorsey.[32] When you considered the sludgy tactics many politicians used to "earn" their reach on Twitter, it was not as noble a gesture as it first seemed, though Dorsey chased the ban with a stab at setting cross-platform standards to limit hate speech, a project called Bluesky. If it didn't help, at least it didn't seem to hurt. Maybe we were finally spying a glint of conscientious platform management.

Brad Parscale of the 2020 Trump campaign complained the Twitter ad ban was "yet another attempt by the left to silence Trump and conservatives, since Twitter knows President Trump has the most sophisticated online program ever known."[33] Trump and allies were the opposite of silent on Twitter, and the ban applied to liberals too, but in the reflexively contentious digital infosphere, the other side was always said to be plotting something.

In early 2020, subscribers to Microsoft Office 365, which gives access to Microsoft productivity software (Word, Excel, PowerPoint, Outlook, *et al*) as an online service with a monthly subscription fee, got an email out of left field: "Welcome to MyAnalytics."

"Your Office 365 account now includes MyAnalytics, a way to discover how you work," declared the email from Microsoft.[34]

In truth this was *Microsoft* discovering how you work, *Microsoft* finding out where your time goes—you probably already know— by observing how you used Office applications. MyAnalytics sent users periodic reports (including incongruous "Wellbeing Edition" dispatches during COVID-19 lockdowns, when a lot of users were likely stuck at home, eating or drinking too much, and cracking up).

MyAnalytics just started happening to people one day. There must be a business case for vacuuming up all this data beyond gifting end users with gratis "personalized readouts" of their email and Skype habits. Multiply this case a hundredfold, and you begin to appreciate how rich, deep and informative the average Joe's consolidated digital data profile is.

In the context of everyday internet use, MyAnalytics is no big deal. Passively strewing personal data in your online wake for the edification of Big Tech has grown unremarkable—at least, that's how Big Tech wants you to see it. Google jots down the news stories you like and uses an algorithm to tune your news feed; it tracks your search history and Chrome surfing habits without really asking. Facebook algorithms curate your conveyor-belt feed of posts from friends, and political and other advertising, in part by watching and responding to your every input on Facebook. Amazon remembers not just everything you order, but every item you glance at; if you consider one stuffed Godzilla for three seconds, but conclude it's too scary for your kid and move on, Amazon will nevertheless dispatch endless entreaties to buy Godzillas of all sorts for months to come.

Big Tech's analytics wizards are too often aided by their own subjects. Your smartphone's geolocation functions know virtually every movement you make, for work or play, whether you visit

Dubuque or Dubai; if there's a gap in the record, the app may ping you and demand to know where you were last Tuesday at 10:45 a.m., and some people eagerly fill in the blank for the sake of a complete map. Driving surveillance is commonplace, whether or not you opt into an insurance company's tracking program and plug a telematics sensor into your OBDII jack. Those indignant folks who told the Axios-Ipsos pollsters there was no way in hell they'd accept a contact tracing effort managed by Big Tech? Some probably let State Farm, Progressive, or Allstate monitor their every Costco run, and maybe also stops at dive bars and no-tell motels, in exchange for a little lower insurance bill.

As part of a privacy investigation, the *Washington Post* tore down a two-year-old Chevy Volt and found GM's onboard computer surreptitiously storing the driver's phone call records, contacts, and route data including all stops. "Some brands even reserve the right to use the data to track you down if you don't pay your bills," it reported—noting also that GM contends it has customers' permission for all this.[35]

It was these capabilities, of course, that looked so ripe for use as coronavirus spread fighters.

Every plugged-in individual emits a bold digital exhaust trail— usually passively. And consciously or not, average digital citizens hack big holes in their privacy boats every day. They strike bad, asymmetrical data deals, deals bad enough to make Monty Hall weep—data swaps wherein people trade away precious knowledge, information that could easily be turned against them, for a literal pittance. They give the store away for the equivalent of a squeezy rubber stress toy from the CES floor. Add up every example of individual self-sabotage, and it paints a picture of a digital population conditioned over time to act against its own interest.

Sites like eRewards and Ipsos iSay—two of many—match market research surveys with willing respondents. For compensation on the order of 30 or 50 frequent flyer miles, worth a few pennies at best, you are invited to reveal your income, your debt picture, all your banking relationships, or confidential health issues from schizophrenia to a leaky bladder. You probably would not volunteer such private things to an unknown seatmate on a plane, but people on the internet cheerfully spill the beans, even though it's usually unclear who the survey sponsor is. Sometimes the instructions promise answers will be anonymous; other times surveys come right out and ask for your street address, "for confirmation purposes." Whatever the terms, individual data, once entered, is beyond the individual's control. It exists somewhere, maybe forever, to perhaps be weaponized against its originator, who bartered it away at a very low price.

More confounding still is the online "sharenting" phenomenon. Parents upload to public websites their kids' intimate medical details and DNA data from 23andMe-type home test kits. Open-source databases like GEDMatch accept genome data from people hoping to find long-lost relatives or others who share rare mutations. Private genetic information gone public can theoretically be sold to marketing firms, data brokers, or insurance companies. Where children are involved, charges civil liberties attorney Nila Bala, this is positively reckless: "Upon a finding that they are at high risk for a disease, children may face negative consequences in school, the workplace and the insurance market—not to mention experience fear and anxiety about their impending fate . . . we should mount an educational campaign that would make disclosing children's DNA information less socially acceptable."[36]

I said earlier I think it's time we ask more of digital citizens—more street smarts, more personal responsibility, more critical thinking. Public skepticism about coronavirus contact tracing shows at least a hint of critical thinking going on. The promise with contact tracing is that you'd be safely anonymous within a big, aggregated database. But in the real digital world everyone is a potential cohort of one, subject to profiling and microtargeting.

Political strategists and marketers have long practiced microtargeting and defined target cohorts. The Silent Majority, the Angry White Male, and the Soccer Mom all obsessed past campaigns. Advertisers trying to peg the appeal of a new car were not so different. They practiced market segmentation, visualizing blocs of buyers with shorthand labels like "I've made it," "Quality matters," or "Just getting around," and tilting media buys accordingly.[37] Today's Big Tech data capabilities, however, let you give up blurry bloc thinking and zoom in on individual personas.

Mark Penn is perhaps America's best-known political strategist, and a former pollster. Politically he has worked both sides of the street, counseling Bill and Hillary Clinton, then Donald Trump. In a prescient 2007 book, *Microtrends: The Small Forces Behind Tomorrow's Big Changes*, Penn foresaw the state we have achieved today: "Today, changing lifestyles, the Internet, the balkanization of communication, and the global economy are all coming together to create a new sense of individualism that is powerfully transforming our society. The world may be getting flatter, in terms of globalization, but it is occupied by six billion little bumps who do not have to follow the herd to be heard . . . Personal technology has become *personalized* technology."[38] Today any party with a ready checkbook can see who's a super-user of Cialis, who's fond of Mazdas or Stolichnaya or L.L. Bean, and who behaves like a high-priority swing voter.

Microtargeting political messages via Facebook has not exactly injected stability into the electoral process. When a campaign wants voters to buy into the power of a shared, common mission, microtargeting may actually make it harder. You and I may both like Senator Sam, but if the messages Senator Sam sends you don't align with the messages he sends me—you like mass transit funding, I like balanced budgets, and Senator Sam sells both data points in separate, individualized pitches—what common ground do you and I have when we meet? Comparing notes over a beer, we might say: Just who *is* Senator Sam, anyway? And that's assuming Sam sticks to the truth. "Some feel microtargeting lets small and more marginalized political voices find their audience in a cost-effective way, since they cannot afford pricier mediums like television ads," Kara Swisher, the Silicon Valley watcher and editor of *Recode,* has said. "Others think that microtargeting allows the powerful to plant millions of lies in the specific ears of the those who are easy to manipulate. Both are true, but by not better policing the practice, Facebook certainly creates an atmosphere of chaos, especially for those interested in more transparent and truthful debate."[39]

How far can Big Tech take targeting analytics? All the way to the end of privacy. A publicity-shy New York City company called Clearview AI claims to have scraped three billion images of people off the internet to create a far-reaching facial recognition app for law enforcement. A cop wearing augmented-reality glasses could walk through a protest march and, conceivably, receive a data display for everyone she looks at. Some police departments have barred facial recognition tech, citing privacy concerns, but Clearview says more than 600 law enforcement agencies already use its product, and some of those agencies say Clearview technology has caught dozens of criminals. Robust facial recognition is, of course, unlikely to remain exclusive to law enforcement. Soon you, too, may be able to look at a stranger on the bus and see their address, employer, and maybe their credit score. "It's creepy what they're doing, but there will be many more of these companies. There is no monopoly on math," Stanford privacy professor Al Gidari told *The New York Times*. "Absent a very strong federal privacy law, we're all screwed." Clearview AI is probably not screwed. The company is well-funded, moving fast, and breaking things. One of its backers is Peter Thiel, the veteran Silicon Valley venture capitalist behind, among other ventures, Palantir and Facebook.[40]

Social media as deliberately designed by Big Tech today—some would say rigged—is inherently performative. When you post or share content, you're putting on a little show for your circle. You hope to impress friends with photos of your trip to Portugal, or your superior take on the news. Campaigning for likes, you might share stories that mirror the world as you see it—or prove (in your view) the depravity of your foes. You might fish for attention or sympathy; some people post video of themselves crying in distress, then turn coy and enigmatic when friends flock to enquire what's wrong. You might attack someone with another political view, knowing that while you probably wouldn't snarl insults like these across a bar or gym, you're in a pretty safe space online.

Newnan, Georgia is a small but growing town about 40 miles from Atlanta. It no longer qualifies as "sleepy," the standard adjective outsiders pin on Southern hamlets, but it's not yet at city scale. In 2018, Newnan suffered a white nationalist rally. The town sought to bounce back and proclaim tolerance and diversity by commissioning and hanging 17 giant, banner-style posters of various Newnan residents on brick buildings downtown—including African Americans, whites, and two Muslim sisters. Reporter Audra D.S. Burch followed what happened next:

> "A portrait of Aatika and Zahraw Shah wearing hijabs was displayed on the side of an empty building in downtown Newnan. The sisters were born in Georgia and had lived in Newnan since 2012, after they moved from Athens, Ga. They attended a local high school in the county. Their father, an engineer, moved to the United States from Pakistan, as did their mother.
>
> "The reaction to their portrait was fast and intense. James Shelnutt was driving through downtown when he saw it. 'I feel like Islam is a threat to the American way of life,' he said. 'There should be no positive portrayals of it.' Mr. Shelnutt turned to Facebook, encouraging residents to complain. The thread quickly devolved into anti-Muslim attacks and name-calling. Some posters referred to Sept. 11 and argued that believers of Islam were violent . . .
>
> "A few Newnan residents protested the sisters' banner in Mr. Shelnutt's Facebook post, questioning whether they were

actual Newnan residents or if they were even American . . . The post drew nearly 1,000 responses, most of them defending the sisters and accusing Mr. Shelnutt and others of being out-of-touch racists . . .

"The backlash made the sisters realize that much of Newnan didn't know Newnan. They said it felt especially painful to be singled out. 'We have been here seven years,' said Aatika Shah, 22, 'and now because they have never seen us and then saw our picture, they somehow think we don't belong.'"[41]

Why have it out on Facebook? Newnan's population is going up, but it's still no Tokyo. You can always take your friends down to Christy's Café on Perry, get the $7 biscuits and gravy (which looks great on Yelp, by the way), and share your views face to face. Except face-to-face dialogue is more complex, more tiring, personally risky, and a less efficient way to get your performance out there. Nothing you tell anyone at Christy's is going to elicit 1,000 responses.

Newnan's Presbyterian pastor, the Rev. David Jones II, fretted to reporter Burch that the town's banner campaign had sparked questions of identity and race requiring more attention: "We need to talk about who lives in our community and if they are different, why does that make us uncomfortable?"[42] But trading one-liners on Facebook isn't talking. Resorting to social media makes life in Newnan both easier—because of social media's insulative properties, and the false vibe of victory that comes when you post a scrap of stylish snark—and harder.

The unique mechanics of social media seem to help coarsen things. Jonathan Haidt and Tobias Rose-Stockwell sought to explain "why it feels like everything is going haywire," and hit on matters of format design:

> "Online political discussions (often among anonymous strangers) are experienced as angrier and less civil than those in real life; networks of partisans create worldviews that can become more and more extreme; disinformation campaigns flourish; violent ideologies lure recruits. The problem may not be connectivity itself but rather the way social media turns so much communication into a public performance . . . outrage can boost your status.
>
> "Citizens are now more connected to one another, in ways that increase public performance and foster moral grandstanding, on platforms that have been designed to make outrage contagious, all while focusing peoples' minds on immediate conflicts and untested ideas, untethered from traditions, knowledge, and values that previously exerted a stabilizing effect."[43]

Social media's architects, the Big Tech innovators who came up with systems of likes and sharing and friending and unfriending, and in Twitter's case character-count limits that interdict complex wordsmithing in favor of little stinging missiles—none of these people set out to rip holes in our real-life social fabric. All they wanted was to be sticky, own eyeballs, and make bank. But the reverberations of their work are much more than they bargained for. They were like the chemist at 3M who accidentally invented the adhesive for Post-It Notes but could not envision how it might ultimately be put to use. Only the internet is somewhat less benign.

Evidence of public disaffection is everywhere. It shows up in authoritative Pew Research Center surveys attesting to the mounting trust crisis staring Big Tech in the face—and the rising belief that technology companies exert a net negative impact on both our personal lives and national politics.

It shows up in international tension over whether and how to regulate technology platforms, how to form defensive cybersecurity alliances, and how to safeguard personal privacy. "Officials across the EU and North America are finally realizing that just as tech companies are breaking down barriers between various industries, so too must policymakers stop living in silos if they really want to come to grips with how the digital economy works," summed up *Politico*'s chief technology correspondent, Mark Scott. "That includes efforts, already started in 2019, to rethink competition rules to take into account Big Tech's use of data, as well as an acknowledgement that online misinformation can only be tackled through a combination of beefed-up privacy standards, online consumer protections and electoral rule changes."[44]

"It definitely won't be pretty. But to take a page out of Big Tech's book, it's time for policymakers to move fast and break things."[45]

Cultural resistance to Big Tech even seems to be emerging among young job seekers. Not so many years ago turning down a Big Tech job offer, even one light on cash compensation, heavy with stock options of murky worth, was more or less unthinkable. But Belce Dogru, a Stanford computer science graduate, told *The New York Times* she detected an increasing stigma around going to work for Big Tech, particularly Facebook. "The work you do at a place like Facebook could be harmful at a much larger scale than an investment bank," she said.[46]

Techlash: It's not just for old fogeys anymore. When I joined the game in the 1990s, we all felt subtle pressure to cheer every putative technology innovation as an undiluted win—Pentium chips, Intel ProShare, Windows 95, USB plugs, and each new CD-ROM edition of Encarta. At CES in Las Vegas in 2020, I saw a lot of that old, ritualistic, muscle-memory oh-how-*cool* energy rolled out once again. It's what they do. But beyond the tech industry's

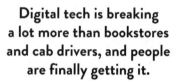

Digital tech is breaking a lot more than bookstores and cab drivers, and people are finally getting it.

walled garden, a broad attitudinal sea change is occurring, and I think the proximate causes are privacy fears—and digital tech's negative influence on the quality and trustworthiness of information. It's breaking a lot more than bookstores and cab drivers, and people are finally getting it.

As the 2020 Consumer Electronics Show vanished into history and I evacuated Vegas—via Uber to McCarran—under the winter desert sun, my old employer, *Slate*, convened "a wide range of journalists, scholars, advocates, and others who have been thinking critically about technology for years" to stack-rank 2020's "30 most dangerous" technology companies. "Which ones might be, well, evil?" pondered *Slate*. "Companies with the potential to do harm can be as distressing as those with long records of producing it."

Airbnb placed 24th on the *Slate* "evil list," accused of disrupting housing markets. 23andMe, the DNA testing company, came in 18th. (One voter said, "The company is quickly building a huge genetic database, and in some cases, sharing that data with partners like GlaxoSmithKline for studies; in coming years, there's no telling how individuals' genetic data might be used, or worse yet, what could happen if that database is ever compromised.") LiveRamp, a consumer data broker, came in 12th. After that it was all the usual suspects. Huawei was 11th, Twitter 8th, Microsoft 7th (for "following Google's playbook in building a business on surveillance and control"), and Apple placed 6th. The top five most "evil" tech players, according to *Slate*: Uber, data analytics giant Palantir, Alphabet, Facebook, and finally—drum roll—Amazon, slammed for *everything*, from worker conditions to its carbon footprint to tax avoidance.

Of Facebook, a *Slate* panelist said: "It's far more powerful than any government. Its products are so varied and far-reaching that neither its users nor founders can keep track of its prying sprawl or purpose. And despite a constant flow of data breaches and upsetting privacy scandals, it has resisted regulation and protected its irresponsible leaders. Most frighteningly of all, the corporation is controlled by a single unelected man who is determined to dodge any kind of ideological stance in the name of higher revenues."[47]

The consumer internet has been running hot for a quarter century, moving fast and breaking things. But while its reach, sophistication, and hardware have evolved at a breakneck pace—at last I can open my hotel room door with my iPhone!—there are three ominous constants. The point of everything is still merely for a very few, very private people to amass insane wealth, at whatever cost to our political and social framework. There is still very little compulsion to sweep up the fragments of broken things, be they the taxi business or our fragile, information-dependent democracy. And to Big Tech, end users are still just marks.

CHAPTER FIVE

UNRELIABLE NARRATORS

The composed, square-jawed 30-something blond woman on YouTube addresses her webcam in calm, assured tones. She's wearing a demure denim top in a nondescript home setting—at a kitchen or dining room table, maybe.

"I do believe that the coronavirus was created by the deep state. I'm sure many of you have heard that Bill Gates owns the patent for it."

Excuse me?

It's former Chicago newspaper columnist and 2020 QAnon mouthpiece Liz Crokin, advising her YouTubers to heed only doctors who are "not cabal-controlled" and ignore the mainstream media's COVID-19 "fear porn." QAnon was the King Kong of internet conspiracy theories at the turn of the decade—an impossibly baroque scenario involving Donald Trump and Robert Mueller covertly joining forces, Justice League style, to take down a global Satanic pedophilia ring. In videos racking up hundreds of thousands of views, Crokin argued the coronavirus was a manufactured cover for the Trump administration to arrest thousands of the rich and powerful for their roles in the Satanic whatever.[1] She also contends Tom Hanks and other "elites" got the virus by consuming adrenochrome harvested from the pituitary glands of children tortured for celebrity enjoyment, but tainted in the covert supply chain by heroic "white hat" conspiracy-busters.[2] (Crokin really, really has it in for Hanks. In pre-pandemic videos, she nailed him for making the '80s comedy *The Man With One Red Shoe*; in her view the movie's title was a secret reference to red shoes made by occultists from babies' skin, and . . . ah, I've given QAnon too much oxygen already.[3])

YouTube delivers this super-embroidered weirdness to the world without caution or comment. No context; no methodical debunking. No editor for Tom Hanks' people to see about a restraining order. Movies have ratings. Every can of soup has a nutrition label so you can judge whether you're up for the carbs and sodium. But here you are online with a QAnon disciple, perhaps taken aback or horrified but maybe curious, with no labels or guidance. You have to judge for yourself whether the QAnon worldview is hinky. The closest YouTube came to a hey-wait-a-minute gesture was to place an enigmatic "Learn More" button at the foot of Crokin videos; clicking it opened the CDC's COVID-19 web page.

Crokin's assured camera demeanor was perhaps no accident, given her stint in legit media. Surely at least some Chicagoland viewers pause to absorb Crokin's QAnon online raps because they recall her old byline in the *Tribune* or *Sun-Times*.[4] The lady doesn't *look* hinky; Crokin looks like she could be doing the weather on TV in Tulsa.

Fake news has been around as long as the free press itself. It burst into the cultural lexicon in the 2010s pretending to be a new pop phenomenon, but that itself was a fake idea. During the pre-1776 gestation of the republic, cranky anti-British pamphleteers jacked up credulous colonists with fact-light diatribes. Samuel Adams of Boston, leader of the Sons of Liberty, went so hard at Crown loyalist Thomas Hutchinson in the pages of the *Boston Gazette*, Adams' readers burned Hutchinson's house down in 1765 for supporting the Stamp Act. (Spoiler: Hutchinson *opposed* the Stamp Act.) Hutchinson complained, to no avail, that "seven eighths of the People" in New England "read none but this infamous paper and so are never undeceived."[5] Adams used fake news to radicalize the citizenry, and he had the legitimizing frame—and distribution might—of the *Gazette*. Hutchinson had squat.

"For colonists aspiring for independence in this Enlightenment era, fake news reports were particularly troubling," according to history writer Jackie Mansky. "Achieving success and establishing legitimacy depended on public opinion, which in turn relied on the spread of information through newspapers." The Founders got the inflammatory potential of fake news. Some had decidedly finite faith in the public's ability to tell fake news from fact. John Adams doubted a free press would mean a more informed public. James Madison held out for letting partisan writers run wild as a byproduct of freedom: "They are the cultivators of the human mind—the manufacturers of useful knowledge—the agents of the commerce of ideas—the censors of public manners—the teachers of the arts of life and the means of happiness," Madison wrote.[6] Madison prevailed, and our free press has come with side helpings of demagoguery, invective, irresponsible conjecture, and weird fringe stuff ever since.

From Stamp Act times to the QAnon era, the main difficulty with fake news tends to be less about the objectively screwy content itself, more about the way it's *framed*. And digital media has killed off most of the important framing conventions we once relied on.

It's remarkable, really, how much framing and signaling assistance we used to get from our physical environment. The conventions of the analog world made classifying and interpreting information much easier. In brick-and-mortar bookstores, titles devoted to QAnon's conspiracy forebears—space aliens, time travel, lizard people, Mothman, moonbase Nazis—were quarantined in the "Speculation" section, not commingled pell-mell with bona fide science. Once you bought the book and dove in, keeping your wits about you was up to you, but at least you left the store having gotten some context. Most storekeepers didn't stand the Loch Ness Monster up next to Henry Kissinger. In the digital infosphere, though, the most outlandish conspiracy theory can cook away on a crank website that looks and feels as credible as *The Atlantic* or CBSNews.com.

Crazy stuff did not make it into Walter Cronkite's newscast or *The Wall Street Journal*. A news digest on television, or in a printed newspaper, was organized and edited before delivery to an audience. Nobody ever claimed *Mad* magazine or the *National Lampoon* bamboozled their readers into questioning reality, or hyped them up to torch someone's house. Works of satire and parody were clearly framed as distinct from the truth. Their packaging and format telegraphed their punches. (Occasionally some uncritical souls do buy an *Onion* story, believing it's true;

China's *People's Daily* resold to its readers an *Onion* dispatch naming North Korea's Kim Jong-un the Sexiest Man Alive.[7] That time, the humorous frame got lost in translation.) If you've been around long enough to remember the glorious *Weekly World News*, the much-missed supermarket tab dealing in made-up banner headlines and paste-up photos ("Space Alien Backs Bush for President!" it scooped in 2000[8]), well, that was some fine fake news, and surely harmless. Its habitat, the supermarket checkout rack, framed its nature; you knew that rack wasn't exactly the home of the *Encyclopedia Britannica*.

Besides, as the comic actor Sasha Baron Cohen has pointed out, humor in general—and satire in particular—depends for success on commonly shared facts. "We have lost a shared sense of the basic facts upon which democracy depends . . . When I, as Ali G, asked the astronaut Buzz Aldrin, 'What woz it like to walk on de sun?' the joke worked because we, the audience, shared the same facts. If you believe the moon landing was a hoax, the joke was not funny."[9] Satiric fake news used to self-separate from the mainstream. Its distinguishing differences used to be plain enough for satire to enjoy legal protection. You could safely lampoon public figures—or rally support for politicians from imaginary space aliens.

We used to have all sorts of framing mechanisms, editors, arbiters—information curators. Their contribution was to classify and substantiate stories. They sidelined garbage, most of the time, and synthesized a shared view of the world that most people trusted.

The establishment media filters had well-documented flaws. The old media machine concentrated too much power in too few hands and displayed too much East Coast elite myopia. It was too eager to reinforce orthodox norms even after they grew stale, and it was far too white and male. All granted. But in our political framework these journalists and editors, almost all honorable and idealistic despite their institutional shortcomings, played the role of reliable narrators.

The unreliable narrator is a staple device of mystery novels and thrillers. It is a first-person narrator who turns out—surprise!—to be untrustworthy. When the story begins you and the narrator set out together on good terms; you are drawn into their confidence and learn secrets; you judge other characters and events through their lens. Only in due course do you realize your narrator is lying, evil, or crazy, and you actually have no clue what's really going on. Edgar Allan Poe and Agatha Christie threw this curve ball like pros, as any middle-schooler freaked out by *The Tell-Tale Heart* knows to this day.

Today's digital infosphere is a Yankee Stadium peopled with unreliable narrators. They look and sound much like the more reliable alternatives perched at the very next URL, and indeed often rip off their legit fellows—twisting, misrepresenting, or undermining original journalism by others. No editor, no authority, has leverage to eject the unreliables from the ballpark—that is, to label their output twisted or fake, sequester them in a special "Unreliable" bleacher, or hold them accountable. When it comes to political advertising, Facebook, as we have seen, refuses to even try. YouTube doesn't do anything about crazed conspiracy videos that can make people lose their bearings. When more reliable voices call out the unreliables, the challenge usually degenerates into a hyperpolarized, he-said, she-said cacophony on social media.

We still have remnants of the old establishment press around, laboring to bring reality into focus. And to a surprising degree, establishment reporting forms the nuclei for a lot of digital output; many new media outlets, particularly those pushing an extreme political viewpoint, simply clip, aggregate, and spin stories from the legacy ones. Even so, those old institutions are much diminished, by their own mistakes as well as the architecture of digital media. Now the old-school outlets are themselves charged with unreliability.

Trust in the mainstream press has collapsed—only Congress gets lower trust ratings. 60% believe reporters are paid by sources to push an agenda. The public is migrating *en masse* away from the old curator-synthesizers—what remains of them—to the splintered, raucous circus of digital and social media.[10] So how did the American public come to distrust its compass? Rebuke its reliable narrators?

I see three ways traditional journalism abdicated its framing role in the digital era: The increasingly aristocratic remove at the top tier of the business; the decay of a talent farm system; and—worst of all—failure to invent a 21st-century profit model.

The Rich are Different from You and Me

First, the aristocracy problem. Journalism has long been a profession with big paydays for the few at the top of the pyramid, poverty wages for lower tiers. Today the gulf between strata is wider and unhealthier than ever. Scan any cable TV news pundit panel; how many on camera do you think are not net-worth millionaires? Establishment political journalists have more in common culturally with the people they cover than those they write for. Washington, D.C., is a tight company town devoted to making, influencing, and commenting about policy; officials and reporters are in the same business, often residing in the same literal neighborhoods. This is not a liberal-versus-conservative thing, it's a shared-bubble thing. At Café Milano in Georgetown, elite journalists sit next to undersecretaries of defense. (Those undersecretaries make nice with those journalists, too, because the connection might mean a steady TV gig after public service.) Conservative or liberal, they raise money for each other's' charities. Journalists greet cabinet members or congressmen at Whole Foods, embassy parties, Kennedy Center premieres, or the service counter at Audi Bethesda. Their children attend Sidwell Friends or Holton-Arms with the kids of White House officials. They marry other elite journalists they courted in the green room, or Citigroup directors, or people they met working at Credit Suisse.

Many are wealthy thanks to TV contracts or getting there thanks to book deals. So many star *New York Times* reporters signed to write books for big bucks in 2019 (about Trump, Russia, the Supreme Court, Uber, and Elaine Stritch, among other topics) and requested time off to finish them, management feared they wouldn't have enough bodies left to put out the paper. "The *Times* has become a book-deal factory," an *NYT* journalist moaned to Vanity Fair.[11]

Every once in a while, a star journalist ventures west of the Hudson River for a glimpse of "real America," gingerly sampling native sentiment like Margaret Mead taking notes in Samoa. But they always look relieved to scamper back to the comfortable ground of Manhattan or Capitol Hill. When the political class and its documenters huddle together in elite, high-income bubbles, it leads not only to isolation but a certain myopic, decadent dissipation.

Strategist Mark Penn said it more than a decade ago: "The elite information circle is dominated by people who live in the world of the top 10 percent, and while in the past that helped drive discussion to more substantive levels, today it does just the opposite. Today, the elites are more fascinated with gossip, and they are driving the debate away from the substantive and toward the superficial."[12]

Things have only worsened since Penn's declaration, made when George W. Bush was president. Establishment TV news is a particularly rarified world, but a shrinking one, and almost certainly less influential than it still believes.

Media tastemakers are fixated on the ups and downs of cable news ratings, obsessing over tiny gyrations, but the real numbers are small. The elite ascribe vast national influence to *Morning Joe* on MSNBC, with Joe Scarborough and Mika Brzezinski, and pundits are thrilled to get dressed in the middle of the night for *Joe* hits. Yet of 330 million Americans, only a million or so watch even some of *Morning Joe.*[13] (And they are concentrated in the east. On the oft-forgotten west coast the *Morning Joe* slot is 3 a.m. to 6 a.m.) By the same token, the liberal media establishment assigns vast, almost supernatural influence to the Fox News prime-time opinion lineup. Within the left's bubble, it is incontestable fact that Sean Hannity and friends single-handedly warp American public opinion. But on a great night, Hannity on Fox draws 4 to 4.5 million viewers, less than 1.4 percent of the country. and he's often the top ratings draw in all of cableland.

Crisis in the Minor Leagues

The second factor that weakens traditional journalism as a reliable narrator: the erosion of a once-robust professional farm system for aspiring journalists. In earlier times, a reporter would break into the business well outside the spotlight, in a small market like Billings or Biloxi, and learn to cover a rate hearing or court arraignment in relative obscurity before maybe ascending to the big time. Small-market journalism was like a medical residency for a new doctor. Today, many small markets no longer have entry-level journalism jobs—the business is that broken—and plenty of well-connected young people start at the top, exerting influence in New York or Washington, D.C. nearly straight out of college. The big networks and papers are often pleased to replace a veteran middle-aged reporter or producer with a noob willing to work for a fraction of the veteran's paycheck.

The casualty in that swap is the shop's institutional memory; a newsroom might oust a 50-year-old national security producer who covered 9/11 in favor of a 26-year-old who takes an interest in national security, but was watching *Mister Rogers* in 2001. Make that trade enough times and the quality of an institution's output declines. Establishment news outlets could have, *should* have, played the experience and perspective face cards against wooly, shambling new media run by neophytes committing grievous errors. They could have programmed steady, balanced content worthy of trust instead of flipping out over breaking stories and running them into the ground for ratings. (Looking at you, Malaysia Airlines Flight 370.) Too often, they didn't.

Will Report for Food

Look below the profitable top tier of the news establishment, at our thousands of daily and weekly papers and TV and radio newsrooms, and the third problem facing institutional journalism is crystal clear. Many if not most metro and regional outlets are dying a slow-motion financial death. The frantic search for a way to not go bankrupt has turned up no magic bullet.

Trace journalism's financial crisis back to bad decisions in the internet's early days. Too many local news outlets dismissed the web as an eccentric outlier channel for geeks and cranks. A typical gambit at newspapers was to give content away on websites as a way of marketing the print product. Regrettably, they trained audiences to expect online news for free, making later desperate efforts to erect firewalls and subscription models that much harder. (As I've said, *Slate* was an early casualty. We tried to charge for access but struck out.) Classified ads had always meant copious, reliable revenue for newspapers, but when Craigslist rolled out free classifieds—entrepreneur Craig Newmark was merely answering Big Tech's call to move fast and break things—papers had no answer.

Online platforms like Facebook pick up and relay local news product without compensating those local newsrooms. Now Facebook faces an ironic content-pipeline crisis. The platform's local news supply is drying up—because people who used to pay for local papers have switched to . . . Facebook.

Facebook's local news providers are dying—because people who used to pay for local papers have switched to . . . Facebook.

Television station groups like Hearst, Sinclair, Nexstar, Raycom, and Gray rolled up network affiliates in medium and small markets, imposing cutbacks and group-wide commonalities to try to keep individual operations above water. Venture capitalists snapped up distressed newsrooms and cut headcount. Alden Global Capital, a hedge fund, acquired and gutted the *Denver Post*, then sought control of Tribune Publishing, owner of the *Chicago Tribune*, the *New York Daily News*, the *Baltimore Sun*, and other important dailies—which prompted an astonishing public S.O.S. from Trib investigative reporters published, not in their own paper, but in *The New York Times*:

> "Facebook and other social media sites give the impression that they offer everything you need to know. But, in reality, most of Facebook's news is generated in traditional newsrooms. If we disappear, its news feed will consist of little more than news releases and opinion-based screeds.
> "Unless Alden reverses course—perhaps in repentance for the avaricious destruction it has wrought in Denver and elsewhere—we need a civic-minded local owner or group of owners. So do our Tribune Publishing colleagues. The alternative is a ghost version of the *Chicago Tribune*—a newspaper that can no longer carry out its essential watchdog mission."[14]

PEN America, the nonprofit free-expression advocate, calls what we're seeing the "collapse of journalism" in America. Since 2004, more than 1,800 local newspapers have ceased publication. The number of U.S. counties with no newspaper coverage at all is climbing past 200.[15] PEN America spent two years probing the slow cratering of local news and concluded, in a report called *Losing the News: The Decimation of Local News and the Search for Solutions,* that it constitutes a national crisis. "That first draft of history is not being written—it has completely disappeared," said PEN America chief executive Suzanne Nossel. In other words, we're losing too many reliable narrators.

On his final broadcast before retirement, Jim Lehrer, the old-school *PBS Newshour* anchorman who died in early 2020, cited nine guidelines for his cautious, conservative brand of establishment journalism:

- Do nothing I cannot defend.
- Cover, write, and present every story with the care I would want if the story were about me.
- Assume there is at least one other side or version to every story.
- Assume the viewer is as smart and as caring and as good a person as I am.
- Assume the same about all people on whom I report.
- Assume personal lives are a private matter, until a legitimate turn in the story absolutely mandates otherwise.
- Carefully separate opinion and analysis from straight news stories, and clearly label everything.
- Do not use anonymous sources or blind quotes, except on rare and monumental occasions.
- No one should ever be allowed to attack another anonymously.
- And, finally, I am not in the entertainment business.[16]

Casually, remorselessly, the post-Lehrer digital infosphere breaks every one of those rules. It has been bent to the agendas of numberless unreliable narrators.

I didn't peg it for what it was at the time—I thought it was just one more development in an engrossing breaking story. But as it turned out, the event heralded the beginning of the end of establishment hegemony over the infosphere. It occurred on January 17, 1998, while I was laboring to make *Slate* more than an experiment on the media fringe.

On that date, a winter Saturday, Matt Drudge's *Drudge Report* picked up a story *Newsweek* had flinched at running, one investigative reporter Michael Isikoff had been pursuing for more than a year. "Newsweek Kills Story on White House Intern: 23-Year-Old, Sex Relationship with President," screamed the *Drudge* banner. The cautious *Newsweek* editors had doubted Monica Lewinsky's credibility and stalled. Drudge had no editor but himself and was anti-Clinton to boot. He got the story of the stalemate within the magazine from an inside source and splashed it wide. It consumed the internet for more than three days until mainstream outlets finally crumbled and conceded the existence of Isikoff's scoop.

In a trice, Drudge and the internet changed the rules. A big story could detonate in public without cautious, lawyerly editing from the analog establishment. All it took was one guy with a gut and a server. The Isikoff story was true—it led to Bill Clinton's impeachment before the year was out—but Drudge could have been no more certain of it than the hesitant *Newsweek* editors who held it. Its release on the *Drudge Report* was expedited by Drudge, an anti-Clinton conservative, *wanting* it to be true. At the time, many saw the Lewinsky story as a kind of declaration of independence from fusty old Ivy Leaguers in cufflinks in midtown Manhattan who controlled the nation's news feed. Looking back, we underestimated the avalanche of trouble to follow. Unreliable narrators *wanting* things, fake or not, to be true, and wanting you to think so, too, are half our problem today.

A few days after the story broke wide, the BBC added: "Love him or hate him, Matt Drudge's report on the Clinton scandal is the most visible sign to date of the changing nature of journalism . . . In the future, academics, politicians and journalists aren't likely to dismiss the internet so quickly."[17] Twenty years later in 2018, the *Drudge Report* was the sixth-most-trafficked media website in the country, attracting more visitors than the *New York Times* or *Washington Post* sites.[18] Drudge links go heavy on UFOs, urban chaos, signs of the apocalypse, exorcisms, and people, often Floridians, running amok. But Drudge sets the agenda for legions of conservative talk radio hosts and is scanned constantly in every newsroom I know. *Newsweek* is moribund.

As internet news exploded, post-Lewinsky, it planted different sensibilities. Format-wise, stories were generally shorter and breezier than traditional journalism, serving screen readers' shorter attention spans. Online media might reflect ironclad standards, loose ones, or none at all. Sometimes it wasn't even spelled right. There was more and more spin—partisan slants on events—and websites began taking political sides in ways American newspapers tended not to. Above all, online news was clickbait-y—crafted to own the eyeballs of casual surfers with a seductive, lurid ferocity that made newspapers and TV look comparatively catatonic.

It was no accident that the 2000s saw the rise of Jon Stewart's *The Daily Show*. Within his fake newscast, Stewart channeled the rebellious, subversive spirit of the internet infosphere. "It is brilliant humor, to be sure, but it is based to a certain extent on how atrocious the official journalism of our times has become," wrote Robert W. McChesney, co-founder of a progressive media reform organization called Free Press and a specialist in the media's role in democratic societies, in an essay published in 2011. "Stewart and [Stephen] Colbert do not need to adopt the asinine professional practices of mainstream journalism, especially the requirement to regurgitate with a straight face whatever people in power say . . . Stewart and Colbert actually demonstrate the idiotic, bogus, and propagandistic nature of what people in power and 'newsmakers' say, in a manner that would be considered 'ideological' and 'unprofessional' were it to come from a mainstream newsroom. By avoiding the absurd professional practices, they can get us much closer to the truth. Fake news becomes real journalism."[19] Stewart and Colbert were reliable narrators masquerading as unreliable ones. A 2007 Pew Research Center survey found Stewart was the fourth most admired journalist in the country—tied with legitimate elites like Anderson Cooper.[20]

In the 2008 presidential campaign Sarah Palin, Republican nominee for vice president, delivered three resounding insights about the digital infosphere that remain her legacy today. One, politicians didn't need branded media channels anymore—they could make direct, unfiltered connections to their public online. "She was a maven on Facebook," remembered Alex Marlow, editor-in-chief of the conservative *Breitbart News*, for a 2020 *Frontline* documentary. "The original politician who saw that you could skirt the media and you could get the message out unfiltered, uncut to the public was Sarah Palin."

Two, in this unfiltered zone, tone and attitude counted for more than mastery of facts. Three, lying worked. Palin proved you did not have to debate data points; you did not have to meet challenges head-on, with reasoned counterarguments. The internet was so fragmented, there was hardly any penalty for just making things up. Without framers, editors, arbiters, reliable narrators assessing information, why not go for it? Say anything.

As Palin dared to do in 2009, you could claim on Facebook that the Affordable Care Act would lead to "death panels"—government boards deciding who lives and who dies—and, untrue as it was, the idea would somehow stick in the infosphere. Health care reform was incredibly complex; the nuances were nearly impossible to grasp online. "Death panels!" was simple. No moral authority, no jointly acknowledged referee, was around to yellow card anyone for repeating it. And even though "death panels" was PolitiFact's 2009 "Lie of the Year," it's stuck around in the margins of conservative thought. For those who *wanted* to believe in death panels, Palin knew tone mattered more than factuality.

"She is the first of a generation of politicians who live in a post-truth environment. She was, and there's no polite way to say it, a serial liar," Steve Schmidt, who helped lead John McCain's 2008 campaign and lobbied to add Palin to the ticket, told *Frontline* ruefully.[21]

Fast forward to our phase of the digital era. Any neat, well-telegraphed distinctions between real and fake news are more or less gone. We've absorbed Palin's insights, however cynical, and gone further. "Once upon a time . . . 'fake news' had a precise meaning. It referred to total fabrications—made-up stories about Donald Trump suffering a heart attack or earning the pope's endorsement—and the phrase burst into the political lexicon as

Any neat, well-telegraphed distinctions between real and fake news are more or less gone.

Facebook and Google vowed to clean up some of the garbage during the presidential election," wrote Callum Borchers of *The Washington Post*. "Since then, conservatives—led by President Trump—have hijacked the term and sought to redefine it as, basically, any reporting they don't like. At the extreme end of absurdity, Trump actually asserted [in February 2017] that 'any negative polls are fake news.'"[22]

Such tactics challenge any remaining broadly held belief in truths we once held to be self-evident. Inventing things to charge up a loyal cohort became bipartisan sport.

The former president of Planned Parenthood, Leanne Wen, claimed over and over that in the years before the 1973 *Roe vs. Wade* decision, "thousands" of American women died annually of botched abortions. This was not true, but Wen repeated the fake stat until *The New York Times* proved it false. She was fired in 2019 for this and other dances with the truth, including revising the Planned Parenthood website to cover health issues Planned Parenthood clinics don't typically treat. The *Times* said, "She had been told repeatedly by her staff [that the 'thousands of deaths' claim was false] but disregarded" the advice.[23]

In 2017, two Republican congressmen from Texas, Lamar Smith and Randy Weber, implicated U.S. philanthropic and political advocates focused on climate change in a chimerical Russian money-funneling plot to hurt the domestic energy industry. The spurious charges against the League of Conservation Voters, the Sierra Club, and Sea Change Foundation got heavy coverage on conservative websites *The Free Beacon* and *The Daily Caller*. Their stories lent a nebulous conspiracy theory the weight of hard fact. Yet it was a baseless smear. A GOP Hill staffer conceded to *Politico* that the charge was really just a "theory, but the reasoning behind it makes sense."[24]

In these cases, and countless more, fake news found favor because partisan sources wanted it to be true, and so did their audiences. And because there were no filters or frames to flag it.

Did you want a world where bleach ingestion advocates get more attention and make new friends? Because this is how you get a world with more bleach ingestion advocates. "Our time has come!" exulted bleach believer Kerri Rivera on Telegram when President Trump mused on live TV that injecting disinfectants might cure people of COVID-19. "This is a MAJOR OPPORTUNITY."[25] With reliable narrators on the wane, it is no wonder that so many people online accept or share so much fake stuff. QAnon enthralls thousands, though not one prediction from the movement's shadowy maximum leader, Q, has come true. Only 45% of Americans know six million Jews perished in the Holocaust.[26] In 2016 one in ten Florida voters said they believed Sen. Ted Cruz absolutely, positively was the Zodiac killer, and another 28% said they just weren't sure.[27] Across the aisle, hard-core online leftists insisted presidential candidate Pete Buttigieg was a CIA plant. ("He's one of the many intelligence community operators working in government," vlogger Steve Poikonen insisted, offering as a dead giveaway Buttigieg's "mesmerizing, hypnotic blue eyes."[28]) And Facebookers of all political persuasions pored over those "Plandemic" videos tying COVID-19 to a shadowy totalitarian plot. "The news media environment is degrading so badly that we're digressing backwards, toward medieval times," said Jennifer Grygiel, of the S.I. Newhouse School of Public Communications at Syracuse University. "People are reading less about medicine from journalists or medical professionals. It's not even Doctor Google anymore. People are becoming more reliant on social media, and Facebook is reaping the benefits."[29]

And so it goes, as Kurt Vonnegut would say.

In 1995, as the World Wide Web arrived on the cultural landscape, Carl Sagan published a warning against superstitious cultism and a plea for more critical thinking. *The Demon-Haunted World: Science as a Candle in the Dark* debunked conspiracies and fringe beliefs, explained away pseudoscience, and cheered for logic. Sagan feared we could easily slide into the intellectual shadowlands, where belief and gullibility overtake skepticism. He dreamed the human species could instead embrace a kind of pocket-reference version of the scientific method for evaluating unfamiliar, unsubstantiated claims. Never mind what you *want* to be true, he might exclaim today. What do you *know* to be true? What can you prove?

Sagan died in 1996. Social media, had he lived to see it, might have extinguished his spirit.

In the cutthroat competition for eyeballs, clicks, and ad revenue, shades of gray lose to screaming gut-punch banners every time. People are less apt to tackle text in archaic, linear fashion. "We skim and scan for the information we want, rather than starting at the beginning and ploughing through to the end," writes Katy Waldman, staff writer at *The New Yorker*. "Our eyes jump around, magnetized to links—they imply authority and importance—and short lines cocooned in white space. We'll scroll if we have to, but we'd prefer not to. We read faster."[30] And we're constantly distracted. Proximate to most online content, fake or real, are parades of clickable buttons promising content that might be better: more fun, clearer, sexier, more aligned with your interests.

The information market feeds the beast with simpler, more absorbable material. In this environment complexity, and centrist equivocation, are much harder sells. Getting you to click on a story is essential to a platform's business model. You're more likely to click on material that validates your beliefs and serves your interests, so that's what the algorithm dishes up.

An infosphere that penalizes nuance, mocks moderation, rewards short, hot takes, and legitimizes fake information is by definition a false portrait of a real, productive political sphere. Nor does it serve us when it portrays us as two rage-fueled blocs, shirts and skins, locked in endless combat. On today's digital battlefield, if you voted for Trump, you are *ipso facto* a racist. How could you not be? You're irredeemable. If you object to Trump on any count at all, if you question his attitude toward the Constitution or Russia, you're a snowflake, equally irredeemable, and no doubt a dangerous socialist in the bargain. (Never mind that neither "team" on social media seems to have a plan for eventually reconnecting with the opposition, which perpetuates the fake, theatrical standoff.)

It's a garish, reductive cartoon of our actual politics, a fundamentally fake view of us. But digital media presents it as real. Even though, contrary to internet wisdom, the thoughtful middle occupies a lot of real estate.

According to the 2016 Cooperative Congressional Election Study, which interviewed 65,000 Americans, only 23% of voters lined up as entirely liberal or conservative on seven major issues: concealed-carry permits, deportation of illegal immigrants, abortion, the Clean Air Act, mandatory sentences for nonviolent drug offenders, the Affordable Care Act, and raising the minimum wage. Only 17% held liberal, progressive views on all seven issues, and only 6% held across-the-board conservative views.[31]

Most people are conflicted on some front or other, but the digital infosphere is unfriendly to gradations. Instead, we get politics as a kind of endless, splenetic athletic championship punctuated with fistfights instead of sportsmanlike hugs and handshakes. Contentious online arguments over journalistic accuracy—or the validity of your beliefs or values, for that matter—devolve into picayune pie fights laced with swaggering whataboutism until one side is teed off or exhausted, at which point the other side declares moral victory and posts a gloat.

Terrible, yes. But for politicians and other influencers, the incentives to leverage the digital infosphere's deliberate, structural distortion can outweigh the lure of sobriety. Steve Schmidt, the Republican strategist, spent much of 2019 advising Starbucks tycoon Howard Schultz on what turned out not to be a centrist presidential campaign. Schultz naturally got no traction in a digital environment tuned for extremism. Schmidt bemoaned the 2020 contenders' failure to lead with "a truth-based, fact-based, reality-based approach which focuses on . . . this system."

"[T]here's this really important debate taking place right now between not just two parties, but between reality and alternate reality," Schmidt told *New York* magazine in fall 2019. "We used to have strong partisan differences in the country, but not two realities . . . We now exist in binary universes."[32]

If you don't like being instructed to pick one universe and live in it, if you contend life and politics are both more complicated than that, you're on the right track.

Here are two tales of unreliable narrators dialing up the extremes.

The conservative online press includes sites that post original reporting and opinion (FoxNews.com, Charlie Sykes' *The*

Bulwark, the *Washington Examiner*, and many more), sites that traffic in mind-boggling, often discredited conspiracies (*InfoWars* is Exhibit A), a big pack of aggregators that repackage and add slant to stories produced elsewhere, and a handful that just make stuff up. AJUANews.com is both aggregator and fiction distributor. It offers mostly unattributed, unverifiable red meat for the alt-right. In December 2019, AJUANews.com posted an account of a Washington press conference starring Democratic Reps. Ilhan Omar and Alexandria Ocasio-Cortez. The two are quoted as vowing to get rid of federal benefits for seniors:

> "They intend to screw over our greatest generation by removing from them everything that we have earned over the years. They do not work for the betterment of the nation. They only look out for themselves . . . The two held a joint press conference yesterday to announce their intention to remove from senior citizens what they termed 'entitlements', such as Social Security and Medicare . . . Omar showed her lack of class and understanding when she stepped up to the microphone: 'America is for the young. It is the youth of this country that work to make it great . . . unlike our senior citizens who only take. Retirees are dead weight.'"[33]

But no enraged Grey Panthers stormed the Hill and beat Democrats' doors down with their walkers, because the story is entirely made up. This fake account of words that were never uttered, at a press conference that was never held—I can't emphasize enough how entirely fake it was—was ultimately traced to DailyWorldUpdate.us, a left-wing troll site that tries to bait conservatives into circulating its made-up "satires." DailyWorldUpdate resembles a lot of half-legit conservative websites (sample head-lines: "With Possible Indictment Looming, Obama Flees to Kenya"; "California Senate Passes Bill That Outlaws 'God Bless America'").[34] It's superficially credible, if you already have an appetite for owning the libs, but complete nonsense. When AJUANews.com reposted the Omar-AOC fiction on Facebook, it was shared more than 18,000 times, according to PolitiFact.

We're lost in the funhouse, here.

Progressive digital outlets can give you a similar case of the whirlies. Take RawStory.com, another aggregator site that mostly repackages stories lifted from establishment outlets—or bits of snark scraped from social media—and sauces everything with a combative, end-zone-dancing, leftward slant. (Partisans on both left and right cheerfully steal from the very mainstream sources they despise.) On any given day in 2020, Trump was "scalded," "mocked," "ridiculed as a big baby," and afflicted by "psychosis" and "narcissistic rage." Kellyanne Conway "goes berserk on Fox News," Rick Santorum was "flattened," and various other conser-vatives were "annihilated," "schooled," "destroyed," "ridiculed," "hammered," "completely wacko," or "stunned" by alleged stone-cold evidence of their own corruption, over and over.

RawStory also takes liberties anthropomorphizing "the inter-net" as a unitary, coherent progressive voice, not the babbling hydra-headed mob it really is. Banner headlines declare various conservative people and assertions have just been "destroyed by the internet." ("Internet mocks Trump for fuming about 'Stable Genius' book.") The thin basis for all this "destroying" is typically a mere six or eight hyper-partisan tweets from nonentities, strung together in a selective, one-sided flurry. But at RawStory, liberalism is in a constant state of glorious, surefooted triumph, and the GOP always looks like the Towering Inferno: engulfed in flames, crippled by ludicrous, stupid self-sabotage, and generally disastrous.

Neither AJUANews.com nor RawStory.com are, strictly speaking, news. Neither source should be part of a balanced information diet. Both sides are dishing up Purina Extremist Chow. It's bowl after monotonous bowl of the same, identically seasoned info-grub, formulated to suit the appetites of particular digital bubble-dwellers.

Both sides are dishing up Purina Extremist Chow. It's bowl after monotonous bowl of the same, identically seasoned info-grub.

The false binary view of American politics retailed online surely exacerbates party polarization. Extreme rhetoric and policy ideas probably not only alienate thoughtful voters, they discourage what could be winning tactics. Conservative commentator Erick Erickson told Bill Maher on his HBO show, "The Democrats don't understand! They would wipe out the Republican Party if you had a pro-life Democrat."[35] But the shirts-and-skins digital infosphere would never accommodate the concept. If any candidate tried it, they'd suffer more than nonstop flaying on Twitter. They'd be written off as fake news.

When the Trump impeachment trial was held in early 2020, it was like the Pro Bowl of extreme, partisan, team-organized online political media. Both sides—and only two sides were evident— were apparently lying. "The Republicans Have Revealed Their Impeachment Strategy—Lying," shrieked *The Nation* online. [C]an anyone stop Trump's Senate enablers from dissembling their way to an acquittal?"[36] From *The Gateway Pundit*, the reliably alt-right rage machine: "Democrats have 'Adopted the Nazi Version of the BIG LIE' As a Way to Impeach the President!"[37] Twitter feeds from one team or the other might as well have emanated from two different planets: "Dems/libs are becoming more unhinged with every passing minute." *Click.* "The entire #GOP are co-conspirators in Trump/Putin's crimes. Traitors all." *Click.* "The House BROUGHT NOTHING. No irrefutable evidence in documents and testimony showing criminal behavior. Nothing." *Click.* "Historians are going to have difficulty explaining how R's could acquit. The answer is that they are as corrupt as Trump."

On Twitter, Schiff himself was either "the greatest defender of the Constitution in the 21st century" (per Lawrence O'Donnell of MSNBC)[38] or "the best white noise out there . . . who needs a sound machine to sleep?" (per Laura Ingraham of Fox).[39] Also on Twitter, it seemed, the American people were finally waking up to the Democrats' sham, or else they were finally waking up to the Trump administration's corruption. The social media brawl raged like a fight in a vintage Popeye cartoon, where you only see fists, legs, anvils, and lightning bolts pop out of a whirling cloud, and there was no earthly way to synthesize it.

Some brave, mostly establishment, crusaders do try to adjudicate truth online. *The Washington Post* makes a little show of awarding "Pinocchios" for whoppers told in the public square. It also claimed to have tallied more than 19,000 Trump lies in the first three and a half years of his presidency. FactCheck.org, PolitiFact, and Snopes all pitch in, trying to red-pencil false rumors and fake news. But their work is mostly retroactive, poking at things already disseminated; if they were promoting aviation safety, they'd be acting not as the FAA, certifying new planes for safe flight, but the NTSB, combing wreckage and pinpointing causal flaws.

Without arbiters and frames in place, the damage caused by misinformation mostly occurs at the moment of distribution. It is pretty fruitless to point back at past distortions or falsehoods and say: Now that those things have caught on in the zeitgeist, we can tell you they're wrong. Anyway, one gets the sense that Main Street America is not exactly convening watch parties to shake its fists at the latest Pinocchio winners.

Fact-checking in this era is noble, but it feels like lonely and quixotic work. And the people and institutions best qualified to do it are under across-the-board assault. Sarah Palin mocked the "lamestream news," and conservatives remain vitriolic today about the big New York media powers (Rupert Murdoch's Fox, *Wall Street Journal*, and *New York Post* excepted). Many liberals also believe those same institutions conspire against popular interests. "Reporters don't have to receive a call from [*Washington Post* owner] Jeff Bezos to know that their paychecks are signed by a billionaire with a well-known personal and corporate agenda— and knowing that agenda exists can shape overall frameworks and angles of coverage," blogged David Sirota, a former reporter advising the Bernie Sanders 2020 campaign.[40] It is open season on reliable narrators.

All this confusion and dysfunction pours gasoline on our gathering trust crisis. It further frustrates our desperate efforts to figure out what's real. How much worse can things get? Much worse. Fact-checking today is mostly focused on misleading language, or videos that take genuine quotes out of context. Wait until ever-more-robust digital technology makes fake news even more convincing.

In the last chapter I mentioned deepfakes: rich, computer-generated synthetic content designed to misinform. During the 2019 British election, an advocacy group worried about the potential for disruption made deepfake videos of Johnson and Corbyn endorsing each other, just to get people thinking about the implications. Coming deepfakes will not be so well-flagged, if the day hasn't arrived already.

For years, public figures have had to reckon with fake Photoshopped nudes of themselves circulating online. It is not so difficult for a troll to take an old Playboy pin-up, graft on the head of a G-rated sitcom starlet, and do (usually, hopefully, temporary) damage to the latter's reputation. Golden State Warriors star Stephen Curry was bedeviled in 2019 by fake nude pictures released on the internet by cranks unknown.[41] Now think what fake media can do to political discourse. Consider the insidious effect of sophisticated fake videos, perfect fake computer-generated voices, fake on-camera pronouncements and promises, fake endorsements, fake concessions, or fake appeals to a candidate's willing loyalists, exhorting them to give up, or riot, or attack reporters. Imagine a campaign war room struggling to bat down an army of online clones, indistinguishable from the real candidate, spouting misdirection and creating electoral chaos.

Imagine a campaign war room struggling to bat down an army of online clones spouting misdirection.

And consider how more robust artificial intelligence and machine learning—the same technologies that enable today's chats with Siri, Alexa, or Amazon Echo—can leverage the wealth of data about you, stored in the cloud by scads of private interests, to design intimate, unique virtual conversations between you and a perfectly simulated politician who lives onscreen, or even as a hologrammatic projection. (The kind Janey Reynolds, 2032 dweller, grew weary of seeing on her kitchen counter in Chapter 1.)

Thanks to the small-d democratization of digital production and leaps and bounds in data personalization tech, all this is not only possible but imminent.

When the 2016 *Star Wars* movie *Rogue One* employed a CGI version of actor Peter Cushing, aka Grand Moff Tarkin, it was an oh-wow moment for fans, and a safe one. Cushing died in 1994. His simulated comeback came with context. CGI Cushing lived only within the well-understood framing device of a familiar fictional narrative. People might prove less receptive to a dead Peter Cushing popping up suddenly on your phone or gas pump screen, calling you by name, demonstrating deep knowledge of your Netflix queue, ex-boyfriends, or favorite cheeses, and trying to sell you things or blackmail you. Yet such interactions are possible in the political arena. If it proves impossible to tell who produces political deepfakes or verify what they say, the effect will be traumatizing.

The Cushing CGI work prompted a thoughtful ethical debate in the movie industry. "[T]he moment is underpinned by some quite terrifying existential questions," wrote British filmmaker Christopher Hooton.[42] Deepfakes raise the specter of a whole new class of identity theft. As for the kinds of forces who would misuse this technology to mislead, and further destabilize politics and elections? Chaos agents tend not to be preoccupied with ethics.

Sens. Marco Rubio, Republican, and Mark Warner, Democrat, have criticized Big Tech for a tepid response to the deepfakes threat. In a 2019 letter, they urged Facebook, Twitter, TikTok, Pinterest, and other big social media players to establish better standards for "synthetic content." "If the public can no longer trust recorded events or images, it will have a corrosive impact on our democracy," they wrote.[43] Meanwhile dead rock stars like Frank Zappa and Tupac Shakur are touring again, as holograms.[44] A CGI James Dean is acting in a new Vietnam War movie, 64 years after getting killed in a car wreck.[45] The *Today Show* is dispensing handy deepfake spotting tips.[46] How long before a convincing deepfake Marco Rubio, shared by an indiscriminate liberal friend, bursts out of your newsfeed advocating abortion on demand and confessing to tax fraud? Perhaps, by the time you read this, it's already happened. And some people online believed it—because they wanted to.

Offshore adversaries of the United States, Russia first and foremost, are always upping their disruption game for the next election. In 2016, they ran circles around Big Tech and hijacked the digital infosphere to accentuate our partisan divide. "Our adversaries, including Russia, China, Iran and others, are persistent: They focus on our politics and try to take advantage of existing fissures and American sentiment, particularly if it may weaken us," Shelby Pierson, who monitors election threats at the Office of the Director of National Intelligence, told *The New York Times*. "They'll try many tactics and can adapt. If it doesn't work out, they try something else."[47]

Does anyone think they won't try deepfakes?

For voters discombobulated by digital media's general unreliability and frequent treachery, the cultural elite have a ready answer. It is the same answer I have seen proffered, over and over, since the wild-west consumer internet first gripped us. It is in no way a solution, and no comfort, but apparently, after a whole generation, it is still the best anyone can do.

The long-standing advice from the big thinkers to the little people is: Be your own editor.

I don't know of any bar that ushers you up to a wall of booze and says: Fix your own drinks. I've never been to a basketball game with no scoreboard. But winnowing truth from fake news online is, say the experts, somehow different.

Farhad Manjoo is, like me, a *Slate* alumnus, then a *Wall Street Journal* and *New York Times* columnist, NPR contributor, and author of a good book called *True Enough: Learning to Live in a Post-Fact Society*. One wants to believe Manjoo is incubating some innovative answers to throw at our unreliable-narrator digital media crisis—which is really just another way to say we can't tell what's true anymore. On New Year's Day 2020, the start of a new and momentous decade, I turned to a new Manjoo column for advice. Here's what I got:

"Only you can prevent dystopia."

Manjoo continued:

"I'm terrified. I enter the new decade with a feeling of overwhelming dread. There's a good chance the internet will help break the world this year, and I'm not confident we have the tools to stop it . . ."

The root of the problem, according to Manjoo, is not the architects, or the profiteering owners, of the digital platforms where the mayhem occurs. Nor is it their abusers, or even a government charged with national security as well as protecting First Amendment rights. The issue, it seems, is you.

"The root of the problem is that humans are weak, gullible dolts; every day many of us, even people who should know better—folks with fancy jobs and blue check marks next to our handles—keep falling for online hoaxes . . .

"There is only one long-term fix: that a critical number of us alter how we approach viral content. Let's all consciously embark on a mind-set shift. In 2020, question anything that everyone's talking about, especially if it fits all your priors . . . If you can't stop sharing, at least slow your roll. The stakes are enormous; there's no room for error. Strive to be better, please."[48]

Oh, things have to get better, for sure. And I do think we can ask digital citizens to do more to protect themselves—more about that later. But this? Telling regular people that decoding our lunatic, fraud-riddled, propagandistic, venom-speckled infosphere is entirely up to them, using whatever time and tools they can muster? You might as well point a man in need of shelter toward a forest, hand him a saw, and wish him luck building a house. Hey, your porch looks crooked. Strive to be better, please.

Shifting editing responsibility from provider to user is not only an audacious dodge. It assumes people have more time, skill, and interest in the task than most are likely to summon. Not everyone camps at a screen and keyboard all day, as elite knowledge workers do. A regular person who drives truck, or waits tables, or lays brick all day might want after-shift assistance flagging the unreliable narrators on their radar. But amid a technology revolution devoted in large part to packaging small conveniences to appeal to prosperous first-world consumers, Big Tech seems to shrink from the really big stuff. We can give you a smart robot vacuum, or an app that ages your selfies for a laugh. We can eliminate the onerous burden of touching your fingertip to a screen by giving you Alexa to shout at. But flagging and framing fake news? Detecting deepfakes and offshore chaos agents? Enlisting patriots and tech titans to come up with systems that elevate truth and restore trust, enabling better voting decisions? Well, *that* sounds like a lot of work. You're on your own.

Manjoo is right about one thing: Free-range fake news can "break the world." But patrolling or repairing the infosphere is not primarily the users' job. Nor is it with *any* failing, potentially harmful infrastructure. (Airport delays? Get out on the tarmac and reorganize those planes, passengers. Deli counter smells rank and gamy? BYO Lysol; sanitation is the customer's problem.)

We must do better, or for anyone who still invests faith in American politics, the penalties on the horizon are too terrible to contemplate.

CHAPTER SIX

ARE YOU BEING SERVED?

Ventilators! When the pandemic hit America, hospitals were desperate for ventilators.

The government's Strategic National Stockpile was supposed to have 80,000 ventilators ready for just this kind of emergency. But when someone checked, it was actually just 16,600, and thousands of those were broken. The feds had let the maintenance contract expire.[1] New York alone wanted 37,000 ventilators.[2] Nobody knew what to do. You can't pick these things up at Best Buy. The White House disclaimed responsibility and told states to fend for themselves. "We're not a shipping clerk," said the president.[3]

Compensating for the federal failure—"At no time in the past 75 years have global leaders so utterly failed to deliver," mourned *Politico*[4]—were private companies.

General Motors CEO Mary Barra took a pleading call from a nonprofit called Stop the Spread. We know *you* guys don't do ventilators, went the call, but what if you hooked up with an outfit that *does*, and throw in what you know about manufacturing at scale?

GM formed an overnight partnership with a small medical device company, Ventec Life Systems. Together they figured out how to make ventilators at ten times Ventec's standard production rate.[5]

Ford and General Electric also joined forces for warp-speed ingenuity. Like the rescue engineers at Mission Control working the Apollo 13 case, they used parts on the shelf, including seat cooling fans from F-150 trucks, for a quick-and-dirty version of a 3M respirator. Ford engineering executive Marcy Fisher landed in a whole new line of work. "We don't have a history with medical devices, but we know engineering, production and supply base," she said.[6]

Car company people worked 14 to 18 hours a day to fill needs the feds couldn't or wouldn't. The main contribution they received from the executive branch of the United States government was attacks. "As usual with 'this' General Motors, things just never seem to work out . . . always a mess with Mary B," and "FORD, GET GOING ON VENTILATORS, FAST!!!!!" tweeted President Trump.[7] The companies did not respond. They were busy.

"As the virus spreads, we're seeing clear fault lines emerge—especially a lack of coordination and government action—that are preventing a collective response," wrote Ken Chenault, the former American Express CEO, and Stop the Spread founder Rachel Romer Carlson in a *New York Times* op-ed pleading for private enterprise to pitch in where the government was striking out.[8] And, oh my, here they came. Bacardi, Anheuser-Busch InBev, and even Exxon Mobil turned to making hand sanitizer.[9] Underwear kings Fruit of the Loom, Jockey, and Hanes churned out face masks. Piper Aircraft made plastic face shields for doctors and nurses. Canada Goose, famed for luxury winter coats, pivoted to hospital scrubs and patient gowns. The lab at Sierra Nevada, the California brewery, turned to making viral transport medium, a mixture that preserves clinical samples, to increase COVID-19 testing capacity.[10] Harbor Freight Tools, the retailer, donated every piece of PPE on its shelves to local hospitals.[11]

Hundreds of companies dropped what they were doing to provide crisis leadership while the government spun its wheels. The story in full felt like a modern counterpart to the Dunkirk evacuation of 1940, in which a plucky *ad hoc* merchant marine flotilla, uncommanded but brave and game, rushed across the English Channel to France to rescue Allied forces trapped by advancing Germans.

Meanwhile federal officials fought with state governors over incoming shipments of medical gear, allegedly commandeering or confiscating some. To outwit FEMA, state-level officials sent incoming cargo flights to out-of-the-way airports and hid medical goods in secret locations.[12] The distraught CEO of a Texas medical supply company, Mike Bowen, testified to Congress that the feds had for years ignored warnings about their woeful unreadiness for a pandemic—then, when COVID-19 became a known threat, also ignored Bowen's offer to jump-start face mask production lines.[13] The CDC told state and local officials in February its testing capacity was "more than adequate."[14] We soon knew better.

As political leaders flailed in zero hour, trusted businesses delivered in their stead. They stepped in to serve. It was a dramatic power shift. But it didn't start with COVID-19.

"CEOs are America's new politicians," proclaimed the trend-framing Axios pundit Jim VandeHei in 2019.[15]

"Today CEOs need to stand up not just for their shareholders, but their employees, their customers, their partners, the community, the environment, schools, everybody," said Salesforce CEO Mark Benioff in 2018.[16]

Online news may be fake, technology untamed and predatory, and government broken, but people still seek trusted leaders. More businesses are giving them new places to look. I know three things:

One, more companies today use their capabilities and reputational equity inventively, in and between national crises, to achieve greater public influence.

Two, there are big opportunities for honorable companies to leverage digital communications in order to serve citizens, earn trust as well as influence, and improve the world. They are equipped to succeed at many things, particularly constituent service, that government struggles at.

Three, the twin engines of this change are unresponsive government, which sends people looking for better service, and the state of digital politics. They not only discourage belief in traditional systems, they suggest new ways for a private company to do and mean new things.

In his landmark study of globalization, the internet, and presidential contests, *The First Campaign,* journalist Garrett Graff wrote, "The people in this tech-savvy new generation—more diverse, more educated, and more interconnected than any before it—yearn for relevant leadership, for political figures who can help bring American society all the way into the twenty-first century. They expect politics to talk to them, because in today's culture everything else does."[17]

Communications in our culture used to be broadcast style. Authority talks, you listen, end of story. Today it's about two-way dialogue, and good companies know it. (A generation ago, an irate customer would type and mail off a letter of complaint. A reply might come back in four to six weeks. Today that customer sends a company a tweet, or opens a live chat, and expects not just a response, but *resolution*, in minutes.) More frequent, less laborious back-and-forth contact occurs. Resolving problems can be a *pleasure* for the customer.

Because the internet has superseded the old channels used by companies and customers to relate to one another, those relationships have changed. Today they're deeper and less superficially transactional. Consumers, especially younger ones, expect more. Increasingly they want to see

Increasingly, consumers want to see evidence of a moral code at work. Activated corporate values.

evidence of a moral code at work—activated corporate values that are more than empty words on the boardroom wall.

Increasingly, they want favored companies to play a political role.

Today's digital platforms make it easier for people to parade their expectations. A 2017 study by Weber Shandwick and KRC Research showed not only that 56% of American millennials thought CEOs have a greater responsibility to speak up on social issues (as did 42% of all Americans), but that 47% of all Americans think CEOs who do *not* speak out risk public criticism.[18] And the hunt for zero-cost, zero-risk public positions is almost always fruitless. A company cowed by fear of reprisals looks lily-livered in the public square, a calculably worse offense today than offending one pressure group or another.

When citizens are repeatedly frustrated by government and politicians owing to their glorious track records of failure and evasion, perhaps they cast their gaze elsewhere. Perhaps they transfer faith to select companies that reward it with dialogue-driven service. Companies that know how to run customer relationships on the internet. In the bluntest of terms, the trust gap in American political life—a gap exacerbated by the internet—represents a market opportunity for the smartest of private-sector operators.

Think where this can lead.

Companies have cultivated brand loyalty since forever, usually in the most apolitical terms they could manage. There was no such thing as a Republican or Democratic beer. "In the past, companies kept their heads down and did their best to never be seen," reminds Jerry Davis, management and sociology professor at the University of Michigan. Anything with a whiff of risk, anything with a chance of kicking the slightest dent in the quarterly dividend, was regarded within the corporate castle walls with something akin to terror. Almost as heart-stopping: the thought of a company taking a position that courted trouble from the government, whose brigades of regulators held nearly every major industry—transportation, banking, energy, agriculture, health care, broadcasting, you name it—on a tight leash.

In rare cases when an old-school brand took on a political slant, it was almost subliminal. An air kiss. The classic Volkswagen Beetle was a peace-and-love, flower-power, Woodstockian ride, gently but indubitably liberal and subversive. You could not see Richard Nixon driving one. Yet VW never pushed that message explicitly—certainly not far enough to dissuade Republican buyers in gray flannel suits who just liked the high MPG. VW did not supply Beetle courtesy cars to lead the civil rights marches. In the 1980s and 1990s, the Benetton fashion label ran traffic-stopping, photo-centric ads tagged "United Colors of Benetton." They referenced HIV, race and interfaith relations, and war atrocities, but always in vague, *you*-think-about-this terms. "We did not create our advertisements in order to provoke, but to make people talk, to develop citizen consciousness," said Luciano Benetton.[19]

You could discern coded conservative values in the Harley-Davidson brand, or liberal ones in Birkenstock. But companies rarely if ever went so far as to publish a political manifesto or lead a campaign for social change. Nor did a company try to convert customer loyalty into much more than frequent patronage.

A smart company in 2020 thinks differently, because thanks to the internet, the potential is different.

It must be said that not every business owns sufficient public goodwill to dive into political or social leadership. In the coronavirus crisis there were business heroes in the court of public opinion—but also losers aplenty. Cruise lines that kept putting to sea as the virus spread, concealing ominous health data from authorities, customers, and crew. ("The Coronavirus cannot live in the amazingly warm and tropical temperatures that your cruise will be sailing to," went a Norwegian Cruise Line sales-center talking point leaked that March to the *Miami New Times*.[20]) Retailers that demanded frontline workers stay on the job without masks, gloves, or hand sanitizer, leading to "open revolt."[21] Giant restaurant chains that snarfed up millions in Payroll Protection Program money meant for small business. Food-delivery apps that urged people in lockdown to "save" their favorite restaurants by ordering takeout, but quietly kept up to 40% of the gross.[22]

Big Tech's leading players won few new friends in the pandemic; their trust stock was trading low to begin with. Edelman reported in May 2020 that only 29% of Americans thought CEOs were doing an "outstanding" job of handling the crisis.[23] Still, only 15% said (in a different poll) they'd rather not hear from companies.[24] And what did people want? From the evidence, genuine empathy. An authentic, altruistic, pro-community social agenda, an ethical backbone with actions that match sentiment, and serious communications chops.

It was golden hour for CEO activism and woke capitalism.

Before COVID-19, Aaron K. Chatterji of Duke University worked with Michael W. Toffel, co-chair of the Harvard Business School's Business and Environment Initiative, on a study of CEO activism—which they saw as a whole new world compared to old-school corporate involvement in politics. The old approach tended to be discreet and clubby, with a lot of K Street lobbyists and expense-account dinners. The new CEO activism played out in public, usually with an internet component. With the pandemic, this view seemed more relevant than ever.

Old-school corporate politics, said Chatterji and Toffel, was mostly grounded in self-interest. The new version has a point of view, a moral center, and risk. "Executives must balance the likelihood of having an effect and other potential benefits—such as pleasing employees and consumers—against the possibility of a backlash," they said. And while in the old days corporate silence was always the safe choice, in the internet era it can be hurtful. Echoing that Weber Shandwick study, they said: "We believe that the more CEOs speak up on social and political issues, the more they will be expected to do so. And increasingly, CEO activism has strategic implications: In the Twitter age, silence is more conspicuous—and more consequential."[25]

The new CEO activism seeds new public expectations. Superficial public relations campaigns no longer feed the bear. When the economy hunkered down because of the coronavirus, how many emails did you get from companies claiming, "We're here for you," "We're all in this together," or even that their corporate "family" was keeping yours in its thoughts? Even my printer ink supplier emailed to ask how I, valued subscriber, was holding up. No break on the price of cartridges materialized, though. How many companies backed up Hallmark-card gestures of empathy with tangible community or customer support?

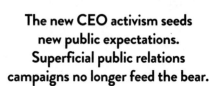

The new CEO activism seeds new public expectations. Superficial public relations campaigns no longer feed the bear.

Which brings us to woke capitalism, meaning a business and communications posture that reflects awareness of social, environmental, and racial justice issues. "Woke" as a modifier was born in the African American community in the 1960s, so far as linguists can tell, referring solely to racism. For better or worse it's been appropriated by the mainstream, its meaning enlarged to bespeak just about any flavor of cultural sensitivity or activism.[26] In corporate boardrooms across the landscape, multitudes labor feverishly to demonstrate wokeness—to display their sensitive new political antennae to customers and the world. (Never more feverishly than in mid-2020, amid the racial justice protests inspired by the death of George Floyd.) Companies angle to compile more social equity across the media spectrum. The results run from authentic expressions of noble values to hollow and desperate virtue-signaling—but I'm getting ahead of myself.

I can name five ways companies are potentially better equipped than government and politicians to capture trust, and therefore influence, in the digital infosphere. Competing for trust, good companies have some natural, structural advantages.

The Trust Reservoir Factor

Yes, big business racks up a low average public trust score year after year. In Gallup's annual measurements of confidence in major institutions, 23% of Americans in 2019 gave big business "a great deal" or "quite a lot" of trust. Since the turn of the century that rating has gyrated up and down from 16% to 29%. (Big business comes out better than Congress, to which a lofty 11% assigned high trust in 2019, but worse off than the military, organized religion, or public schools.[27])

But 23% doesn't tell the whole story. Only 34% of us have "very little" or "no" confidence in big companies. Almost everyone is a superfan of at least one or two companies. The top global consumer brands that cracked the code in 2019 and earned high public repute, according to Reputation Institute: Bosch, Netflix, Michelin, Canon, Sony, Microsoft, Adidas, The Walt Disney Company, Lego, and Rolex.[28]

If you're the only gas station for fifty miles around, trustworthiness need not be job one. (Nor low prices, nor restroom hygiene.) But few businesses have their customers really, truly cornered that way. Most brands benefit from rewarding public trust: They can quantify the business value of a good reputation and the cost of a broken one. Compared to politicians and government, businesses pay a higher real price for betraying or squandering trust. Those tagged with scandals or deception can get dragged around the internet like Vichy collaborators dragged through French villages after Berlin fell. Companies judged to have misbehaved, or been overly selfish, during the pandemic might face similar music; one sensed that a crisis-sharpened public was compiling a shitlist.

Private sector agencies don't collapse or get taken over because they're not trusted. They plow on regardless. Congress is the least trusted major American institution, yet at least 95% of incumbents are typically reelected.[29] But successful companies know the value of a trust reservoir—cultivating it, maintaining it, and tapping it when they need customers' forbearance. In a digital world where trust is in decline, that puts them ahead.

The CRM Factor

The best private companies are configured, intrinsically, to respond to customers. They pride themselves on being "customer-driven"; they have robust systems to support customer relationship management (CRM) and, if you get mad at them, retention. Such responsiveness is not exactly a prerequisite for political institutions. You write to your incumbent congressman, he or she might write back, might not. If a member of Congress is tackling an issue close to your heart, but you reside outside their district, you might not even be able to reach them online. (Translation: You can't vote against them, so they care less about what you think.)

Campaigns are more responsive, but Daniel Bennett of the Institute for Politics, Democracy, & the Internet has pointed out that incumbent officials treat constituents differently. "First, campaigns and elected federal office have rules that keep them separate. They have different budgeting, different calendars, and different traditions . . . Members of Congress, in their official capacity, are involved in literally hundreds of different issues . . . and honestly, if a topic that interests a voter is off-message, they do not want to talk about it anyway."[30]

And as I've already discussed, companies leverage mounds of customer data to drive more relevant, productive dialogue with customers online. As long as they don't cross into creepy or stalker-ish territory, that gives them another edge over politicians. Travis Bullard is brand practice leader at APCO Worldwide, the global corporate communications consultancy. In an end-of-2019 letter to clients, he pointed out that as "companies will move towards a greater granularity in their understanding of customers" using digital analytics and microtargeting, "The key here will be building trust, and whether a company can successfully manage this will be a make-or-break moment in the world of the near-future."[31]

The *Kaizen* Factor

Leading companies self-analyze and invest in continuous improvement—*kaizen*, in Japanese. Not even the best government agencies think like that. *Kaizen* is how Great Western Bank turned a 34-step process to set up a new checking account into a 24-step one. It's how Herman Miller, the office furniture company, learned to produce an Aeron chair in 17 seconds instead of 82.[32] Competitive forces in the private sector mean there's a new, improved Apple iPhone every year or so. "Success breeds complacency. Complacency breeds failure. Only the paranoid survive," warned Intel CEO Andy Grove in the 1990s, when Intel had 85% of the x86 PC microprocessor market. If any American CEO could afford complacency, it was Grove.[33] Yet Intel never relaxed into easy hegemony.

Government, on the other hand, is typically a quart low on *kaizen*. Elected officials are focused on getting and retaining power, not necessarily performance improvement. Public-sector agencies work to justify their budgets and angle for increases. Pressure to innovate ruffles feathers and discomfits incumbent forces.

A paranoid competitive outlook dosed with passion for *kaizen* is a better foundation for internet-era influence.

The Crisis Chops Factor

If the tale of how H-E-B, the San Antonio-based grocery chain, managed through the pandemic doesn't become a landmark crisis response case study, it sure ought to. The retailer had maintained a pandemic-and-influenza playbook since 2005, when the H5N1 epidemic hit China. It had a full-time director of emergency preparedness, Justin Noakes. In January 2020, as the U.S. government was publicly wishing COVID-19 away, H-E-B was in dialogue with retailers over in Wuhan and holding tabletop exercises plotting its response to a hypothetical outbreak in Houston. When Texas had its first positive test on February 12, H-E-B activated its emergency response center and already knew exactly what switches to throw to keep the shelves stocked and employees safe. "We're here to take care of our partners, take care of our customers, take care of our community," said Noakes.[34] You kind of wish someone in Washington had not only said that, but known how to do it.

But when it comes to super-competent disaster response by private interests, H-E-B has company. If a flood or hurricane levels part of the United States, the nearest Anheuser-Busch brewery might shut down its beer lines, switch to canning drinking water, and speed donated truckloads to disaster zones, sometimes running rings around FEMA. Since 1988, Anheuser has produced and donated more than 80 million cans of water on short notice. The company now shares a key function of government and NGOs; it has disaster assistance down to a science.[35]

When trouble strikes, UPS, Walmart, and other private-sector logistics virtuosos complement FEMA on the ground. Procter & Gamble sends mobile laundry trucks with the Tide logo on their sides. Home Depot and Lowe's wrangle building supplies to the scene. All these are organizing and humanitarian functions we once expected from public relief agencies.

The political message: Government can go MIA in a crisis; companies can deliver. When that perception takes hold, people can look to the public sector to supplant or even overshadow government in other urgent arenas.

The Keeping it Real Factor

Shrugging off old allergies to going off script or speaking boldly, more companies are getting good at deploying authentic, engaging voices on social media—real people with real voices and real agency.

For some reason, the Twitter personas of food brands, like Pop-Tarts and Steak-umm, score particularly well in this department.

During the pandemic, Steak-umm's Twitter guy, Nathan Allebach, took to dispensing sage advice on how to assess and analyze health data. "We're a frozen meat brand posting ads inevitably made to misdirect people and generate sales, so this is peak irony, but hey we live in a society so please make informed decisions to the best of your ability and don't let anecdotes dictate your worldview," went one tweet. A pretty unorthodox public communications strategy for a convenience food, but it worked. (Response tweets: "You have the support of this vegetarian. Steak-umm bless." "Just had a Steak-umm sandwich for the first time in 15+ years in your honor."[36]) Authenticity and relevance promote trust and loyalty. When a company

Authenticity and relevance promote trust and loyalty. When a company speaks with a genuine voice it gains more influence.

speaks with a genuine voice it gains more influence—and distinguishes itself from every political leader who deflects a sharp question or flees a tough town hall.

The keeping-it-real play need not wait for a national emergency. Southern Rail, a British commuter rail operator called "beleaguered" or "most hated" in the press for erratic performance, took a great leap forward in terms of authentic public voice when it installed a funny 15-year-old boy called Eddie at the controls of a Twitter feed normally used to announce service delays:[37]

- @SouthernRailUK: Hi, Eddie here! Here on Work Experience and ready to answer your questions!
- @TheRunningBug: Eddie, if a jogger runs at the speed of sound, can he still hear his iPod? #askeddie

- @SouthernRailUK: He wouldn't be jogging anymore. Eddie
- @bookslinger: What's the biggest animal you could single-handedly cling film to a lamp post?
- @SouthernRailUK: Probably a sloth. I can't picture them running away. Eddie
- @RobStewart4: I think Eddie is secretly the CEO and Southern have just been fooling us all along #askeddie #conspiracy
- @SouthernRailUK: If I am, it is the greatest cover-up story the world has ever known. Eddie

Eddie, unpaid intern and temp fill-in, earned heavy retweets, social media stardom, and admiring national press. "He never expected that he would end up . . . labelled a national treasure and hailed as Southern Rail's 'saviour'," marveled *The Telegraph*.[38] The beneficiary was the brand. Eddie was no bot or corporate lackey. He was cheeky, surreal, and authentic. He broke the mold. Possibly overheard at Waterloo: "Why on *earth* is a not-terribly-good rail service having a *child* answer questions about *sloths*?" "Perhaps they're better chaps than we thought!"

"This is the age of ambient corporatism," technology journalist Molly Roberts has observed. "The trick to self-promotion without self-immolation, at least on Twitter, is to play human—to make clear, for example, that there's someone behind the MoonPie handle, riffing with company accounts but also perhaps going a little crazy . . . Brands: They're just like you!"[39]

Most politicians and government agencies, however, bring less to the table in this department—usually much less. Wooden, tardy, dense, or suspect communiques, or none at all.

Earned trust, better customer relationship systems, a culture of continuous improvement, knowing how to respond in a crisis, and an authentic human voice: All five factors, demonstrated on the internet, can cause people to turn to companies first for authority, advice, and assistance. They can turn fair-weather customers into citizen-evangelists.

Business Roundtable is a U.S.-based agglomeration of elite CEOs and a synthesizer of conventional corporate wisdom if ever there was one. Since 1978 the Roundtable has issued periodic, jointly devised Principles of Corporate Governance, meant to set priorities for—well, for corporate priorities. And for decades those statements basically stated and restated one core idea: Corporations exist mainly to serve shareholders. It was economist Milton Friedman's vintage doctrine, and a cornerstone of establishment CEO thinking: Start with shareholder primacy and everything else falls into place. "The social responsibility of business is to increase its profits," said Friedman in 1970[40]—not, by implication, to raise money for breast cancer or clean up the ocean or make sure hospitals have enough face shields.

In 2019, the tune changed.

Call it a new appreciation for woke capitalism; call it recognition that the internet heightens customer expectations. Call it jitters over keeping favor with judgy millennials. Maybe it was a quiet way to acknowledge the opportunity for new kinds of leadership when government and politics strip their gears. Whatever the motives, the new-and-improved 2019 Principles of Corporate Governance explicitly demoted shareholders.

"Americans deserve an economy that allows each person to succeed through hard work and creativity and to lead a life of meaning and dignity," the statement read. "We commit to delivering value to our customers . . . Investing in our employees . . . Dealing fairly and ethically with our suppliers . . . Supporting the communities in which we work . . . embracing sustainable practices across our businesses . . ." And coming in *last:* "Generating long-term value for shareholders." *Long-term* value. They didn't even mention quarterly dividends.

Business Roundtable members extolled the revised priorities. "The American dream is alive, but fraying," said Jamie Dimon, CEO of JPMorgan Chase and Roundtable chairman. "These modernized principles reflect the business community's unwavering commitment to continue to push for an economy that serves all Americans."

The 2019 Principles of Corporate Governance explicitly demoted shareholders. . . that clatter in some comfy afterlife clubroom was Milton Friedman dropping his martini.

"CEOs work to generate profits and return value to shareholders, but the best-run companies do more. They put the customer first and invest in their employees and communities," said the CEO of Progressive, Tricia Griffith.[41]

That clatter in some comfy afterlife clubroom was Milton Friedman dropping his martini.

181 Business Roundtable members endorsed this topsy-turvy new worldview; that is, most of them. A few big member firms like State Farm and Alcoa waved the signing pen away, but still, the new Principles amounted to an emphatic restacking of American business values. 25 years of internet culture—constant online

dialogue and public feedback—had scrambled the old hierarchy. "Delivering value to customers"? That could mean anything, depending on what customers wanted from a business—maybe not just low prices, but values, ethics, altruism in a pandemic, perhaps even political surrogacy. Maybe customers wanted favorite companies to amplify their voices—to be warriors for things they cared about.

A vague inkling in the boardroom that charitable or social-conscience actions were nice to do—sometimes gotta-dos—had been supplanted by a conviction that social or policy activism was . . . smart. Smart customer relations, but more than that. A smart strategy for maximizing a company's meaning.

Like a recipe that lists ingredients but no measurements, Business Roundtable's new Principles lacked a little critical guidance. Go forth and create value, it said; give customers what they want, serve your communities, embrace sustainability. But how, exactly? Without organizing principles, companies tried all kinds of gestures, from the smart and strategic to the desperate and unstrung, to show the world they got it.

But there are endless ways for a company to bobble a social equity strategy. There were rampant examples of virtue-signaling companies grasping clumsily for their own slice of that woke capitalism pie and getting fragged for their efforts.

In 2017, Pepsi released a commercial in which celeb-without-portfolio Kendall Jenner, daughter of Kris, defused a racially charged street standoff by handing a riot cop a can of soda. The furious backlash on social media went supernova within hours—globally. "When you portray a can of Pepsi solving the entire problem of police brutality, the entire problem that the black people have had with the state . . . it undermines the grave seriousness of the issue at hand," complained Hrishkesh Athalye on the India-based Youth Ki Awaaz youth media platform.[42] The spot was pulled.

Gillette posted a two-minute ad in 2019 that sought to leverage the #MeToo movement to sell razors. It showed a montage of boorish, bullying mansplainers and urged viewers to "say the right thing" and "act the right way"; "It's only by challenging ourselves to do more, that we can get closer to our best," went the tag. Dislikes swamped likes; social media accused Gillette of "gender-shaming" men. "Stop trying to emasculate men!!" tweeted @angelsvoice66. An avalanche of scathing comments got that spot pulled, too.[43]

A lot of the failures had in common not only what-were-they-thinking? tone-deafness—who thinks a Kardashian makes a great race-relations ambassador?—but a fundamental disconnect from the company's business mission. Tone-deafness suggests inauthenticity of the sort normally associated with squirming establishment politicians, which on the internet suggests death. The more empty or opportunistic the gesture seems, or the murkier the connection between the host brand and the message, the more trouble results.

A company can even be attacked from within for its political positions. Social media enables this, too. When Amazon threatened to fire employees critical of company environmental policies, more than 400 criticized Amazon right back on *Medium* in daring defiance of corporate rules. ("It is unconscionable for Amazon to continue helping the oil and gas industry extract fossil fuels while trying to silence employees who speak out," posted an Amazon business analyst. "Amazon's main principle is Customer Obsession, it is time to broaden it and get obsessed with Humanity," wrote someone in Payments.[44]) Oracle workers walked off the job in protest when CEO Larry Ellison hosted a fundraiser for President Trump, complaining that, as *Recode* put it, Oracle's "conservative culture . . . has not been touched by the current bouts of workforce activism sweeping major tech companies."[45]

And then there are the fear-driven corporate cave-ins in response to exterior pressures, or merely the threat of same. Given the velocity and ferocity of internet sentiment, these little dramas hardly ever end well. In 2019, for example, the owner of the NBA Houston Rockets, Daryl Morey, tweeted a note of solidarity for pro-democracy protesters in Hong Kong: "Fight for freedom, stand with Hong Kong." League bigwigs, terrified of offending the lucrative mainland Chinese market, denounced Morey, calling his defense of democracy "regrettable." Whereupon Americans of all political stripes, from Ted Cruz to Beto O'Rourke, linked arms and turned on the NBA. "The only thing the NBA should be apologizing for is their blatant prioritization of profits over human rights," tweeted O'Rourke, knowing an opportunity when he saw it.[46] Morey deleted his tweet, but Chinese sponsors pulled the plug on Rockets deals, and for the NBA the optics were death. The league looked more interested in those deals than democratic ideals. He shoots, he misses.

What separates meaningful corporate social action from wide-of-the-net shots? Neville Isdell knows.

Isdell was CEO of The Coca-Cola Company from 2004 to 2008. He launched an ambitious campaign to make Coca-Cola operations water-neutral—a laudable social good, but also prag-matic. Abundant clean water is essential to Coca-Cola's business interests. In a 2019 op-ed, Isdell took gentle issue with the sweep of the Business Roundtable declaration, suggesting that successful social action hinges on a absent but simple organizing notion.

> "I propose that every business has two responsibilities: to make money and to address those societal issues central to the business. It's a far more multilateral view of the world than Friedman's, yes, but hardly a green light for scattershot social activism that can drain resources and muddy a compa-ny's public profile. On this middle ground we find a prudent litmus test for assessing potential engagements.
> "Thoughtful, strategic corporate social activity may serve an even bigger cause: salvaging capitalism itself. I agree with the former Unilever CEO Paul Polman, who argues that companies putting short-term profit ahead of long-term sus-tainability may not survive in the 21st century. "Companies with a strong sense of purpose are better able to grow not only revenue and profits but also create additional value," says Polman. I'll add an asterisk: Without profit it is far harder to create other kinds of value."[47]

Companies can earn public credit with social campaigns that not only resonate with their loyalists, but have line-of-sight rele-vance to their brands and businesses. That's where authenticity lies.

Lloyd Blankfein, senior chairman of Goldman Sachs, is among many corporate leaders working to liberalize LGBTQ rights; he's building social equity for a lot of Goldman clients and employees. Before the Paris climate accords were reached, food companies around the world from Nestlé to Ben & Jerry's pressed government leaders for meaningful action; the warming climate matters to their businesses as much as clean water matters to Coca-Cola. The IMF and major central banks are advocating for policies cutting greenhouse gas emissions; the Bank for International Settlements warned in 2019 that climate change could cause "potentially extremely financial disruptive events that could be behind the next systemic financial crisis."[48] When the Trump administration sought to relax auto emissions rules, Ford, VW, Honda, and BMW struck a deal with the state of California setting tougher standards for themselves.[49] The White House was outraged, but it rang the right bell with other influencers.

Chatterji and Toffel, the duo behind that study of CEO activism, agree with Isdell. "To influence public policy, the message has to be authentic to both the individual leader and the business. There should be a compelling narrative for why *this* issue matters to *this* CEO of *this* business at *this* time . . . Because the credibility of business leaders rests on the perception that they make decisions after careful analysis, CEO activists can be effective only if they really understand the issue under debate."[50] In the internet era, companies accrue power and influence not only by passing that relevance test, but through dialogue, authenticity, and responsiveness.

What do companies do with that influence?

Levi Strauss, REI, Patagonia, and Sweetgreen are among U.S. companies lined up to boost election turnout by convincing Americans to vote early. "With changing rules and options like mail and in-person voting gaining significant attention due to public health concerns around COVID-19, we believe it is more important than ever for businesses to use their platforms to share current and accurate voting information with their audiences," said Vote Early Day, the campaign those companies support, told Axios.[51] It's billed as a nonpartisan push, but only Democratic and progressive factions labor to increase voter turnout. Those companies are taking an explicit political stand.

Starbucks could be an effective leader in trade and climate policy. Ally Bank and Sofi might be better than the Department of Education at solving the student debt crisis. I don't see why Anheuser-Busch, Procter & Gamble, and Walmart shouldn't play a bigger role in disaster recovery policy; they're good at logistics, they move faster than government, and the public trusts them. Maybe Johnson & Johnson, whose management of the 1982 Tylenol-poisoning crisis is still taught in business schools, could outdo the government's shambling coronavirus response.

The inspiring London-based business thinker Umair Haque pegs responsiveness as a new cornerstone of prosperity for private enterprise. In *The New Capitalist Manifesto: Building a Disruptively Better Business*, Haque calls out a range of corporations engaging in more enlightened capitalism—many not exactly corporate Young Turks, either, but fixtures such as Unilever, Lego, Walmart, and Nike. The best companies, says Haque, see the potential to play new roles and evolve.

"These firms are now all utilising resources by renewing rather than merely exploiting resources, shifting from value chains to value cycles. Value propositions are being replaced by value conversations and competitive advantage is now increasingly seen as a matter of long-term philosophy rather than short-term strategy."[52]

If he weren't already gone to his reward, you'd have to bust out the defib paddles for Milton Friedman.

In early 2020 the unelected, totally-not-governmental Greyhound bus company took a political stand—on federal immigration policy. The company told the U.S. Border Patrol that federal agents were no longer routinely permitted to run surprise, warrantless passenger credential checks aboard Greyhound buses. Nor would Greyhound allow warrantless searches in parts of depots passengers need a ticket to access, such as boarding gates.[53]

With its tactics to apprehend undocumented immigrants, a non-trivial portion of Greyhound's customer base,[54] U.S. Customs and Border Protection raised a lot of eyebrows. The ACLU called warrantless Border Patrol bus searches "dragnets," argued they violated the Fourth Amendment and sued.[55] U.S. Rep. Peter Welch of Vermont, in full deplore mode, said, "The correct course of action is for Congress to get off the sidelines and undertake a comprehensive reform of immigration laws that provides an appropriate path out of the shadows to citizenship."[56]

But comprehensive federal immigration reform was about as likely as a catered three-course meal on Greyhound. On immigration, as with coronavirus response, Washington was gridlocked, forging no consensus, and sapping public confidence and trust. Surprise searches upset passengers and delayed trips. Poor Greyhound was caught in the middle. In olden times, Washington lobbyists cozy with Capitol Hill would have been tasked with twisting arms to modify policy. Now, in the era of CEO activism, Greyhound changed things for itself, not on K Street but at the El Paso bus station. Demonstrative policy stands used to be the province of political leaders, but it's a new world.

All political action comes with inherent risk. Weber Shandwick advises would-be CEO activists: "Develop a thick skin. Expect the pitchforks to come out. As much as there will be genuine support and admiration for a CEO's activism, the criticism can be stinging as well. Learning how to not flinch will be critical."[57] The pitchforks came out for Greyhound, all right. The head of the Border Patrol Safety Council, Brandon Judd, went on *Fox and Friends* to charge the bus company was "putting profit above the safety of the American people."[58] It was surely putting customer privacy first while perhaps advancing its business interests. Backed by loyal customers cultivated in the digital infosphere, Greyhound could gain influence over immigration policy. Clearer laws, if they result, would benefit both the company and its riders.

The power shift underway, opening up new leadership roles for trusted businesses, is a natural dividend of the new digital dynamics. The internet teaches us to expect to be served what we want when we want it. If old sources of leadership screw up, lie, or otherwise abrogate trust, we the people now have the freedom to transfer faith and loyalty to institutions that give better service.

It sure puts a fresh spin on the old Greyhound slogan: In the internet era, leave the driving to *us*.

CHAPTER SEVEN

I CAN SEE CHAOS
FROM MY HOUSE

Aidy Bryant, the *Saturday Night Live* star, has seen the future of digital politics. No fool, she bailed.

Bryant played White House press secretary Sarah Huckabee Sanders on *SNL*. For putting herself out there, she was brutally eviscerated by online political extremists—on both sides. "The thing that always blew me away was that when I would play her on the show, I would be inundated with tweets saying I was a fat, ugly pig who didn't have the right to play someone as 'brave and smart' as Sarah Huckabee Sanders. The other half were tweeting at me saying I was too 'beautiful and good' to play someone as 'vile and fat' as Sarah Huckabee Sanders . . . It wasn't good for any reason," she told an interviewer.

Bryant deleted her Twitter account—one of numerous women performers, like Leslie Jones and Lindy West, harassed into retreat—and vowed never to return.[1]

Ms. Bryant, meet U.S. Army reservist Maatje Benassi. You two have more in common than you might think. Baselessly fingered by a YouTube conspiracy theorist as American coronavirus patient zero, Benassi endured waves of death threats from manic comment thread posters. "It's like waking up from a bad dream, going into a nightmare, day after day," she told CNN. Nothing she could do about it, either. YouTube deleted *some* abusive comments, but only after CNN covered Benassi's story.[2]

While I'm at this, say hi to writer and reformed internet political troll Therin Alrik, for whom provoking outrage is no longer job one. "I started an argument I knew I could win on every political post," recounted Alrik, in a confessional he published on *Medium*. "I dropped friends like flies. I spent hours doing this on Facebook . . . I relished the feeling of declaring victory over my opponent not by changing their mind, but by making them look dumb.

> "The purpose of argument, it seemed, wasn't to engage in a mutually constructive conversation, to deepen my understanding of an issue or the people on the other side of it. It was more like a video game, where the goal was to collect as many gold coins as possible, in the form of likes and shares, which were only granted each time I intellectually humiliated someone."

Shedding friends, getting blocked by family members, and finally realizing his online activity "didn't actually matter," Alrik beat his flame war addiction in 2019. Some in his circle didn't get the memo. When he posted about donating to Planned Parenthood, a relative accused him of "murdering babies." "I promptly ended the conversation," he wrote.[3]

This is our dominant political information system today: riddled with nonsense, reflexively cruel, rains of death threats flung as casually as beads in a Mardi Gras parade, allergic to empathy and complexity, distilling no consensus view of true facts or events, and driving its users to extremes. Not to mention exhaustion. In mid-2019, 46% of adult social media users said they felt "worn out" by political material online, up from 37% a year earlier, according to the Pew Research Center; 68% found it "stressful and frustrating" to broach political topics on social media with people they disagree with; only 27% said they found such interactions "interesting and informative."[4] Imagine the stress meter at the height of coronavirus quarantine season, when stay-at-homers had little more to do than pick online fights about hydroxychloroquine.

We greet every new communications medium with an initial flush of optimism. Television launched in the late 1940s with idealistic as well as commercial aspirations. TV would be a "university of the air," making viewers more erudite and worldly, and early series like *Playhouse 90* and the *Kraft Television Theater* aimed for high cultural ground. (As late as the 1970s and '80s, blockbuster TV miniseries produced with noble *and* moneymaking intent, like *Roots* and *The Winds of War*, brought the country together, and genre producer David Wolper insisted that any successful miniseries must have "sociological significance."[5]) There was always drivel on TV as well, and it grew more profuse as TV economics changed and the viewer base scattered to hundreds of cable channels plus streaming options and the internet. Somehow, though, it was . . . *trustworthy* drivel. Safe drivel. And political coverage on TV? Flawed and insufficiently diverse, as I've already discussed, far too enamored of its own conventional wisdom, but not fiction. Not made up out of whole cloth. And irate neighbors didn't surround your house with torches and pitchforks because your family was Huntley-Brinkley people instead of Cronkite people.

It was imagined that digital media, also, would lead to a sort of second Age of Enlightenment. In 1997, journalist Jon Katz predicted in *Wired* that "[t]echnology could fuse with politics to create a more civil society."[6] I expected the same, back in my *Slate* days. But the precise opposite has happened. Journalist Joseph Bernstein has been tracking the social and political impact of digital media for years. "The feelings of powerlessness, estrangement, loneliness, and anger created or exacerbated by the information age are so general it can be easy to think they are just a state of nature, like an ache that persists until you forget it's there. But then sometimes it suddenly gets much worse," he says.[7]

You want to know how much worse it can get? When you combine the natural lawlessness of the digital infosphere with always-advancing digital marketing and targeting capabilities, plus legions of calculating, unreliable narrators working to mislead you? Let's talk.

I see the digital ice cream shop serving up seven distinct flavors of decline, in ever-larger, more indigestible jumbo scoops. All seven forms of trouble are already evident. But as current trends continue, I see them morphing from annoyances into severe, perhaps fatal threats to electoral integrity, therefore public acceptance of the mechanisms of government, therefore democracy itself.

Noam Chomsky, the progressive social critic, derides "manufactured consent"—the idea that corporate-controlled mass media diabolically programs rank-and-file citizens to support elite agendas. But what the splintered, atomized digital infosphere provides us is orderless, manufactured *chaos*—an environment in which informed consent becomes impossible.

Disinformation, Lies, and Deepfakes

"America Leads the World in Testing," proclaimed White House victory banners in mid-May 2020, a moment amid the pandemic when the America certainly did not lead the world—not in a proper per capita ranking. Hardly any state was hitting even the bare minimum health experts recommended.[8] But as the administration knew, the internet had made it safe to assert para-truthy things as fact, and some believed it—just as some believed President Trump "won the popular vote," as he told bemused congressional leaders at a get-to-know-you reception in the first days of his presidency.[9] The cellular, subdivided, personalized echo-chamber structure of digital media made believing such things a whole lot easier.

When we have no reliable truth detectors at hand, faith and preconceptions take over. People become absolutely certain a ring of pedophiles works out of a Washington, D.C. pizza joint, or Pete Buttigieg is a CIA mole. Charges of rigged elections or voter fraud sound more plausible, all the more so if you're on the side of the victim. Lost in the fog, we fall back on what we want to be true, gripping our beliefs ever more fiercely.

In a more or less unmoderated sphere, it is a snap to manipulate people by manipulating the system running in the background.

Unreliable narrators wear many guises. *VICE News* caught Google Maps directing women in search of abortion counseling to pro-life centers and the National Memorial for the Unborn in Chattanooga, Tennessee; anti-abortion centers in Arkansas and Alabama had manipulated Google into categorizing those sites as abortion clinics.[10] Fake local news websites powered by Locality Labs, a conservative group, sprouted by the dozen from Maryland to Wisconsin; they purported to offer small-town coverage but delivered unbylined, unsubstantiated, slanted articles urging readers to vote down high school funding measures or support right-wing congressional hopefuls. "In the fractured media environment we're operating in now, if you're just scrolling through your Facebook feed or your Twitter feed and you see an article, you click on it and you might take in the information from there without really ever wondering what the source actually is," said Matt Gertz of Media Matters.[11] Russian-backed disinformation sites like *Sputnik News* and RT.com get a legitimacy boost from programmatic ad algorithms that plant banners for Geico, Walmart, AARP, and Disney among fake, divisive agitprop.[12]

All the counsel in the world to "be your own editor" won't surmount obstacles like these. When you make people embark on scavenger hunts for good data or force them to decode puzzles to pick truth out from drivel, it's like forcing hungry people to pick the real meatballs out of a giant bowl of red-sauced ping-pong balls. It's a callous and humiliating meal, and there has to be a better way to avoid starving.

Technology to make spookily convincing deepfakes is getting more accessible all the time. It's not just for big-budget movie-makers with the cash to reanimate Peter Cushing and James Dean. At the economy end of the scale, smallball digital artists produce really good deepfakes singlehandedly. One, called Shamook, modifies classic movies for a lark—replacing Harrison Ford with a circa-1980 Tom Selleck in *Raiders of the Lost Ark*, for example. (*Raiders* co-writer George Lucas wanted Selleck, but he became unavailable when CBS television took Selleck's *Magnum, P.I.* pilot to series. Selleck must wonder to this day how Indy's fedora would have fit. Now he doesn't have to wonder. He can click on Shamook's YouTube channel and see himself trapped on the rope bridge with Short Round and Kate Capshaw, or trading quips with Sean Connery.[13])

To the casual observer, these images are acceptably real—and more convincing still when presented by someone they trust. President Trump retweeted a deepfake showing Joe Biden with a lizardlike CGI tongue.[14] Moving images can be more convincing than written text. Think how casually most everyday voters regard political advertising. Imagine what people can be made to believe in future.

Just as bad: Imagine not believing anything any more.

No More Secrets

"The surveillance state's got brand new tricks," went a lyric in a jokey 2020 Super Bowl commercial for Snickers, sung by a sad-eyed old man alone at his kitchen table while smart home devices assure him they're not spying, and you were meant to laugh.[15] With matter-of-fact rhetoric as well as laugh lines, Big Tech has for decades sought to make targeted surveillance seem inevitable—to reposition the dystopian dynamics of *1984*'s all-seeing telescreens as a benign cultural norm. Way back in 1999, Scott McNealy of Sun Microsystems famously declared, "You have zero privacy anyway. Get over it."[16] It was a resistance-is-futile message. And whether people actually liked the idea, struck a weary bargain with it, or just got worn down over time, the campaign seems to have softened us up. Henry Mance at the *Financial Times* nailed the attitudinal sea-change:

> "It is not simply that information is being collected on us; that information is now often high-quality video and audio, which can precisely identify our every move . . . employers can track our sleeping habits, retailers can follow us round the aisles, car parts suppliers say that they can identify drivers' emotions. The resulting data are training complex algorithms, which then nudge us towards certain behaviours. "Twenty years ago, if a supermarket had asked to put a microphone in our houses, or a landlord had asked to put in a camera, or a train company had asked our whereabouts in the station, we would have said no. Now we buy Amazon Alexas, rent Airbnbs and use London Underground's free wifi. And then we cross our fingers."[17]

If you were crossing your fingers that all the data-gathering technologies probing your life are staying in their own lanes and not comparing notes, guess again. It happens all the time. The Electronic Frontier Foundation reported that the Android app accompanying Ring, the smart doorbell from Amazon, was compiling a "plethora" of tidbits about what's going on inside its customers' homes and other networked devices—and forwarding summaries to analytics and marketing companies such as AppsFlyer and MixPanel. MixPanel even gets Ring customer names and email addresses. "All this takes place without meaningful user notification and consent and, in most cases, no way to mitigate the damage done," said EFF.[18]

Exceptional case? I wish. Avast, the big antivirus company, was found to be harvesting data from 100 million customer devices and reselling it via a subsidiary called Jumpshot to deep-pocketed corporate customers. Users who allowed Avast access to their browsing history were promised their data would be "stripped and de-identified." But according to an investigation by *PCMag* and *Motherboard*, at least one Jumpshot customer, Omnicom Media Group, got individual device IDs anyway. Even without them, a big company can do a little triangulation, compare Jumpshot data to its own records, deduce that it was *you* who purchased that red wheelbarrow online at 11:35:17 last night, and suddenly see your entire online life. "What should be a giant chunk of anonymized web history data can actually be picked apart and linked back to individual Avast users," concluded *PCMag*.[19]

Sometimes, reported *VICE*, the stuff relayed included minute, screen-by-screen records of a user's PornHub sessions: "It is possible to determine from the collected data what date and time the anonymized user visited YouPorn and PornHub, and in some cases what search term they entered into the porn site and which specific video they watched."[20] Thus was it theoretically feasible for Omnicom, or any Jumpshot client, to deduce an Avast user's kinks. For science, no doubt.

When *PCMag* and *Motherboard* caught Avast, Avast wound down Jumpshot hurriedly and . . . apologized. Yeah, there's a lot of that going around.

I would love to tell you the Avast case is unique, but in truth if I gave you a page on every case like it, you could use this book for weight training. We've talked for years about the not-fully-activated value of your grocery-buying data, compiled by your supermarket chain's loyalty-card program. A health insurer would naturally like to know when its policyholders start buying more Scotch or red meat, but such insight is typically siloed, leveraged only by the store, which might slip you a coupon for half-price ribs. Now we see those silos crumble as new data technologies and analytics strategies assert themselves. Any data, once surfaced, is abusable.[21]

The Chinese government used mass-scale facial recognition to identify pro-democracy street protesters in Hong Kong, and help track and control COVID-19 transmission—even with people wearing face masks. Perhaps you've seen ads for the Shen Yun dance company that tours U.S. cities; Shen Yun is a fundraising and propaganda tool of Falun Gong, which opposes the incumbent Beijing regime. What if Beijing records the faces of American Shen Yun ticket-buyers as they file into auditoriums and concert halls, identifies them, and targets them with digital propaganda of its own? Or denies them entry to China when they attempt business trips or vacations?

Stick with me here. Could a U.S. political campaign made aware of every journey you make in the physical world—every bar, church, pharmacy, or bank you visit—base a more effective, or invasive, personal pitch on that information? Could a political cause that discovers your embarrassing browsing history reach out and propose silence in return for loyal activism?

We used to court gettable voters by ZIP code, then by home address. But these digitally aided targeting strategies, increasingly plausible and therefore increasingly likely, make the old ways look like the Flintstones. If only that were as alarming as the digital surveillance story gets. But now comes Neuralink.

Neuralink, an Elon Musk company, was planning 2020 trials for a device to be implanted in people's brains that could read and transmit thoughts. The first primitive expressions of the technology will likely have medical angles, such as helping paralyzed people control physical devices with mental effort alone. But Musk is said to believe that in order to keep pace with artificial intelligence, we will all inevitably get these implants. His thinking on this subject is blocks ahead of government regulators (though perhaps not government surveillance agencies). There are no laws preventing the National Security Agency from collecting your thoughts, surreptitiously or not, or a future Jumpshot-type outfit packaging up your brain data and selling it to third parties.[22]

Musk isn't even first on the moon, here. China is said to be already deploying brain-reading technology to monitor the mental and emotional states of people in mission-critical jobs, like train operators.[23] As part of its autonomous-vehicle push, automaker Nissan is incubating a technology that lets Nissan cars read brain signals from their drivers; it "delivers more excitement and driving pleasure by detecting, analyzing and responding to driver's brainwaves in

Never mind peeking at your browsing history. Now we're talking about third parties getting access to your entire consciousness.

real time."[24] Never mind peeking at your browsing history. Now we're talking about third parties getting access to your entire consciousness—not just your preferences in wheelbarrows, but your loves, fears, dreams, desires, and political preferences.

If legal brain spying is perfected, then hacked—and *every* digital system is hackable—the implications are profound. Knit these new technologies with agenda-driven politics, and the result looks like an unprecedented, disruptive form of societal chaos.

"I've come to the conclusion that because information constantly increases, there's never going to be privacy," pronounced David Scalzo, an investor in Clearview AI, the facial recognition solution serving law enforcement. "[Y]ou can't ban technology. Sure, that might lead to a dystopian future or something, but you can't ban it."[25]

Maybe yes, maybe no. But to Big Tech's satisfaction, we have so far not mustered the focus to even try.

Extremists Gonna Extreme

82% of Republicans in October 2019 believed the Democratic Party had been taken over by socialists; 80% of Democrats meanwhile believed the Republican Party had been taken over by racists.[26] Neither is remotely true. But the digital infosphere's sharpened, caustic, bumper-sticker-simple formats help cement the impression that there are no longer any centrists out there—or at least that their puny numbers are safe to ignore.

This is not the case. Not dissuaded by Bernie Sanders' primary defeat in 2020, liberal activists dominating Reddit threads continued to claim the United States harbored broad-based, pent-up demand for Scandinavian-style social democracy. But socialism is actually not that popular: In a February 2020 NBC News/Wall Street Journal poll, 19% of Americans view it positively. 53% viewed socialism negatively. And while progressives on social media noisily celebrate the imminent death of capitalism, only 18% of Americans overall viewed capitalism negatively; 52% liked it.[27] 87% of Americans actually have a positive view of the term "free enterprise."[28] The loudest voices in chat rooms are not a fair sounding of overall public opinion. They just want you to think so, and ye who dare to differ are corporate dupes or maybe even fascists.

Fair play: Right-wing activists excoriate their challengers in terms at least as childish and pestilential. Republican candidates go to market claiming a vast majority of the public loves the conservative agenda, and the rest are anti-American saboteurs. But in 2018 the party's own internal survey data showed "increasing funding for veterans' mental health services, strengthening and preserving Medicare and Social Security, and reforming the student loan system all scored higher than Trump's favored subjects of tax cuts, border security, and preserving the Immigration and Customs Enforcement agency."[29] In other words, the broad public was way out of alignment with right-wing voices hogging social media, too.

Each extreme, left and right, assures its adherents they're right and the other team is lying, evil, or insane. Each side positions itself online as the voice of the majority and acts like the big, giant, nuanced middle doesn't exist. (The GOP's 2018 data found its own voters refused to believe the Democrats could possibly win back the House in that year's midterms, which of course happened.) "It feels like the moderate middle is melting like late-winter snow in Maine," said Republican Sen. Susan Collins, a Mainer struggling for her political life amid disdain from left and right alike.[30] As one internet disinformation cowboy said during the 2018 election, "The more extreme we become, the more people believe it."[31]

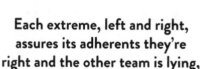

Each extreme, left and right, assures its adherents they're right and the other team is lying, evil, or insane.

In truth, in January 2020, per Gallup, only 27% of voters called themselves Republicans. An identical 27% identified as Democrats; 45% said they were independent.[32] (Keep those numbers top of mind next time you hear someone allude to "overwhelming" Democratic or Republican support for something.) The Cook Political Report concluded in September 2019 that something like 30% of the public qualify as "swing voters," genuinely undecided or only "probably" going to vote for one presidential candidate or the other. Cook also reported that these swing voters "tend to be younger, more moderate, and less engaged in politics compared to those who have decided and to the overall electorate." Their flags don't fly very high on the internet. The architecture and incentives that define the digital infosphere promote more outrageous, extreme, performative content. Information providers fight for eyeballs on a second-by-second basis, so there's little room for subtlety. Social media rewards audacity; measured, equivocal essays don't score so many clicks.

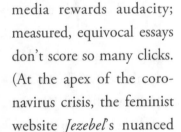

Social media rewards audacity; measured, equivocal essays don't score so many clicks..

(At the apex of the coronavirus crisis, the feminist website *Jezebel*'s nuanced contribution to national unity and civility was an essay titled "I Will Personally Be Thrilled If Stephen Miller Dies of Covid-19," Miller being the controversial White House adviser whose new wife contracted the disease.[33]) Social media even demonizes evolution. A changed mind telegraphs weakness. (Look how progressives combed Donald Trump's old tweets for ancient pronouncements that contradict new ones, while the Trump campaign excavated debatable votes Senator Joe Biden cast during the Ford administration—both held up as examples of mendacity if not idiocy.)

Through this distorted glass, our politics look ever more partisan and simplistic, a false and misleading portrait of us. And if you, a thoughtful citizen of nuanced or undecided views who may have changed your mind a time or two, don't see yourself reflected in the internet media mirror, you might be tempted to conclude, sadly and however inaccurately, that you no longer exist.

Mainstream political media could have chosen to exert a mature, countervailing force against online extremism. Instead it has too often emulated the trend. Once middle-of-the-road media outlets quote out-of-context tweets to bolster a partisan case and stage televised shoutfests that valorize extreme soundbites. The dissolution of middle ground in media is on trend and affects how politicians communicate. Trump in the first three years of his presidency gave 70 interviews to Fox News—no other network news organization got more than five.[34] And certain Democratic senators decorate MSNBC so often, you could swear they're getting their mail delivered to the green room.

The "pro-reason, pro-individualist" political essayist Robert Tracinski has written that buying into such a warped, hype-driven caricature of our political environment can help destroy us. "We have a tendency to catastrophize about the state of the world and gravitate to the most pessimistic view. Yet this tendency raises the risk that we will cause the very disasters we're trying to avoid. If we look at a society that is historically well-off, peaceful, and orderly, and we imagine—with help from the latest hysterical rantings on social media—that it is all collapsing into chaos, then we are likely to precipitate the collapse of the institutions that brought us our freedom and prosperity."[35]

The Rage Dial Goes to 11

The digital infosphere is not only a rotten substrate for complex ideas and dialogue, it is a rage accelerator. When you trade views with friends out on the sidewalk about the imminent mayoral election, gentle contradiction is not automatically read as persecution. Not right there in front of the nail salon. But online, an arms race of insults and personal attacks often ensues. As the rage dial gets turned up, you can watch people shed grammatical skills as well as their inhibitions.

When screaming, profane, misspelled, unmoderated fights among anonymous strangers cruising for likes acquire such prominence in our political discourse, our systems naturally degenerate. Abject terror of partisan animus surely plays some role—how big is hard to say—in elected leaders' relationships with constituents, therefore their decisions. "It's the difference from a representative democracy to a direct democracy," said Illinois Senate President John Cullerton, a Democrat. "So, the old model (for voters) is, 'I'm busy. I'm hiring you. Go down to Springfield. Listen to testimony. Make your informed decisions. Every two years, I'll check on you,'" he said. "And now, you just go directly to the legislator (who says), 'We don't need to listen to any testimony. I got 500 emails and 5,000 tweets retweeted saying I've got to vote for this bill.'"[36]

Fear of amplified rage on digital media may help explain why Republican senators like Ted Cruz and Lindsey Graham evolved from blunt critics of Donald Trump to ingratiating courtesans. The mere threat of internet abuse was said by some Washington observers to have influenced the denouement of the Trump impeachment trial. "I've had numerous retiring [Republicans] talk warily—sometimes fearfully—about the 'cult' of Trump supporters back home," said journalist Tim Alberta, author of *American Carnage: On the Front Lines of the Republican Civil War and the Rise of President Trump*. "They worry about harassment of their families, loss of standing in local communities, estranged relationships."[37]

With violent rage a sanctioned form of expression in the digital infosphere—Twitter has a "hateful conduct policy" and "abusive behavior policy," which can result in time-outs, but it's selectively applied—online influencers of all stripes field death threats in response to relatively minor acts. In the hours after basketball star Kobe Bryant's death in a helicopter crash, *Washington Post* reporter Felicia Sonmez had a security detail assigned. Why? She had tweeted about Bryant's checkered, albeit distant, past, which included sexual assault allegations. In calmer conventional media channels, the same point about Bryant was made without fuss. Sports journalist Bob Costas raised it during a CNN roundtable the night of Bryant's death, and no other panelist dove across the desk at him. Say it on Twitter, though, and Sonmez found herself living in a hotel in an undisclosed location, not daring to return to her own home, while *Post* editor Marty Baron suspended her and wrote her, "A real lack of judgment to tweet this. Please stop. You're hurting this institution."[38] Why were Costa and other TV commentators allowed to mention Bryant's controversial history, while Sonmez caught hell for a tweet? Fear. The unpredictable online rage factor.

None of this is good for us, our ability to understand let alone respect each other, or the quality of our government, and if we continue on this course, I see things only getting worse.

The Death of Trust

What naturally follows when people no longer believe what they read or see? People no longer trust anyone, or any claim, that does not conform to what they want to be true.

Political scientists eke out full-time careers charting the collapse of public trust in once-esteemed institutions. Congress? Fuhgeddaboudit. Public schools, labor unions, big business, health maintenance organizations, journalists? None are trusted "a great deal" or "quite a lot" by more than 29% of Americans.[39] Solid majorities believe both the federal government and news media withhold information important to the public.[40]

When the population catches the low-trust bug, three bad things happen to political discourse.

First, tribal thinking takes charge. You make allowances for your tribal fellows and, especially, leaders. During President Trump's impeachment, *Politico* editor John Harris invited Trump supporters to write in and provide "an honest illumination of what defenders would think if the essential facts . . . were the same except for one—Hillary Clinton were president." He got this back: "Consistency is certainly an essential standard of logical argument, but it is, in my opinion, very overvalued as a measure of judgment. We live in 'scoundrel times' and when both sides prove themselves to be scoundrels, you may be forced to 'pick your poison.'"[41]

Voter suppression happens—indubitably. But it is hardly ever read objectively. Without trust in essential systems, voter suppression is either a right-wing plot to maintain power or a liberal invention to persecute the right wing. In the 2018 Georgia race for governor between Democrat Stacey Abrams and Republican

Brian Kemp, Kemp, Georgia's secretary of state at the time, closed hundreds of polling stations in predominantly black districts and suspended 53,000 applications to vote for miniscule infractions, such as hyphens missing from surnames. African Americans comprise 32% of the state's population, but 70% of the suspended applications. Kemp, white, defeated Abrams, black, by a hair—in what was either a "homegrown corollary of the Administration's xenophobic rhetoric" (per the left-leaning *New Yorker*)[42], or faithful enforcement of voter-ID laws and "election officials making adjustments based on the changing ways people are voting" (per the right-leaning Heritage Foundation).[43] I expect one or the other rationale may have raised your pulse rate just now, if you belong to one tribe or the other.

Election irregularities did not end in Florida with the 2000 Bush-Gore hanging-chad recount. Whether the cause is nefariousness or incompetence, we keep getting questionable outcomes, always interpreted through the internet's tribal prisms. In my state, Washington, the 2004 gubernatorial race was such a debacle, conservative election-watcher John Fund called it "Florida with rain." Republican Dino Rossi's 3,000-vote lead on election night melted in a seven-week storm of recounts, newly discovered absentee ballots, admission of unverified provisional ballots, and on-the-fly rules changes by Democrat-controlled authorities. Although a conservative computer consultant later showed King County had counted "more votes than voters," when a tally finally showed Democrat Christine Gregoire ahead, she was declared the winner shortly before Christmas.

With such clearly untrustworthy results—the totals seesawed all the time during November and December—you thought this mess was either a solemn quest for truth and justice, or a ham-handed campaign to subvert the peoples' will. A majority of Washingtonians wanted a revote, but Gregoire unsurprisingly said that would be "ridiculous." In January, King County election supervisor Dean Logan admitted he didn't know who had really won the "messy process" of an election. "Are voters supposed to trust an election merely because it can't 'clearly' be shown to have been hopelessly tainted?" wondered Fund.[44] No, but in a world where wanting things to be true replaces trust in data, the rules—and outcomes—change.

The second bad thing: People angling for power use the low-trust environment to their advantage. A losing candidate can refuse to concede, deny the numbers on the tote board, and some tribal loyalists will fall in line. Kentucky Gov. Matt Bevin lost narrowly to Democrat Andy Beshear in his 2019 bid for re-election but would not admit it for more than a week, claiming a slew of election-day irregularities. Little or no evidence emerged to support him, a statewide recanvassing showed almost no changes in the vote count, but Bevin stuck to his guns. When he finally conceded, he sowed fresh if unsubstantiated doubts about electoral integrity: "If the people lose confidence in their ability to actually know that the vote they cast is the one that was tabulated for the person they intended it to be for . . . we lose something in America," Bevin said.[45] Irony keeled over and died right there.

President Trump has routinely sought to reduce faith in election systems, encouraging rally crowds to "Watch other communities, because we don't want this election stolen from us!" It's catching on. Law professor Richard L. Hasen calculates that election litigation has nearly tripled since 2000: "It's not clear that we can rely on responsible leaders of both parties to assure democratic transitions and acceptance of election results."[46]

The third bad thing: As the political divide over COVID-19 proved, a society this skeptical of any and all information in the public square is less equipped to survive systemic shocks. In a close election where even the principals become arguably unreliable narrators—and sequels to the Kemp-Abrams or Rossi-Gregoire dramas are inevitable in this divided nation—will we ever accept that the victor was indeed the victor? Who's left to referee these contests believably?

The fog is so thick now, I believe a successful, verified exterior cyberattack on a big American election would be denied by some, embraced and leveraged by some, and debated to death by others—no matter the weight and clarity of the evidence. Michael Daniel, the former cybersecurity coordinator in the Obama White House who now runs the Cyber Threat Alliance, told *Rolling Stone* he isn't sure the country would ever be the same. "How do we deal with that?" he asks. "How do we recover from that?"[47]

In our current state, not well.

When these trends play out in the foreground of increasing economic inequality, in which a giant preponderance of citizens run up against nonporous barriers to upward mobility, it just makes everything worse. "As they become poorer, people begin to distrust each other—and then hate each other," reasoned Umair Haque, author of *The New Capitalist Manifesto*, "Why wouldn't they? . . . As distrust becomes hate, people who have nothing to give anyways end up having no reason to even hope to give anything back to anyone else . . . Why give the very people who denied you healthcare and education anything?[48]

"This is how a society dies," concluded Haque.[49]

Godwin's Law says the longer an online debate careens on, the greater the probability of someone bringing up Hitler.[50] (It was coined a quarter-century ago by Mike Godwin, staff lawyer at the Electronic Frontier Foundation.) This is not an online argument, and we're seven chapters in without hitting the Hitler button, which Godwin said usually terminates the debate, with the invoker the loser. But as a one-time indulgence, it is worth recalling what Hannah Arendt had to say about the tactical efficacy of lies and propaganda.

The German-born Arendt was a young woman when Hitler took power. She was briefly imprisoned by the Gestapo before fleeing to the United States in 1941, where she studied the Nazi regime, and Stalin's, from a safe distance, resulting in her keystone work, *The Origins of Totalitarianism*, published in 1951. Arendt examined the role of bad information—fake news—in generating a "mixture of gullibility and cynicism" among citizen-consumers:

> "In an ever-changing, incomprehensible world the masses had reached the point where they would, at the same time, believe everything and nothing; think that everything was possible, and nothing was true . . . The totalitarian mass leaders based their propaganda on the correct psychological assumption that, under such conditions, one could make people believe the most fantastic statements one day, and trust that if the next day they were given irrefutable proof of their falsehood, they would take refuge in cynicism; instead of deserting the leaders who had lied to them, they would protest that they had known all along that the statement was a lie and admire the tactical leaders for their cleverness."[51]

Today we call it gaslighting, and it works in and out of politics. Make stuff up, assert the opposite of what is true, target receptive people, pump the narrative out through pervasive channels, sideline the reliable narrators—or propagate a platform with no frames, editors, or filter—and a lot of people will buy it.

This is not a right-wing thing, necessarily, or a left-wing thing. It's an across-the-spectrum perversion of political discourse greatly enabled by the digital infosphere. It transforms a population, and it murders trust.

Walled Gardens Make a Comeback

The consumer internet dawned as a metroplex of controlled fortresses such as CompuServe, Prodigy, and AOL. Like theme parks, they provided a self-contained, patrolled experience. There were virtual gangplanks leading out to the wild and woolly free-range internet, but you ventured outside the park walls at your own risk.

CompuServe and Prodigy are long gone, but paid premium experiences are back with bells on—partly as fashion or status statements, partly as strategies for users to avoid the low-rent mosh pit. "Free apps like Twitter and Facebook have become extractive mass-surveillance tools," wrote Kevin Roose, technology columnist for *The New York Times,* in 2019. "And once the Internet became the primary place where our identities are forged and performed, it was inevitable that some people would want to pay their way out of the panopticon—that escape from the very services we lusted after in recent memory would become a premium good."[52]

So today you pay not only for online journalism (well, if you don't, please consider supporting some outlet you trust—the more local, the better)—but for premium password keepers, premium email handling, premium security, premium Fortnite character skins, Spotify and Netflix, podcasts, maybe ad-free YouTube. You can spend yourself silly insulating yourself from the baseline, everyday internet.

But there's a political problem with the resurgence of walled gardens. Privacy and personal data may be at increasing risk on the "free internet," but if you've got the funds, you can buy up into a more secure experience. The net result is quintessentially undemocratic: a two-tier virtual world in which, as Roose wrote, "The programmers simply built the machines that let big corporations, powerful politicians, and savvy media manipulators tell other people what to do, and they are letting rich people pay to turn those machines off." It reminds me of the Jodie Foster sci-fi movie *Elysium*, in which rich people pay to migrate off a ruined, dangerous Earth and go live in a cushy orbital space cruiser, leaving the rabble with low credit scores to slug it out down below. We're better than that, or should be.

Sundar Pichai, CEO of Alphabet and its ubiquitous subsidiary Google, has said: "Privacy cannot be a luxury good offered only to people who can afford to buy premium goods and services." Ironically, he was taking a shot at Apple, which was rolling out updated, premium-priced iPhones with a new privacy pitch.[53] And while he's right, walled-garden syndrome has implications beyond privacy. It suggests a virtual world with socioeconomic tiers, a world that eventually mirrors some of the worst aspects of the real one—where it's the haves versus the have-nots, and the haves get better news and information, better security, more highbrow discourse, better everything. Yet the United States of America is not a jumbo jet with first-class suites up front for the Sapphire Platinum crowd, butt-punishing basic economy in back for low rollers. Our politics and elections depend on equal access to trustworthy information.

The Arena Empties

Like fair-weather fans of a mediocre rock band having an off-key night, voters sick of all this noise can be expected to depart the arena—especially if they make unrewarded investments in the process and come to feel ignored. If too many give up on politics, they leave behind only the hard-core faithful, those with an appetite for punishment, and self-interested combatants who know the more participants exit, the more power flows to those who remain.

Aidy Bryant can close her Twitter account and feel great about firewalling herself from all the ragey madness, so how many Americans will eventually react to digital dysfunction by quitting politics and binging Animal Planet on election night—and feel at least as good?

In Chapter 1 I mentioned *Exit, Voice, and Loyalty*, Albert O. Hirschman's landmark 1970 treatise on how people react to unsatisfactory organizations or political environments. Hirschman's thesis was that a displeased citizen has only three rational options: move somewhere else, complain, or grit your teeth and deal. I suggested that our politics have now evolved to give people a fourth option uncited by Hirschman: denial. Stay where you are, but stop paying attention. Switch over to Animal Planet, groove on some lemurs, and let those lying, foul-mouthed politicos continue bombarding each other without you.

Denial may not have crossed Hirschman's mind as a reasonable choice half a century ago, but in a 21st-century infosphere where nobody knows what's true, the atmosphere is simplistic and abusive, and politicians no longer do much of what a majority of the public wants anyway, I think abandonment is tragically rational. We risk driving millions of potential voters out of the political arena, leaving it in the hands of elites, hobbyists, and comparatively small knots of aggrieved grudge-nursers.

Demographic analysis shows denial has in fact been quietly trending for years, especially among younger Americans more tuned into digital media, less invested in—even disdainful of—traditional establishment media. Of course, many a "reform" presidential candidate of the past, most of them liberal Democrats, pinned hopes on the activist "youth vote" but lived to regret it. Fred Harris in 1976, Jerry Brown in 1980, Gary Hart in 1984 and '88, Howard Dean in 2004, and Bernie Sanders in 2016 and 2020 were a few of the candidates who bet on a "youthquake" to shatter conventional wisdom and sweep them to power, but none were nominated. Young voters have long been vociferous in the media but elusive on voting day, while older voters show up to cast ballots more reliably. What we are promised on social media is a "youthquake" perennially just around the next curve. But what we actually get is a gerontocracy, a country run by older people, which is perhaps another inducement to young people to give politics a pass.

In the 2018 midterms, touted at both ideological extremes as "the most important midterms of our lives," overall voter turnout was 53.4%. But voters under 30 underperformed at 36%, while those 65 and up overperformed at 66%.[54] Activating the youth vote is a chicken-egg dilemma—it's hard to convince them the effort is worth it until they observe results, and there won't be any results to observe until they exert serious effort.

Left-leaning young voters online in election season are as strident as ever. You could spend all day getting into slap fights on Facebook with half-remembered high school classmates over the true definition of socialism. But when you zoomed out to look at the whole country the story might have been different. In the last days of 2019, an *Economist*/YouGov poll reported only 36% of Americans were paying "a lot" of attention to the 2020 campaign. The percentage of respondents 18 to 29 paying a lot of attention was a sobering 22%; 50% of young voters were paying "only a little" attention or "none at all."[55]

Social media, partisan digital news, and cable TV pundits made American politics look all-consuming, like a sport with 350 million rabid, full-throated superfans rooting for one of only two teams. Reality was almost certainly different. The actual, engaged participant base across the country may be smaller than anyone wants to believe, and the digital infosphere may be causing more and more to throw up their hands.

To those aspiring to control things, though, this state of affairs was more than fine; it was helpful. The fewer hands fighting for the political throttle, the better. Social critic Umair Haque believes a worst-case state of atrophy is already upon us: "Politics [in the United Kingdom and United States] has become a sclerotic Soviet affair. Anglo-American societies aren't really democracies in any sensible meaning of the word anymore. They're run by and for a class of elites . . . In America, that class is a bizarre coterie of Ivy Leaguers pretending to be aw-shucks-good-ole-boys on the one side, like Ted Cruz, and Ivy Leaguers pretending to be do-gooders on the other, like Zuck and Silicon Valley. In Britain, it's the notorious public-school boys, the Etonians and Oxbridge set."[56] It only *looks* like a populist revolution. Cast your gaze up from the internet and the distribution of power and influence is different.

Some think all this, rolled up, points to the end of democracy. An eminent "political psychologist" named Shawn Rosenberg sparked an uproar at a 2019 professional conference by presenting a paper saying so. The internet and social media, he said, cause information overload and a burgeoning trust crisis. People don't invest enough energy in good governance. They abandon reliable narrators, in part because those narrators are remote elites with whom they have nothing in common. In their absence, without a compass, more people think authoritarianism looks pretty good. "In well-established democracies like the United States, democratic governance will continue its inexorable decline, and will eventually fail," said Rosenberg.[57]

Alarmed as I am about the mounting chaos in the digital infosphere, Rosenberg makes me look like Kimmy Schmidt. But I think he's being too dire. Rosenberg's argument requires us to believe we're all strapped in aboard a doomed, rudderless high-speed clipper heading for the rocks, and none of us below deck have the strength to break free, bust down the bridge door, and steer to a safer heading.

I think we do. There are actions we can take: technology improvements, regulatory changes, and a long-past-due revolution in civic consciousness. They would result in pervasive uplift. They'd ignite new hope for our politics and our country. They might coax Aidy Bryant back to social media. And they begin on the next page.

CHAPTER EIGHT

TRY MY AMAZING FIVE-STEP PROGRAM

So here's that agonizing reappraisal you ordered.

Long before the pandemic, the trends I've mapped were swimming into ominous focus. COVID-19 threw everything into HD clarity. Literally overnight our digital connections, flawed and sometimes ugly or frightening as they were, became sole lifelines for work, news, family check-ins, scoring Clorox wipes and take-out dinners, and—especially—politics.

As I said off the top, I was shaken by so much of what played out online in the coronavirus crisis, from noxious Twitter fights between national leaders to waves of lunatic misinformation. But the spectacle left me feeling that we have to link arms and make change, More, that positive change is eminently possible.

Throughout my career I have tried not only to work at the edge of the envelope, pushing it outward and trying for more, but to remain an optimist. Despite recent events, I am optimistic now.

They're straight shooters, I think, at the Pew Research Center. Their loyalties lie with truth, data, and wisdom; Pew does not tolerate alternative facts. Working with Elon University's Imagining the Internet Center, Pew in the second half of 2019 asked nearly 1,000 influencers how they thought technology would affect democratic institutions through 2030.

The Pew study was released in early 2020, when the coronavirus was still seen as China's problem. It did not make for reassuring reading. 49% of tech innovators, business leaders, and assorted movers and shakers surveyed thought tech would "mostly weaken core aspects of democracy and democratic representation in the next decade," which, if you've caught my drift in these pages, already happened in the *past* decade. But one-third of the voices in the mix—33%—said the reverse: that technology will actually "strengthen" our political systems. (18% predicted no significant change.)[1]

33% of influencers predict technology will actually strengthen our political systems in the 2020s.

I'm with the 33%. Really.

The pessimists expected disinformation, invasive data harvesting by Big Tech platforms, and heightened digital surveillance will torpedo what trust remains in democratic systems. The minority of optimists told Pew effective solutions will evolve, "because people always adapt and can use technology to combat the problems that face democracy." Paul Saffo, chair for futures studies and forecasting at Singularity University, told Pew: "There is a long history of new media forms creating initial chaos upon introduction and then being assimilated into society as a positive force. This is precisely what happened with print in the early 1500s and with newspapers over a century ago. New technologies are like wild animals—it takes time for cultures to tame them. I am not in any way downplaying the turbulence still ahead . . . but there is a sunnier digital upland on the other side of the current chaos."[2]

If I wasn't a net-net optimist I would not be writing at all. I'd be holed up with my family in the intellectual equivalent of a '50s underground fallout shelter, seeing if we've stockpiled enough canned peaches to survive both pandemics and the digital apocalypse. But we got beyond nuclear dread—the global thermonuclear war form of dread that colored my childhood as an Army brat—and we can fix this, too. Or so I believe.

The scholar Shoshana Zuboff, emerita professor at Harvard Business School, has ably covered the techno-social-economic waterfront for years. Zuboff coined the term "surveillance capitalism" for what we're watching happen. It's old hat to remind consumers that when they're not paying for online bonbons, from Google Maps to Facebook gifs, *they* are the product. Actually, Zuboff says, at this point tech users are neither customers nor products, but a kind of Soylent Green to be munched on by a growing, momentum-driven economic juggernaut, "the raw material for new procedures of manufacturing and sales that define an entirely new economic order: a surveillance economy."[3]

"Its success depends upon one-way-mirror operations engineered for our ignorance and wrapped in a fog of misdirection, euphemism and mendacity," says Zuboff.

But she also reminds us: "Anything made by humans can be unmade by humans."[4]

So here goes some unmaking. In five categories: regulation, voting, journalism, civics, and internet anonymity.

Regulation Time

It seemed I was not the only one in the digital world for whom the coronavirus crisis clarified the stakes. As things got worse in 2020, Big Tech's leading lights seemed to sense it, too, and hustled to seem human.

"We just realize the seriousness of the moment and the importance of getting it right at a moment when our services are really needed," Facebook vice president Molly Cutler told Axios.[5] Here, maybe, was a chance to model more responsible, public-spirited behavior—and perhaps head off a corrective regulatory reckoning.

A morass of new regulatory legislation was piling up on Capitol Hill, including measures to protect kids' privacy, ban ads targeted at minors, and create the country's first data protection agency, complete with subpoena powers.[6] But in the throes of the COVID-19 outbreak, Facebook—whose head told a House panel just months earlier that fake facts weren't his problem—was suddenly yanking posts promoting anti-quarantine protests, calling them "harmful disinformation;"[7] laying on a new artificial intelligence program that used text and image matching to find and delete hate speech;[8] and daring to pull down a Trump 2020 campaign ad for violating hate-speech policy. (The ad featured an upside-down triangle similar to a symbol used by Nazis to classify political prisoners.[9]) Google and YouTube were trying to steer users to better-quality information from the World Health Organization and CDC and away from garbage search results. Twitter labeled misleading coronavirus tweets, including some blaming 5G mobile networks for spreading the disease,[10] and advanced Bluesky, the company's push for open, decentralized standards that might link various social media platforms and reduce disinformation and abuse.[11]

No doubt these new virtue signals did some good. But Big Tech's signature response to the virus was to produce money. Oh, boy, was there money. Netflix created a $100 million relief fund for the entertainment community. Apple pledged $15 million to virus relief. Google announced $800 million in cash and ads to fight the virus. Yelp promised local businesses $25 million in free ad space. Tech's move-fast-and-break-things leaders were like a classroom of insolent small children who, when their teacher threatens to cancel the field trip. turn abruptly, uncharacteristically—perhaps desperately—angelic.

Beside gestures against COVID-19 misinformation, the internet powers rolled out new anti-fake news measures for the 2020 election.

YouTube fielded "information panels" meant to tip viewers when content was produced by government-funded organizations; Facebook provided a "context" option that added background on the sources of newsfeed articles, and tried having professional fact checkers call attention to false content. (Although a team of cognitive psychologists, Drs. Gordon Pennycook and David Rand, ran a study and found these efforts mostly ineffective. "Emphasizing sources had virtually no impact on whether people believed news headlines or considered sharing them," they concluded.[12])

Twitter rolled out a new "manipulated media" label it planned to apply to posted video, photos, or audio it deemed erroneous, "significantly altered or fabricated." Kind of like the supermarket leaving rotten eggs out for sale but affixing "ROTTEN" stickers to the cartons, but anyway. The first time Twitter deployed the label, on a misleadingly edited clip of Joe Biden tweeted out by White House social media director Dan Scavino and retweeted by President Trump, it mysteriously disappeared after a while. The deceptive clip stayed up, so millions of online Americans watched Joe Biden tell supporters "We can only re-elect Donald Trump," and perhaps believed it. "The platform is working on a fix," reported *Politico*.[13]

We can't go on like this. We shouldn't have to.

The comic actor Sasha Baron Cohen, of *Borat* fame, says: "By now, it's pretty clear that [the social media platforms] cannot be trusted to regulate themselves. In other industries, you can be sued for the harm you cause: Publishers can be sued for libel; people can be sued for defamation . . . But social media companies are almost completely protected from liability for the content their users post—no matter how indecent . . . That immunity has warped their whole worldview."

I want a stronger regulatory hand asserted in three areas: accountability for content, data privacy, and algorithmic transparency.

Americans know they're being micro-targeted by political actors, bombarded with uncanny data-driven precision, and they don't like it. A Gallup Organization survey conducted with help from the Knight Foundation in early 2020 found 72% believed "Internet companies should make no information about its users available to political campaigns in order to target certain voters with online advertisements." This strong opposition was consistent across party lines. It came from 69% of Democrats, 72% of independents, and 75% of Republicans, even though online microtargeting was likely the winning tactic that put Donald Trump in the presidency.

59% of Americans thought a website ought to disclose who paid for a political campaign ad, how much it cost, and who it's aimed at. Only 16% thought political ads should not be regulated. Firm majorities wanted misinformation banned from online political ads, though that is easier said than done.[14]

Sad to say, the Federal Election Commission has been asleep at this switch for years. There's a strong case to be made that the FEC has power here, as any situation in which money influences politics is technically in the commission's wheelhouse. But the last time it updated its rules for online political advertising was in 2006—before Facebook was even a thing, and when the default impulse was still to let the internet thrive as a small-d democratic, no-seat belts bazaar of ideas. So online political messaging is virtually free to go where it wants. Some FEC commissioners at least know we have a fake-news, dark-posts disinformation crisis, and want to require more disclosure on digital political messages. But past overtures of that kind drew—you guessed it—death threats from internet mobs. ("Die, fascist, die!" wrote one critic to reform-minded commissioner Ann Ravel.[15]) And in any event the FEC was powerless in 2019 and 2020, with half its six seats vacant—so, not enough commissioners to take any action. Those remaining were reduced to asking the platforms themselves to please try to figure something out.

Congress could grant the FEC greater power to review and set standards for online political ads. Another, more dramatic move would be to yank back years of legal protection that insulates the big internet platforms from editorial responsibility—particularly a loophole that protects them from liability for content users generate.

Section 230 of the Communications Decency Act is Big Tech's get-out-of-jail-free card. It lets the platform providers claim they're closer to public utilities than broadcasters or publishers, though they're now the highest-trafficked news content providers. It's how Facebook gets away with delivering political disinformation while explaining, "We don't have a policy that stipulates that the information you post on Facebook must be true."[16]

Congress passed Section 230 in 1996, just as the consumer internet got rolling, to help first-generation platforms survive. The main help they got was immunity from the liability exposure regular publishers had to accept. The new guys weren't really *publishers*, went the reasoning; they were *distributors*. They could hardly be expected to keep tabs on everything they were distributing, any more than UPS knows what's in every box on the truck.

The tech powers grabbed the ticket and ran. They have as much liability for what happens on their digital real estate as a wireless provider has for phone sex.

1996 was a lifetime ago. The fledgling internet platforms Section 230 was meant to protect—Prodigy and CompuServe—are long dead. Compared to them, today's incumbents have insane power and influence. At tremendous cost to the cause of trustworthy information and reliable narrators, government wanders in their wake playing catch-up. "The gap between technological advancements and the mechanisms intended to regulate them—often called the "pacing problem"—is only growing wider," Travis Bullard, APCO Worldwide brand practice leader, advised clients. "There's a disconnect between the speed of technological innovation and existing regulatory structures . . . As emerging technologies drive new business and service models, governments must rapidly create, modify, and enforce regulations."[17]

In mid-2020 President Trump mulled a review of Section 230 in an attempt to prove social media bias against him. Twitter fact-checked baseless presidential tweets calling vote-by-mail systems "substantially fraudulent." The president viewed Twitter's "Get the facts" links, pasted in by management below his tweets, as "completely stifling FREE SPEECH."[18] If social media platforms edit user posts, do they forfeit freedom from responsibility? Trump wanted the FCC to decide.[19] While I don't think Trump presented an ideal basis for overhaul, it's nonetheless past time for Section 230 to be revised to make the internet powers more responsible for the material they distribute so profitably.

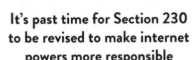

It's past time for Section 230 to be revised to make internet powers more responsible for the material they distribute.

As Sasha Baron Cohen says, "Here's a good way for Facebook to 'live up to' its responsibilities: Start fact-checking political ads before running them, stop micro-targeted lies immediately, and when ads are false, don't publish them."[20]

The big platforms say they couldn't possibly do that—that rearguard reviews of fake or pernicious content are all they can manage. But they'll have to deal with harsh new rules in Britain, where social media platforms are to be held responsible for harmful content in a revised, unforgiving regulatory framework.[21] What if the platforms became as liable in the U.S. for poison content as

NBC is to the FCC when an *SNL* sketch player blurts the f-word? I'm sure Big Tech would figure it out. Just as broadcasters figured out the seven-second delay.

Former Facebook lobbyist Adam Conner, now overseeing tech issues at the liberal Center for American Progress, has additional worthy regulatory ideas: de-concentrate power from the current handful of behemoths and promote competition. Prevent social networks from acquiring each other. Get more digital experts serving in the public interest.[22] All worth discussing, for sure—but let's close that giant Section 230 liability loophole.

The second regulatory hurdle is digital data privacy.

California set a fresh regulatory benchmark in 2020 with sweeping new rules. The CCPA (California Consumer Privacy Act) gave people at least some rights over data harvested by Google, Facebook, and various data brokers, and required companies to tell consumers what personal data they were amassing, and for what purpose. But the new law was controversial. Some predicted it could hurt businesses not intended as targets. Many regarded it as a good-faith first stab at taming an invisible and impossibly dynamic world, but by no means the last word.

"I think CCPA is well-intentioned, but not well thought out in terms of its unintended consequences," my friend and former work colleague Chuck Davis told me soon after the law took effect. Chuck's a pioneer in behavioral biometrics and online measurement. He's worked for the Department of Homeland Security and Wells Fargo. Data protection and regulation are his business.

"In principle, it's a good thing. It makes companies accountable and establishes clear penalties for non-compliance. The problem is that practically every marketing firm nowadays falls under CCPA. If you have 50 or so employees, you'd spend about $50,000 to be

CCPA compliant. If you've got 500, the number may be as high as $2 million. So, we're already seeing several amendments being considered to CCPA."

Chuck suggested next-level transparency regulations could allow motivated individuals to see their own personal data utilization maps: "I think that that is the ultimate in transparency, and will make it easier for people to understand how their personal data is organized and who it's shared with, color-coded so you can understand it at a glance. I think that's a real business opportunity."

"A personal data map sounds like a genealogy tree," I replied. "Someone could log on, put in their Social Security number, and see a visual readout of where their data goes."

"Right," said Chuck. "Then you get into deeper issues: What's the value of that data? Data has the most value of anything in the world today—more valuable than gold, oil, the dollar, even Bitcoin. But how valuable? Is my data more valuable than your data? If a millionaire's data is worth more than a grocery clerk's, doesn't that just worsen our problems with social inequalities?"[23]

But virtually everyone's data is worth *something*, although as I said earlier in this book, most trade it away for next to nothing. If internet users ever quit spilling details about their mental illnesses or bankruptcies to earn four cents' worth of airline miles, it'll signal major consciousness-raising going on, and Big Tech will have a whole new think coming. In fact, the futurist George Gilder believes Big Tech's end is nigh. "Whereas Google now controls your information and uses it free of charge, you will be master of your own information and charge for it freely . . . Whereas Google envisions an era of machine dominance through artificial intelligence, you will rule your machines."

What is Gilder talking about? A next-wave, fundamentally different, security-first computing environment he believes will replace the current, intrinsically insecure one. Gilder believes most of us have it all wrong. Big Tech is no insuperable monolith, he says. In the late 2010s it actually represented "an industrial regime at the end of its rope," crippled by after-action, bolt-on security measures: "The crisis of the current order in security, privacy, intellectual property, business strategy, and technology is fundamental and cannot be solved within the current computer and network architecture . . . centralization is not safe." Gilder predicts a blockchain-based "cryptocosm": a new, security-first network that sweeps aside the status quo. "A network whose private keys are held by individual human beings, not by government or Google."[24]

With the cryptocosm's ETA still TBD, though, competing proposals jockeyed for air on Capitol Hill—proposals for nationwide privacy protections patterned after California's. Six weeks after CCPA became law, Sen. Kirsten Gillibrand proposed creating a new federal agency, the Data Protection Agency, which would have power to make rules for Big Tech, issue orders, "investigate, subpoena for testimony or documents, and issue civil investigative demands." The DPA would have three core missions: give people control over their own data by enforcing protective rules, ensure fair competition, and upgrade the U.S. government for a digital era. (Shoshanna Zuboff was on board, saying the DPA idea promised "to assert democratic governance over commerce in the digital age."[25])

Gillibrand had plenty of company in Congress, and not just from Democrats. New data privacy rules had bipartisan appeal. Republican Sen. Josh Hawley moved to overhaul the Federal

Trade Commission to put the big hurt on Big Tech: "The FTC has stood by as major corporations have consolidated their power and stifled competition. The agency as presently constituted is in no shape to ensure competition in today's markets, let alone tomorrow's," Hawley said. "Google and Facebook have acquired hundreds of companies in the last two decades, yet the FTC never once intervened to try to block any of these acquisitions." This was a serious free-market conservative talking.[26]

Harold Feld of Public Knowledge, a public advocacy group, also proposed forming a whole new federal agency—a bigger one, with more far-reaching authority to regulate digital platforms via fierce content rules, consumer protections, and enforcement powers. (Lest a giant new regulatory agency seem like overkill, Adam Conner points out that we've done it before at the federal level to stabilize new technologies that rocked American life: The Federal Railroad Administration and the Food and Drug Administration didn't always exist.)

There were anti-Big Tech, pro-privacy heads of steam building all over Washington. Something seemed bound to emerge from the clouds, and not a day too soon.

Finally, let's look at a related issue: proprietary algorithms—mathematical formulas that serve as the secret cogs and levers of artificial intelligence.

Facebook algorithms determine which friends, ads, and news stories are omnipresent in your feed, and which never scroll into view. Amazon algorithms drive your cross-shopping offers. Algorithms decide what ads you see on your smartphone, what new songs Pandora offers you, and—more portentously—what political content you see. Algorithms decode your history and render all kinds of decisions about you, from trivial to pivotal.

And you have no idea how they do it. The makeup of high-value algorithms is as zealously guarded as the WD-40 formula or the KFC recipe. They deliver vast competitive advantage for their owners, but their innards are a mystery to their subjects.

There's obvious tension between corporate intellectual property rights and the public's arguable right to know how and why A.I. decisions are made. Advocates for algorithm transparency seek to force software powers to drop their towels and expose the little engines that exert such big influence on human choice and behavior. Big Tech, in the main, is not in a sharing mood. "They will tell you, 'Oh no, this has nothing to do with public policy, it's about competitive advantage,'" said Burcu Kilic of Public Citizen's Digital Rights Team. "Whoever controls the data controls the future, right? So, they want to control the future."[27]

A realistic algorithm accountability measure could be modeled after the Sarbanes-Oxley law and phased in gradually. Sarbanes-Oxley (SOX for short) set up an oversight framework to drive more transparent, honest financial reporting by businesses. It was born in 2002 in reaction to mind-bending financial scandals, resulting in criminal charges, at Enron, WorldCom, Tyco, and other firms. SOX promulgated a checklist of accountability measures for business, with audits for those who fall short. Algorithm oversight can work the same way, with regulators weighing potential for trouble or abuse and scoring for risk. If tech powers react the way public

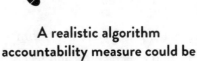

A realistic algorithm accountability measure could be modeled after the Sarbanes-Oxley law and phased in gradually.

companies reacted to SOX, they'd police themselves so as not to court sanctions.

Giving regulators that kind of visibility into private algorithms could mean the government gets a consolidated, God's-eye view of peoples' personal data at some future point. The Big Brother concern is worth raising. But Chuck Davis told me that horse has fled the barn. "I think to a certain degree, we're naïve. We're already there. Legislatively, we're starting to catch up. The government already has so much metadata on us; they can stitch it together when there's a reason to. If I become a target and something needs to be ascertained about me, then all the pieces come together. But the mechanism and the data are already there to do that."[28]

"The public has a right to know the data processes that impact their lives so they can correct errors and contest decisions made by algorithms," insists the Electronic Privacy Information Center. "Without knowledge of the factors that provide the basis for decisions, it is impossible to know whether government and companies engage in practices that are deceptive, discriminatory, or unethical. Therefore, algorithmic transparency is crucial to defending human rights and democracy online."[29]

We should take a crack at it. Do we want Big Tech compiling more data on us in secretive fashion? Are we better off shedding more and more privacy to serve ever finer microtargeting—without knowing how it's done? Are we helpless? We're not. Half of Congress is working up good counters. Remember, Shoshana Zuboff, the "surveillance capitalism" coiner, said anything made by humans can be unmade by humans. She also says: "The choice to turn any aspect of one's life into data must belong to individuals by virtue of their rights in a democratic society . . . In support of a new competitive landscape, lawmakers will need to champion new forms of collective action."[30]

That's what I'm for. Responsive, informed lawmakers who understand the stakes can indubitably tame Big Tech and lead us to healthier politics. If we need more, elect more. The movement we need is on our shoulders, not Mark Zuckerberg's.

Evolve the Vote

Election integrity and secure voting may not have been the top American vulnerabilities exposed by COVID-19, but they were right up there.

In April 2020, as virus cases spread, the Wisconsin primary election forced voters to leave home, line up at live polling stations, and risk exposure to COVID-19. Within weeks more than 50 who voted in person or worked the polls tested positive.[31] Perhaps with that terrible example in mind, back in Washington the House gave itself unprecedented permission to vote on legislation remotely, work-from-home style, instead of risking infectious confabs on Capitol Hill. (Speaker Nancy Pelosi was initially against it but came around.[32])

Arena rallies were replaced by streamed speeches; Democrat Joe Biden campaigned via webcam from his Delaware basement. Voter town halls moved to Google Hangouts.

Rumors festered on social media that the November vote could be delayed or even called off—constitutionally murky territory, but a predictable fear in the paranoiac digital infosphere. "The prospect of some 138 million Americans (as voted in 2016) converging on about 116,990 polling places amid a national pandemic is inconceivable," said the progressive outlet Truthout.org.[33] A coalition of state and local election officials told Congress COVID-19 posed "unprecedented challenges . . . as we work to balance public safety and the sacred right to vote."[34]

The obvious fallback strategy amid a full-blown pandemic: transition to a vote-by-mail system, hammer and tongs. Contrary to claims from critics like President Trump, vote-by-mail fraud, like the incidence of fraud with any voting method, is extremely rare. A multi-university study of the 2012 election found just 0.02% of votes cast were proven bogus.[35]

But nationwide vote-by-mail was no walk in the park, either. Ideological opposition to mail-in balloting was fervent in some quarters. Only a few private contractors print and mail ballots, and they warned they didn't have the bandwidth to service the whole country. Voters completing ballots at home often don't follow directions. Ballots can be lost, stolen, or destroyed. Counties switching to mail-in ballots would need more tabulation time; many prohibit any processing before election day, so laws would have to be changed fast.

Electronic scanners used to tally paper ballots can fail or be hacked. In some states, volunteers are permitted to deliver ballots to polling places in big stacks, making authentication difficult. Hand recounts of paper ballots are far from error-free.

"Rolling something as complex as this out at large scale introduces thousands of small problems—some of which are security problems, some of which are reliability problems, some of which are resource-management problems—that only become apparent when you do it," Matt Blaze, a Georgetown Law School election security expert, told *Politico*.[36] On top of all this, the U.S. Postal Service itself was in dire fiscal shape in 2020. COVID-19 widened its operating losses. Voting by mail requires a functional, universally accessible mail service.

The pandemic made it plain: We had no national fallback plan for electioneering and voting.

In preceding pages, I have called out some of the failures associated with efforts to take elections digital, from the Iowa caucus app disaster, to blithe Big Tech execs minimizing the security risks of e-voting, to the hacking risks presented by disparate, rickety systems. There have been a lot of cases to sap confidence. Yes to all that.

But here's my idea: Proceed anyway. Ramp up digital elections. We've got to go there.

I consult on mobile voting initiatives with a startup in Washington state called Democracy Live. The goal is not to whitewash the ham-fisted mistakes of the past, including secrecy, arrogance, and lack of foresight. The goal is to modernize voting technology slowly and soberly, in compliance with international standards, and test carefully. "As election officials grapple with how to allow for safe voting in the midst of a pandemic, the adoption of more advanced technology—including secure, transparent, cost-effective voting from our mobile devices—is more likely," said Democracy Live's chairman, Joe Brotherton. "In the near term, a hybrid model—mobile-phone voting with paper ballots for tabulation—is emerging . . . We should expect that option to become more widespread."[37]

Tech investor Bradley Tusk's nonprofit Mobile Voting Project, which works with Democracy Live, has funded a series of e-voting experiments by state and local governments. Just before the coronavirus upended everything, a small-scale, pilot-style electronic mobile voting exercise I worked on with Tusk and Democracy Live proved pretty gratifying.

In stark contrast to the Iowa caucus debacle, we operated in a puny, unglamorous electoral arena: a race in King County, Washington for a seat on the King County Conservation District's Board of Supervisors. (The board consists of volunteer officeholders who manage natural resources.) The Iowa app guys worked in secret, did scant load testing or user training, and debuted their product on one of the biggest nights in a presidential campaign. We worked in the sunshine, liaised with the Department of Homeland Security, got our work checked by an independent lab and the nonprofit National Cyber Security Center, and stayed unassuming.

We did not use an app. We did not store votes electronically. Our e-voting window lasted three weeks in early 2020. Voters could submit marked ballots via the web, as PDF files, or choose to print and mail; 94% opted for electronic. Turnout nearly doubled, confirming the view that once people trust it, mobile voting encourages more to take part in elections. ("It's not that people inherently hate voting," says Bradley Tusk. "They hate doing it on a random Tuesday, trying to find where to go and drive there and wait in line."[38]) Blind and disabled people got a low-effort way to vote: "I was able to vote and submit my ballot entirely independently for the first time in my life," affirmed blind King County resident Douglas Bright.[39] And a post-vote audit by the National Cybersecurity Center vouched for the security of the process. "With top-notch platform development, effective election official training and voter education, mobile voting can be accomplished securely," said the Center's Forrest Senti.[40] The COVID-19 crisis generated new inquiries about e-voting from heretofore skeptical election officials.

Not everyone was a fan. Charles Stewart III, a director of the CalTech/MIT Voting Technology Project, looked us over and said, "At this particular moment, we need extreme caution in putting these systems out in the wild, and we, the public, need to be very careful in what we conclude from these pilots."[41]

I agree with Charles, though. Slow and steady. Bold but not reckless. The appropriate conclusion from King County: E-voting is worth working on. E-voting can innovate past old mistakes and swim in larger waters, provided we keep working transparently and justifying public trust. At any rate, unbeknownst to many, we have been adopting electronic voting in small ways since 2010, when Congress required electronic balloting for military and overseas voters. Some states now require e-voting channels accessible at home for blind and disabled people. We can scale up eventually. I think we have to, given the proven fragility of other election systems. But we must never move recklessly.

Sustain Local News

"It could be the end," posted the chief executive of the *Sacramento News & Review* as he announced the paper, and affiliates in Chico and Reno, were suspending publication.[42] Three of many.

One of the darkest ironies of coronavirus times was that as Americans became more desperate for credible information, the crisis edged the tottering local news business closer to collapse. Advertising dried up overnight. Some papers lined up for emergency government loans—the *Tampa Bay Times* got $8.5 million from Uncle Sam, the *Seattle Times* $9.9 million—and begged readers to trust their journalism wouldn't be compromised.[43]

From 2004 to 2020, one out of every four newspapers in America was shut down or merged up, according to research from the University of North Carolina.[44] One of five Americans already dwell in a "news desert," with no access to reliable local media. Many papers still hanging on are sad, thin remnants of former glory. The pandemic deepened their economic misery. It particularly ravaged lively alternative weeklies dependent on street and newsstand distribution. Big dailies furloughed staff, cut hours, or iced their sports and social-event coverage. For many metro and small-town reporters covering the story of their lives, the eventual reward for their risky, heroic work would be a pink slip. Some small-town weeklies soldiered on with everybody working for free.

The nation's remaining handful of powerhouse papers sold more subscriptions amid COVID-19 and drew hordes of new online readers. National cable news and financial channels saw ratings spikes; on the broadcast networks the venerable evening newscasts attracted their biggest audiences since the 2000s.[45] At the apex of the journalism pyramid life was survivable. But below the apex the coronavirus looked potentially fatal, and not just medically.

Audiences seem not to get this. 71% told Pew researchers in 2018 they thought local news outlets were actually doing well financially, but only 14% had paid for access to a local news source.[46] (It might startle them to know how many energetic young reporters putting in marathon hours at small or medium-market TV stations cannot afford to go out for dinner much, despite being locally famous. Getting recognized at Taco John's out on the arterial is nice, but it doesn't buy the nachos.)

People complain nonstop about bias and selective coverage decisions by the national press. At the top level, though, you have a spectrum of options; read something else or change the channel. Local news options are severely limited, and narrowing further, yet they are among the last remaining reliable narrators.

In communities without reliable local news, residents turn to suspect social media rumor mills or opinionated national outlets. A *Journal of Communications* study suggested more partisan, less informed voting behavior occurred in news-starved localities.[47] News deserts also saw increased city-level corruption, fewer candidates for public office, higher borrowing, costs and more violations of pollution rules. "Someone might be tweeting from the city council chambers," said *Governing* magazine, "but far fewer people are being paid to ferret out and synthesize enough information to give citizens in many communities solid, ongoing information about what their government is up to."[48]

This is nuts. We need credible, non-partisan local journalism—not just as a trustworthy counter to online misinformation and propaganda, though that is vital, but as a critical cog in our checks-and-balances mechanism.

Even before COVID-19, bipartisan recognition had dawned in Congress that Big Tech was quietly, mercilessly decimating local news outlets, distributing their stories without paying for them. A bill was cooking to exempt local news organizations from antitrust laws, so they could negotiate survival terms *en masse* with Google and Facebook. "I am a free-markets guy and have fought against the idea that just because something is big it is necessarily bad," said Rep. Doug Collins, Republican of Georgia. "But look, I'm a politician and live with the media and see its importance. These big, disruptive platforms are making money off creators of content disproportionately."[49]

I don't think opening a little antitrust loophole is enough. Nor are the niche experiments on the news landscape, such as forming co-ops with reader money, or converting to nonprofit tax status. I have another idea.

In the United States, we used to have state-level News Councils. They were independent, civic-minded, nonpartisan organizations, usually dependent on private foundation money, that conducted independent reviews of media coverage when members of the public raised concerns. Councils were typically a mix of journalists and members of the community. For a time, I served as president of the News Council in the state of Washington, founded in 1999 by *Seattle Times* columnist John Hamer and funded by the Bill & Melinda Gates Foundation. It closed in 2014, the last example of its kind in the country, though they still work overseas.[50]

The councils' old investigative mission may not make much practical sense anymore. But suppose we had News Councils with community roots overseeing a fund to sustain local newsrooms?

Federal block grants to support local journalism are worth considering. Washington underwrites the Corporation for Public Broadcasting; most of the money goes directly to public TV and radio stations. The United Kingdom and Germany fund public media generously. Perhaps the U.S. is overdue for an analogous financial lifeline for local papers. New Jersey is testing the idea with a new Civic Information Consortium to shore up local news, seeding the project with $2 million in taxpayer funding.[51] I'm more partial to public-private partnerships, which could include digital expertise from efforts like The News Project (whose partners include the Associated Press) plus money from foundations like the Facebook Journalism Project, Newmark Philanthropies, or the WordPress Foundation.

Facebook has begun to understand the local news crisis, which it helped create by diverting audiences and not paying for local stories it relays, ultimately hurts Facebook, too. In March 2020, Facebook announced $100 million in grants to support local coronavirus coverage. Mid-tier papers like the *Southeast Missourian* and *El Paso Matters* were among the first recipients.[52] Good, but corporate largesse doled out from a single source on high, with invisible criteria and no community filter, is no solution to the business-stability problem in local news.

In the long run, do smaller outlets really want to be wards of the biggest internet information force? What if the folks with the deep pockets grow bored, or take offense at critical stories?

Local news would be better off with diverse local people channeling the money. It would be best if Facebook needs local reporters more than they need Facebook.

In the best of all possible worlds, tech companies provide technology for local news to flourish online as print editions inevitably go gentle into that good night. Government money flows to communities from federal, state, or local sources. Reconstituted non-partisan News Councils, comprised of journalists and local leaders, distribute the funds and perhaps undertake ombudsman-slash-watchdog duties when grantee organizations generate public criticism. Maybe regular citizens could help fund this model at the state level as well, in the same way the IRS asks each year if you want to contribute $3 to the Presidential Election Campaign Fund.

If we can designate a lot of public money to run dispiriting elections—in 2020 there was $357 million sitting in the Presidential Election Campaign Fund, awaiting takers[53]—perhaps we can designate a little to rescue inspiring, high-value journalism.

Civics at the Center

Since the squalling birth of the mass-market internet, it has treated users as consumer-customers. This is fine when all you want from the web is Dove bars delivered at 2 a.m. It is much less fine when you depend on the digital infosphere to hold society together, as we do now.

Consumers have certain rights. Citizens have rights plus responsibilities. They earn the former by living up to the latter. It is past time for a broad campaign to inculcate a culture of digital citizenship.

Board a commercial airliner and you have a right to professional pilots and mechanics and a seat nobody has puked on. But you also bear responsibilities. You agree not to smoke, and to keep your seat belt on, and to not try opening the cabin door inflight. Beyond the explicit statutory requirements of Flight 329 citizenship, chances are you also observe unstated cultural rules to co-create an amicable airborne mini-society. It is not normal to be crammed in with so many strangers, but you adjust. You help the senior citizen stow her criminally large rollaboard in the bin. You do not refuse to rise from your aisle seat when the guy by the window needs the lavatory. You work out some wordless, civil deal for armrest-sharing. Most of you do not trim your toenails inflight (if only to avoid internet shaming). The crowded cabin works only because almost everyone plays their citizenship role.

Think what a bobsled to hell air travel would become if passengers—not to mention the airline—brought the worst, appetite-driven internet behavioral norms to basic economy.

"Beginning with television," wrote Roger McNanee in *Zucked*, "technology has changed the way we engage with society, substituting passive consumption of content and ideas for civic engagement, digital engagement for conversation. Subtly and persistently, it has contributed to our conversion from citizens to consumers. Being a citizen is an active state; being a consumer is passive. A transformation that crept along for fifty years accelerated dramatically with the introduction of internet platforms. We were prepared to enjoy the benefits but unprepared for the dark side. Unfortunately, the same can be said for the Silicon Valley leaders whose innovations made the transformation possible."[54]

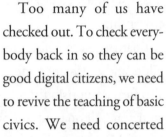

Too many of us have checked out. We need to revive the teaching of basic civics.

Too many of us have checked out. To check everybody back in so they can be good digital citizens, we need to revive the teaching of basic civics. We need concerted endeavors to instill information literacy, so people are more skeptical of crazy stuff. And we need to reward community solidarity, online and off.

First, civics. It's been withering for years as a secondary-school staple. No wonder Bernie Sanders' vaunted youth vote underperformed in the 2020 Democratic primaries; too many young Americans either dismiss the power of their vote or were never taught it in the first place. Visit any social media venue where younger people hang out, and you'll see an amazing range of excuses for not voting—from "I have to work" to "All candidates are the same anyway" to "No candidate worked hard enough to appeal to me personally." That last one is the voice of a consumer, not a citizen. She might as well be car-shopping. *You didn't earn the sale.* "It may take years or even decades for millennials to be proportionally represented in the halls of power," says the author of *The Ones We've Been Waiting For: How a New Generation of Leaders Will Transform America*, Charlotte Alter.[55]

The civics vacuum goes beyond young people. Shawn Rosenberg, the political psychologist I mentioned earlier who thinks people aren't constitutionally suited for democracy, believes "Americans are generally unable to understand or value democratic culture, institutions, practices, or citizenship in the manner required . . . As a result they will interact and communicate in ways that undermine the functioning of democratic institutions and the meaning of democratic practices and values."[56] Rosenberg and I stand far apart on the optimism-to-pessimism spectrum—remember, he thinks democracy is doomed, and I don't—so I interpret his words as a warning, not an inevitability. But damned if he isn't describing bad anti-civic behavior in the digital infosphere.

Eric Liu's Civic Saturdays, however, give a man hope.

Liu, a former Clinton White House policy official, organized his nonprofit, Citizen University, to "cultivate a culture of citizenship," he said. Civic Saturdays borrow the format and syntax of faith gatherings, but celebrate American civic "religion" with strictly nonpartisan readings, "sermons" on the meanings and duties of citizenship, and discussions. They offer "a creed of ideas and ideals, and what it takes to actually live up to and to fulfill the promise of our democracy," said Liu.[57] He knew he'd tapped into something when he booked a Seattle bookstore for the first Civic Saturday expecting 40 or so, and 220 showed up.[58] Civic Saturdays instill connectedness and inspire engagement. Since 2016 they've spread across the country. I love it. So might Shawn Rosenberg.

For young people we might require proficiency in American civics by 8th grade or so, the way some schools make you prove you can swim fifty yards before you get a diploma.

"It's not that young people are disengaged, it's not that they don't care about the issues at hand; it's just that they really struggle to follow through," said John Holbein, co-author of *Making Young Voters: Converting Civic Attitudes into Civic Action.*[59] Holbein argues—and I say right on—that the answer is civics education that gives new citizens "knowledge and experience grounded in awareness of the factors that shape voter participation."

The second pillar of our digital citizenship campaign should be an information literacy drive.

In 2014, in a move I very much admire, Finland launched a national push to teach its population, particularly students, journalists, and politicians, how to spot and counter false information engineered to confuse or divide them. Finland shares an 832-mile border with Russia. Its leaders know exactly what's coming over the fence. Watching the Kremlin mess with the 2016 American election, the UK Brexit vote, and contests in France and Germany, the Finns labor to inoculate everybody against fake news. The drills begin in kindergarten.

"It's not just a government problem, the whole society has been targeted. We are doing our part, but it's everyone's task to protect the Finnish democracy," said the prime minister's communications chief, Jussi Toivanen.[60]

Making information literacy a national priority has paid results. By some measures, Finland has the highest media literacy rate in Europe, and Finns trust their media institutions the most, which makes them less apt to glom onto squirrelly alternative sources. Ironically, the Finnish leadership imported American experts at first to help them craft anti-fake news countermeasures. A little later America was drowning in misinformation, with COVID-19 myths and deception sometimes literally dying of it, and Finland was doing OK.

In the United States, the nonprofit News Literacy Project is trying to recruit 20,000 "news literacy practitioners" to teach students along the same lines; it reports enhanced news literacy boosts trust in local news.[61] Another nonprofit, Senior Planet, holds workshops at senior centers, teaching the elderly to be more skeptical about online content. (Facebook users 65 and up post fake news to Facebook at a rate seven times that of adults under 29, say researchers at Princeton and NYU.[62]) Benedictine University offers a fun evaluative tool for suspect content called the CRAAP test, heh heh.[63] (Currency, Relevance, Authority, Accuracy, Purpose.) There are lots of these piecemeal good-faith efforts popping up, and they're great if they happen to cross your path. But an information literacy campaign should become a national priority with federal backing. If the United States could produce and distribute ubiquitous wash-your-hands PSAs for every media channel in mere days as the coronavirus blew up, it can do this.

The third pillar of digital citizenship is empowerment.

The sad truth is that we accede to so many bad things happening to us in the digital realm—if only by ticking AGREE on dense Terms of Service language we never read. A citizens' lobby should demand a cultural revolution for Terms of Service agreements: Make them shorter, sharper, and clearer. (Before Big Tech tells you that's impossible, remember similar clarity campaigns of the past simplified new car window stickers and credit card statements.) We should mandate a purge of negative opt-in offers, so users don't authorize subscriptions and so forth without realizing. We should demand plain-as-day cancellation buttons for online propositions involving recurring payments.

We need "Unsubscribe" buttons that actually work, so you don't keep receiving unwanted appeals or propaganda in your inbox long after you lose interest. I'm sure you can think of more online irritants you'd like to cut out of your life.

We also accept, even reinforce, social media conventions that make political discourse worse. Upvotes, likes, sharing functions: They are all double-edged swords. Jonathan Haidt and Tobias Rose-Stockwell suggest "demetrication"—obscuring likes and upvotes, eliminating the popularity-contest overlay—in order to "reduce the frequency and intensity of public performance." It might even help to make content-sharing a less impulsive one-click act: "[T]he less friction impedes transmission of social media content, the more toxic it seems to get; more friction, less toxicity. An 'Are you sure you want to post this?' query has been shown to help Instagram users rethink hurtful messages. Experts could audit recommendation algorithms for unperceived harms and biases—essentially injecting an editing function into sharing tech."[64]

Yes, the big content providers and social media operators can be forced to make these changes, via legislative fiat. But it is also up to us as digital citizens to rally for these things. We don't. We should.

Washington Post TV critic Hank Steuver looked over a 2020 *Frontline* documentary on Amazon airing on PBS, found it pretty scathing, but identified a key missing ingredient—us.

> "What 'Amazon Empire' lacks . . . is a wider reflection on the consumer's complicity in all this. Are we really so tech-besotted that *anything* goes? No one forced us to hand over all our personal data and install Amazon's listening devices or surveillance cameras in our homes—we just did, because we,

too, want the future to be cool. We rationalize our immediate need for its delivered products against environmental impact or any other effect, be it physical or psychological."[65]

A consumer asks: Where are those Tide Pods I ordered, Amazon Prime? A citizen asks: What is my role in this system, and how might I act to improve things?

My fourth and last pillar of digital citizenship is community.

The dismaying mid-pandemic demonstrations against face masks and social distancing seemed to me to be militant anti-community gestures. Cooperative protective measures adopted on a mass scale should have been framed as acts of solidarity. But they were scorned and mocked in some enclaves as symptoms of weakness. A real American sneezes where he wants. What communications medium of ours could possibly have conditioned people to rage against community interests and present as self-interested nations of one? Any guesses?

Despite the stress and spectacle of 2020, my fellow optimist Joel Kotkin, geographer and futurist, believes our current track will nonetheless lead to a better society. "The America of 2050 will be radically transformed, but it will still reflect the basic ideal that has driven its evolution from the beginning—a rejection of the fatalism and hierarchy characteristic of most older societies. The central government and giant private institutions can play a critical role in helping meet what will no doubt be daunting obstacles, but basic faith in the individual, family, and community will remain the fundamental instruments for securing the country's future."[66]

George Gilder, who wrote an entire optimistic book entitled *Life After Google,* believes our technology is due for a paradigm shift—and we will see a "new system of the world" focused on blockchain-enabled trust, security, and a sense of community sweeping aside paranoia and fear: "The Google system of the world focuses on the material environment rather than on human consciousness, on artificial intelligence rather than human intelligence, on machine learning rather than human learning, on relativistic search rather than on the search for truth, on copying rather than creating," says Gilder. "The new system of the world must reverse these positions."[67] The digital building blocks for this new world are all around us today; blockchain transactions propel the cryptocurrency movement led by Ethereum and Bitcoin, and Gilder tells us to anticipate the day when blockchain inhabits every strand of our digital DNA, with pleasing, empowering, privacy-protecting effect.

That would halt internet bombardment altogether.

When the decade turned and the coronavirus to Americans was still a distant offshore obscurity, David Brooks used his *New York Times* column to publish a fanciful, fictional retrospective on a decade that had not yet begun to happen—"A Ridiculously Optimistic History of the Next Decade." By March a lot of Brooks' optimism seemed cruelly out of date. But as he looked back at the 2020s from 2030, he did invent some developments that ought to transcend COVID-19:

> "The most important cultural change came to be known as the Civic Renaissance. During the first two decades of the century, hundreds of thousands of new civic organizations came into being—healing political divides, fighting homelessness,

promoting social mobility and weaving communities. But these organizations were small. They did not grow into the big national chapter-based structures that had repaired America's social fabric a century earlier—the Y.M.C.A., the Rotary, the Boy Scouts.

"By the 2020s, philanthropists and community builders realized the only way to change culture and weave the social fabric was by creating an A.F.L.-C.I.O. of civil society, with big national voices and large, decentralized national organizations so that people across America had easy and practical pathways to get involved in community revival."[68]

No matter how distant Gilder's new system of the world may be, we should use the internet for that starting now.

Time to Drop the Masks

There are about 400 million social media users in India, a good chunk of the country's 1.3 billion citizens, and they are all in line to lose their online anonymity. New government rules floated in late 2019 required Facebook, YouTube, Twitter and TikTok to reveal user identities to Indian government agencies upon demand, no warrant or judicial order required.

A trade group representing Big Tech players complained the requirements "would be a violation of the right to privacy recognized by the Supreme Court." Other tech interests warned of "automated censorship" and "increased surveillance." The government was going ahead anyway.[69]

To which I say: Good. Anonymity can be liberating, but it can also serve as *carte blanche* to abuse, bully or coerce innocents online, or commit criminal acts. The United States should consider the same move.

Inability to identify social media users is a big law enforcement problem in India. Terrible rumors and disinformation crackle online and spark catastrophes. Mob violence and dozens of lynching deaths were traced to a false story of rampant child abduction and organ harvesting on WhatsApp, and still WhatsApp would not work with authorities to catch the rumormonger.[70]

User privacy is paramount, but there is a big difference between state spies snooping through a user's Visa transactions—and protecting an anonymous snake's right to stalk, threaten, or lie to others online. In debates like these, Big Tech has gone to strenuous lengths to confuse different kinds of personal rights. (Pitted against Indian law enforcement, or for that matter American agencies trying to unlock criminals' mobile phones, tech interests that routinely spy on their users suddenly become zealous defenders of their privacy.)

It is not legal to take out a credit card, rent a car, or apply for a passport using a false name. The internet is awash in dual-factor authentication protocols to confirm your identity before you can check your bank balance or pay your insurance premium. Financial providers in particular have made it harder to commit identity fraud online. Yet there is not much to stop you forging fake Facebook or Twitter accounts and harassing an ex, a classmate, or any public figure. Ask Aidy Bryant, or virtually anyone in her position, how that feels.

The silo-style, cellular structure of the digital infosphere encourages delusions and bad behavior, and so does the cloaking effect of anonymity. I think it's time for social media account applications to be assessed with at least the same scrutiny the TSA gives you at LaGuardia.

Users seeking to join Facebook *et al* should have to present a valid form of identification. (Minors can piggyback on the ID of a parent or guardian, just as they sometimes get credit cards backed by a parent's FICO score.) The big social media platforms could co-manage a joint verification system linked to DMV and law enforcement databases. There would obviously be an appeal process for those flagged by the system, but a vetted, approved user could receive an equivalent of the TSA's Known Traveler Number—that code that says you've been vetted and gets you into the PreCheck queue. Call it the KDC code, for Known Digital Citizen. When applying to post on more platforms, enter your KDC code for faster service. Maybe Twitter's push for cross-platform standards, Bluesky, leads to a world where your KDC is propagated for you as you hopscotch around the web.

If approval takes a couple of days, it's no major trauma; heck, TripAdvisor takes days to vet every Hampton Inn review you submit. A *pro forma* three-day waiting period for a permit to post, such as some states impose on handgun sales, might even be good for community karma.

In India, the government seeks to force tech providers to reveal user identities only on request. What if we went further, and attached every social media username to a real name, searchable by anyone? How much less abuse and deception would we see in social media spheres if everyone had to attest to their identities? How many extreme, delusional subcultures founded on folkloric or false information would dry up, or at least shed some crazed intensity? (What if we all knew who Q of QAnon was?)

How much less bad advice would infect the digital zone if every contributor had to sign a real name to each post? How many fewer married people would patrol Tinder or Ashley Madison? And how many bots and trolls would vaporize if new accounts had to be linked to a known identity?

I saved the drop-the-mask recommendation for last, because I know it will make some recoil. But I think the damage done online by depraved anonymous people is so great, and the costs of changing the game so comparatively manageable, it's time to retire anonymity.

It would be a mighty incentive to reduce the digital bombardment. It would be a great step forward for a responsible digital nation. It would require all of us to stand by our words and actions, which would lead to better political discourse.

Near the close of a book with dollops of politicians and CEOs, polls and data points, I will now zig when you might expect a zag and haul in two . . . philosophers.

Michael Schur, creator of the brilliant heaven-and-hell situation comedy *The Good Place*, said the intellectual engine of the show was the question: What do we owe one another? What are our obligations as citizens of a community? The lead character, Eleanor Shellstrop, arrives in the afterlife decidedly imperfect—an admitted "dirt bag" who spent her earthly days dodging her bar tabs, snatching the last cookie, and ghosting on friends. She clearly has work to do.

As he plotted his show Schur borrowed heavily from a real, operating philosopher, T.M. "Tim" Scanlon, and his key work,

What We Owe to Each Other.[71] (Result: Scanlon's ideas got heavy play on a hit network sitcom, a break never accorded Descartes or Kant, so far as I know. Descartes never came up on *Punky Brewster*.) Scanlon's is an essentially moral, ethical inquiry. His answer, boiled way, *way* down, is that you ought to design rules that couldn't be rejected by the people you share space with. In the series, Eleanor and her afterlife pals devise a moral society that works.

Dare to talk this way in a Silicon Valley white-board session, and for that matter most political campaign war rooms, and you'll likely have your visitor pass torn off your lapel before you can say Eleanor Shellstrop. I'm asking anyway. What do we owe each other? At the intersection of politics and digital tech, a heartfelt and truthful answer is tricky. The truth might threaten profits. It might obstruct exploitation and deception campaigns that preserve status quo power. It might make people reconsider cavorting for viral fame or inflicting sick burns for likes and lulz.

From Big Tech oligarchs down the influence chain to drive-by trolls, so many in the digital realm squelch any inkling of obligation to the community. They're consumers, not citizens. They are self-interested Eleanors, operating as if the digital infosphere is no community at all—merely a strip mine for opportunists. Particularly in politics. In their very slight defense, the internet is built to make them feel that way.

In an age of fear and chaos, of COVID-19, will we really choose an infinity of rage and misinformation—misinformation that kills some of us? Here's my second philosopher, Jan-Werner Müller. He reflected, "A common affliction demonstrates that our feeling of individualism is illusory. Digitally connected isolation is predicated on fellow citizens producing and delivering food, and anyone along the delivery chain, forced to work because they live paycheck to paycheck, could be contagious . . . Nobody can buy immunity, let alone immortality; nobody can wash his hands of conditions that make the United States look more like a failed state than a functioning democracy."[72]

Well. As *The Good Place* unfolds, self-absorbed, me-first Eleanor and her friends figure out what they owe each other. She becomes more connected and so more human. Now is a good time for we in politics to attempt the same—and revitalize our democracy in the process.

In the digital infosphere we owe each other more. If some people believe swigging bleach protects them from COVID-19 or voting by mail is inherently illegitimate, we owe them as much true, objectively verifiable information as possible. We owe each other honesty. We owe each other truth, honorable campaigns, and fair elections in civic systems that reward faith—elections with credible results everyone accepts. We owe each other a political arena that beckons people and validates their efforts at citizenship, not sickens and discourages them. We owe each other an effort to improve civic life instead of lapsing into red-faced, spittle-flecked screaming fits at the tiniest challenge.

"We owe each other a certain amount of reasonableness and respect in society," said Andrew Cuomo, governor of New York, during the pandemic.[73] He was talking about wearing face masks in public and I am talking about politics and digital media, but the point stands either way. In and out of politics, we have an ethical responsibility to try to improve each other's lives, not make them worse, or wreck them for sport.

And it is all possible on the internet. Every word of it.

CHAPTER NINE

CITIZEN JANEY

I hinted we'd revisit Janey Reynolds.

Nothing in the future is preordained. Free citizens make choices. The "butterfly effect" in chaos theory suggests small incidents have power to beget big impacts. Election night 2032 need not unfold as imagined in Chapter 1. With a few non-radical changes between now and then, Tuesday, November 2, 2032 could be very different.

Janey Reynolds voted at sunset, walking home from St. Patrick's Church, and felt great about it.

Janey was too old to have been born with the civic habit, or to have had it drilled into her in secondary school. That graduation requirement was a key post-pandemic reform of the 2020s. The young teens who went through the new two mandatory years of civics training (there was a name for this next generation of American youth: Gen C, the C standing for coronavirus) were likened by many to Israeli youth, for whom mandatory national service forged passionate patriotism. Gen C was a new breed of citizen, engaged and idealistic. Most were kids, it would be years before they reached voting age, but still, they were growing up as reformers, already dedicated to building a more responsive, inclusive democracy.

Janey had 15 years on the oldest Gen Cers. She had sailed blithely through school with only the merest exposure to government, civics, or politics. She'd endured losing her father to the first coronavirus eruption in 2020. She graduated from college without him—or her classmates, for that matter. Janey blamed terminally unserious, unresponsive leaders and institutions, plus an internet freighted with falsehoods and ignorance, and resolved to steer through life without them.

At the height of the medical and economic conflagration caused by COVID-19, Janey entered the workforce anxious. But she was lucky to be hired quickly by a Colorado meat processor, which made her a supply chain coordinator. In the early going she'd been proud to work on a small team that figured out how to restart beef jerky distribution, and a fierce thought had flashed across her mind: *My little crew did this, we jump-started a whole processing center from nothing, but when my father needed one goddamn ventilator, the whole United States government was too busy congratulating itself on TV to come up with one.*

It took half the 2020s to rebuild the stricken U.S. economy. A flurry of probes and panels and commissions formed in the aftermath of COVID-19, but Janey barely noticed. No probe would bring Dad back. The fractious 2024 election, with widespread revenge-voting against incumbents, came and went without her caring. She heard about fundamental changes to health care but didn't bother learning more, and in any event nothing big seemed to have happened. Janey got promoted at work, made and kept friends, binge-watched her infoslate shows, haunted the Royal

Horse when it was allowed to reopen, kept her antibody passport current, and did her best to ignore the government.

One of those federal commissions ignored by Janey addressed the quality of public information during COVID-19. It concluded that internet disinformation, fake news, and unedited rumors had in themselves posed significant secondary threats to public health. Credulous Americans had drunk bleach and died, partied at Mardi Gras, laughed at social distancing, made fun of face masks, even occupied state capitals with swastikas and assault weapons—all thanks to propaganda they'd soaked up in the digital infosphere.

The sharp, sweeping legislative response came in 2025. A bipartisan congressional majority enacted SIMPRA—the Social and Internet Media Platform Responsibility Act. President Harris, in office for only a few months, signed it with a flourish.

The SIMPRA acronym rapidly became part of the American vernacular, as common and familiar as TSA or FDIC. SIMPRA had several positive effects on internet life.

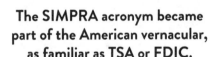

The SIMPRA acronym became part of the American vernacular, as familiar as TSA or FDIC.

First, it closed the loophole social media platforms had used for decades to evade responsibility for the content they delivered: Section 230 of the Communications Decency Act. Once Big Tech became legally culpable, after years of insisting it could not possibly police all these systems, it began doing just that. The platform owners discovered they could engineer A.I. filters to zap haters, stalkers, and bullies before their social media posts saw daylight.

As for fraudulent content masquerading as news, the big platforms found they could catch and kill most of it with impressive speed and efficiency, just as cybersecurity defense weapons neutralized malware threats before they could cause havoc. The fake-news problem receded dramatically. Janey slowly noticed the change. She found herself reading up, casting around for additional sources, and trusting the material more.

Under SIMPRA, proprietary algorithms used by Big Tech to subdivide and micro-target the population had to pass muster with a newly formed regulatory agency: IUDA, for Internet User Defense Agency. Like the Consumer Financial Protection Bureau, IUDA's mandate was to advocate for mistreated individuals—here, by safeguarding personal data profiles and sanctioning abuse. IUDA didn't stop all microtargeted marketing, only the most sinister or unnerving efforts. But it had the welcome effect of eliciting better, more respectful voluntary behavior from analytics wizards. Users told polls they were more confident in the internet. They felt less spied on.

IUDA also had the power to sanction deceptive trade practices on the internet, from negative opt-in snares to impossible-to-cancel subscriptions. Janey used to spend hours disentangling herself from terrible, one-sided e-commerce relationships; she loved that one.

SIMPRA's most controversial pillar was to require proof of identity from all who registered for social media accounts. Anonymity was over. First Amendment advocates fought this part of SIMPRA, declaring infringement on freedom of speech. In 2026 the challenge went all the way to the Supreme Court, which rejected it, ruling 6-3 that "freedom of speech does not mean freedom from consequences," as Chief Justice Gorsuch wrote for the majority. Legal scholars said the decision breathed new life into the precedent case *Scheck vs. United States* more than a century earlier, the one where Chief Justice Oliver Wendell

Holmes opined that "falsely shouting fire in a theater and causing a panic" did not qualify as protected speech.

Ending online anonymity did not extinguish hate speech altogether, but it banked the social media flames considerably. Trolls and bots were virtually wiped out. Multiple accounts were done for. Extremists had to own their words; they were surprisingly responsive to community pressure to civil up. For Janey, discarding anonymity wasn't that big a deal. She hated trolls. She

Trolls and bots were virtually wiped out. Multiple accounts were done for. Extremists had to own their words.

verified her identity with the platform she used most and received a KDC (Known Digital Citizen) number; thereafter, she entered her KDC in online situations where she had to prove she was who she said she was. When holdout critics saw the new burden was about as terrible as typing in a credit card's CVV code to buy socks, and the public applauded less cruelty and deception online, those critics shrank very small on the internet landscape.

Finally—the last big thing—SIMPRA addressed online political advertising by directing the FTC and FEC to collaborate on designing big, simple, inescapable disclosure messages. What they came up with was surprisingly successful: an overlay preceding all political ads that was formatted a little like the "Nutrition Facts" chart on a cereal box. The nutrition label disclosed calories, carbohydrates, and sugar. The political ad label revealed who paid for an ad, the outcome the ad was designed to produce, the method used to present it to a particular cohort, and how to complain about it to the FEC. Best of all as far as Janey was concerned, the presentation protocol required every user to proactively trigger the ad before it could play; they had to touch or click on the overlay to get past it and view the content. No auto-rolled ads, no uninvited pop-ups. The advertiser had to secure permission from the viewer every time. Campaigns chafed at the new disclosure norms. Most voters liked them.

Thus was Janey Reynolds coaxed into the American political process. There were no invasive ads from candidates who seemed to know everywhere she roamed, everything she ate, drank, or bought, and everyone she kissed. No surprise holograms on her kitchen counter. She wasn't spooked or vexed by internet politics anymore. When e-voting spread to more states in 2028 including Colorado, she actually voted for the first time. She found it vaguely, unaccountably satisfying—even though her candidate, President Harris, whom Janey regarded as the lesser of two evils, got blown out.

2032 brought one more convulsive change to American politics.

For years, a majority of likely voters had self-identified as neither Republican nor Democrat, but independent. The militant extremism that dominated the pre-SIMPRA internet, where the loudest voices belonged to the alt-right or hardcore progressives, painted a false, distorted portrait of America. The SIMPRA reforms literally moderated the digital infosphere. It became safer to occupy the big, thoughtful, grayscale space between angry extremes. In the revamped digital world, it looked like there was an opportunity for a new centrist political movement—one built to attract the stateless majority.

The 2028 election installed Republican House Speaker Kevin McCarthy in the White House and Rep. Elise Stefanik in the vice presidency, even though that year's Gallup poll of party preferences found just 22% of voters still called themselves Republicans. In spring 2029, a coalition of moderate Republicans and center-left Democrats formed the Unity Restoration Party. They had plotted in secret; the rollout was a thunderclap. Janey had never heard of most of the new party's key players—Bill Kristol, Claire McCaskill, Sean Patrick Maloney, John Brennan, Rick Wilson, Justin Amash, Krysten Sinema, Tim Scott, Adam Schiff, and others. Intrigued, she got busy Googling. The more she absorbed, the more she realized what courage it took for this vanguard to sever lifelong links with their old parties, even if those parties were mean and exclusionary and wracked by infighting. And the more she understood the renegades' motives.

On the old internet, the Unity Restoration Party would have been shouted down and marginalized by hardcore ideologues plus trollbots. In 2032, the new party held virtual primaries via the internet, staged an efficient virtual convention Janey attended from the comfort of her living room couch, and ran profuse but respectful online ads, all overlaid with that disclaimer thing Janey was getting used to.

In the run-up to the general election, Janey signed onto a useful series of live, open internet issue forums hosted by the three major-party candidates or virtual proxies. They were organized in virtual pods of 50 or 75 attendees whose political inclinations were deliberately commingled by A.I. assigners—an intentional hedge against the old echo-chamber problem that, pre-SIMPRA, had made internet discourse unbearable. Since everyone's identity was plain, almost everyone behaved. All the forums were free, presented by the least biased major news organizations—bias scores having been assigned by a national-level News Council. To gain admission, Janey simply tapped in her KDC number.

Years before Janey voted on her way home from church so enthusiastically, Judith Donath, founder of the Sociable Media Group at the MIT Media Lab, suggested there were two possible scenarios for Janey's 2032. In one, she said, "democracy is in tatters." Disasters created or abetted by technology would spark the "ancient response"—the public's fear-driven turn toward authoritarianism. In the more optimistic alternative, she predicted, "Fairness and equal opportunity are recognized to benefit all . . . Investments in education foster critical thinking and artistic, scientific and technological creativity. . . New voting methods increasingly feature direct democracy—AI translates voter preferences into policy."[1]

The reformed world Janey inhabited now would have made Donath smile.

On November 2, 2032, NBC's Brian Williams was in Rockefeller Plaza having the election night of his life. It felt like the Super Bowl, Oscar night, and a royal wedding rolled into one; the network's production values were dazzling, over the top in every way. The purpose-built set with Williams and Lester Holt at its center took over the whole 30 Rock skating rink. There were 3-D holograms dramatizing voting data everywhere you looked, and thousands of rubberneckers gazed down from the plaza. Best of all, election night was back on the broadcast network. No more downgrades to the LiveStream ghetto while regular NBC aired old *SNL* sketches. Williams was on his game, voluble and wry. He sensed a huge, engaged audience returning from a terrible season in the wilderness.

Janey, her friend Anita, and everyone they knew mobbed the Royal Horse to watch the returns. They had to line up outside to use the UV scanner and flash their antibody passports, and when they got in there was no place to sit, yet nobody whined, let alone went home. People tracked state returns on their phones and called out results, sometimes ahead of Williams' projections on TV: "McCarthy takes Kentucky!" "Duckworth takes Illinois!" The old bar and grill had seen nothing like it since coming back from the '26 coronavirus shutdown, maybe even since life changed in 2020.

Janey stole glances at her phone, too. The three-way race was close—so close. Third-party challenges in prior elections had always come to naught; Ross Perot had carried not one state in 1992, John Anderson not one in 1980, George Wallace just five southern states in 1968. That was why smart money said third parties never had a chance, Janey knew—because they never had before. Because they split the opposition. Because people fear wasting their vote.

She liked the old Kristol guy, though. She'd sat rapt through his nominating speech at the Unity Restoration virtual convention. He seemed to know what he was doing. If he had a feeling, and if he and people like him were willing to try building something new to succeed something broken, Janey was finally willing to trust.

With a few quick taps on her smartphone, walking home from lighting a candle for Mom on election day, Janey, heart swelling, had voted for the Unity Restoration ticket.

At midnight Mountain Time, Brian Williams projected Janey's candidate would win Colorado. Nine electoral votes. In the bar Janey leapt to her feet, hard seltzer flying, hugging Anita, transported for the first time in her life by the open-nerve thrill of democracy when it breaks your way. The place was shouting itself hoarse.

Janey was transported for the first time in her life by the open-nerve thrill of democracy when it breaks your way.

But it was nothing compared to the roar that rocked the block two hours later. At four in the morning in New York, Williams cocked his head toward the camera and called the game: Unity Restoration candidate Sally Yates of Georgia, the former Justice Department attorney, and her running mate, Florida's Francis Xavier Suarez, the former mayor of Miami, had captured 278 electoral votes. Yates-Suarez had carried the Pacific coast, Georgia and Florida, Virginia and North Carolina, Colorado, and just enough other states. A demographically transformed Texas had put them over the top. The Unity ticket edged out incumbent President McCarthy and Democrat Tammy Duckworth. Sally Yates would be the 49th president of the United States.

NBC dissolved away from Williams, not to campaign headquarters awash in glee, shock, or rage, but to the thousands crowding Rockefeller Plaza. They had hung in there all night. It was cold with nowhere to sit—the wind whips hard through that canyon—yet here they stayed, totally invested, and now . . . now they were *singing*, strangers arm in arm . . . there was no knowing who had voted for whom, but here they swayed together, thousands of tiny green CoviCop health-sensor LEDs winking across the space, reclaiming the night.

At the giant desk in the well of the plaza the anchors and pundits knew enough to stop talking. The crowd mics were jacked up full and drone cams panned the masses. The people were singing *America the Beautiful*.

Citizen Janey Reynolds welled up. She could hardly see the screen over the bar.

My God, she thought to herself. *It works.*

EPILOGUE

MALAYSIA

At the hub of the main international terminal at Kuala Lumpur International Airport—KLIA, they call it—they've installed an honest-to-goodness rain forest. It's a calming, lush, green oasis, a literally cool counterpoint to the gleaming L'Occitane and Ferragamo outposts dotting the concourse. The airport rain forest is not huge, exactly, but it's genuine. Heartening and hopeful. Shuffling off a long-haul flight in the closing months of 2019, I walked past the rain forest and it made me felt better. I pushed on toward the passport check and the outside world.

This was not my first visit to Malaysia as what you might call a modest, under-radar political missionary.

Part of my life now involves traveling overseas to train political parties, candidates, and activists—brave people trying to advance democratic ideals in their own countries. Despite the problems I've regaled you with in this book, they still see America as a role model. I run workshops on fair electoral mechanisms, ethical use of technology to influence the outcomes of campaigns, and digital strategy and messaging. Frequently, I go under the auspices of the International Republican Institute, a noble non-governmental outfit conceived in the Reagan era to help export democratic ideals. IRI has worked in more than 100 countries since 1983. Name notwithstanding, IRI is not a stealth arm of the Republican Party—it's strictly nonpartisan. It's funded by the National Endowment for Democracy, foundation grants, and the U.S. State Department.

I owe my IRI connection to Mike Connell, vendor of record for digital operations at the Republican National Committee when I was there too, many moons ago. Mike knew people at IRI, and when he passed away around 2010, I met some of them at a memorial reception. A couple of years later, I got a call asking if I'd like to do some volunteer training. Over and over, my professional life has proven that you never know where a chance meeting is going to take you.

IRI recruited me for what you might call servicing its Malaysia account—first in 2013, returning in 2017. This was my third trip. Since my last visit, Malaysia's political landscape had changed, and it seemed possible that IRI and I had played the tiniest role.

I flashed my passport, hefted my bag off the carousel, spilled into the big buzzy arrival hall, and caught the purple KLIA Ekspres, the fast train into Kuala Lumpur. Stand the Newark Airport monorail up next to the Ekspres and tell me who's winning the global science fair. The Ekspres was virtually silent as it accelerated like hell—a sobering reminder, for an American, of the relative woefulness of transport infrastructure back home, and the home-grown political gridlock that perpetuates a crumbling, often embarrassing status quo. Most Americans want better trains, roads, bridges, and airports, but not nearly enough happens. The sad contrast is almost enough to make a visitor to Malaysia forget he's observing a semi-democracy at best. Freedom House, an independent watchdog organization, rates Malaysia "partly free," with an "Aggregate Freedom Score" of 52 out of 100 points.[1]

We hurtled through flat exurban farmland. Humidity fogged the train's big rectangular windows. As I took in the view, I thought about the unlikely political resume I'd compiled in this distant place. I was about as far away from the Old Executive Office Building as a man can get and still be on Earth.

The Malaysian political system is interesting and, for most of recent history, represented a preference for authoritarianism, security, and pragmatic economic progress over real multilateral democracy. With authoritarian governance gaining more popular favor in the West—and with certain regimes learning to use digital tools and tactics to gain and maintain power—Malaysia's a relevant political laboratory, and a justifiable place for IRI to spend time and effort.

After the Federation of Malaya became independent from Britain in 1957, one party, the United Malays National Organization (UMNO), maintained power for decades, presiding over an untidy multi-faction coalition. From 1981 one UMNO prime minister, Mahathir bin Mohamed, held onto power for 22 years, winning five straight elections on a growth-and-modernization platform. But Mahathir was not great on civil liberties; he took robust advantage of the country's Internal Security Act allowing detention of regime critics. He was a confirmed, voluble anti-Semite and maintained prickly relations with the West. Scandals and infighting raged in Mahathir's ranks. Anwar Ibrahim, a deputy prime minister who demanded a corruption crackdown and hinted support for relaxed civil liberties, was ejected from UMNO and himself jailed on trumped-up sodomy charges.

Mahathir quit the premiership in 2003. UMNO and its Barisan Nasional coalition kept power, but in the ensuing decade looked increasingly embattled. Freedom House, dedicated, like IRI, to expanding democracy around the world, did not think much of Malaysian elections: "The political playing field is tilted toward the ruling party through measures such as gerrymandering of electoral districts, unequal candidate access to the media, and restrictions on campaigning, in addition to election day fraud."[2] Despite all this, in 2008, a ragtag opposition led by Ibrahim racked up unprecedented gains.

Religious tensions rose. (Freedom of religion is constitutionally guaranteed, but about 60 percent of the population practices Islam and some, Mahathir included, have called Malaysia an Islamic state.) In 2013, the year of my first workshop with Malaysian opposition parties, the government attacked rogue Filipinos laying claim to remote, disputed Malaysian territory in Sabah state. In short, after decades of authoritarian stability, things were hotting up—but also increasingly uncomfortable.

On that first 2013 trip, I didn't even get as far as Malaysia. IRI operatives were forbidden to set foot there at the time, for reasons that now seem obvious. As a fallback, I met the opposition representatives in Bangkok. The feedback was good, I was thanked politely, but on my way home I concluded the account was closed. That was that.

Events kept moving, though. Mahathir bin Mohamed renounced UMNO. In 2016 he founded his own splinter party, the Malaysian United Indigenous Party. From the strange-bedfellows files, he struck a deal with Anwar Ibrahim to join forces in an opposition bloc, Pakatan Harapan ("Alliance of Hope"). Together they might finally gin up enough horsepower to give UMNO and Barisan Nasional a real run for their money in the 2018 general election. It was hard to say how that might go over with UMNO or its own powerful coalition. But Mahathir ended up in the driver's seat at Pakatan Harapan, raring to take down his old UMNO machine.

Anti-West, anti-civil liberties, and an anti-Semite Mahathir may have been, but when opposition officials invited IRI and me back in 2017, to Kuala Lumpur itself this time, I was cautiously interested. I had to look myself in the mirror. Was I really committed to democracy *qua* democracy, whether or not I favored the contenders and their ideals?

> **Was I really committed to democracy *qua* democracy, whether or not I favored the contenders and their ideals?**

I was pondering this when another, heavier shoe dropped: As a condition of teaching the opposition digital political strategy, I had to meet in person with designates from the incumbent UMNO party, too.

Gulp. Obviously UMNO knew I had done more on my 2013 visit to Bangkok than tour the elephant sanctuary. I was not certain what "meet with" might be a euphemism for. Malaysia's Internal Security Act had been repealed some years back, but a successor law, the Security Offenses (Special Measures) Act, had been used in 2016 to arrest civil rights activists.[3] Double gulp.

I said I'd go.

Before departing the States, I emailed my father:

I was asked to conduct another training for International Republican Institute (IRI) in early June, in Malaysia. Jennifer will join me and the kids will stay with Sally.

As long as I don't become a political prisoner it should be a good trip!

When I travel abroad on gigs like this, I sign an IRI waiver confirming I understand the risks and chance of harm. The standard list of possible pitfalls is enough to make Mom's eyes water. IRI has thorough lawyers. I signed now, too, but in all honesty did not know precisely what I was marching into. I felt I understood the Malaysian political framework, but from a distance; these would be my first footsteps in the country itself. I was wary.

When you lay eyes on it for the first time, the Kuala Lumpur skyline is spectacular—if you go, check out the twin Petronas Towers—but on that trip I forgot to savor the view. I was preoccupied.

My IRI handler, Matthew Hays, met me at my hotel with a driver. We motored out to a bustling area 30 minutes from the center of Kuala Lumpur. We had agreed to a rendezvous in a very public coffee shop and, when we arrived, chose an outdoor table surrounded by spectators. Our interlocutors had provided no advance agenda, so while we waited for them to show up, Matthew and I prepped for possible questions. I told Matthew I wouldn't speak on behalf of IRI, only about my experience as a digital strategist.

I could not taste my tea. (I don't drink coffee, though Malaysian *kopi* is excellent.) My stomach churned. Did my belief in exporting digital democracy really extend to being interrogated by Malaysian officials in a random coffee shop on the outskirts of the city? I had no idea where I was, really; I had paid no attention to our driver's route. What would I do if the meeting went sideways? I felt like an impostor in a Jason Bourne movie, lacking Bourne's self-preservation chops.

I looked up. Here came the two government functionaries. They cast long shadows across our table before we shook hands and sat down together. They were nondescript, middle-aged men with saturnine complexions. One of them did all the talking.

"So, you're the American who came here to overthrow our country," he began.

> "So, you're the American who came here to overthrow our country," the Malaysian official began.

I searched his face and tone for a hint of irony, or wry humor. I saw none. Matthew, next to me, drew a sharp breath. It was an inauspicious way to kick things off.

Not the case, I responded with what I hoped came across as calm, respectful confidence. I was a neutral broker, I said. I traveled the world to help political operatives apply some of the digital techniques used by American campaigns. I had no direct interest in advancing any cause beyond democracy.

I lurched on.

Something Matthew or I said defused the situation. I concentrated on selling myself as an experienced tactician, no fanboy of any ideology, left or right. To this day, I do not know if our two glowering friends really thought I had turned up to conspire against them, or if the whole encounter was some cryptic litmus test. Whatever the truth was, I gambled that if I positioned myself as an advocate of democracy, the ruling regime could not lock me up or throw me out. That would define them as anti-democracy.

After an hour they shrugged, stood up, shook hands and departed. Matthew and I unclenched during the ride back to the hotel in the center of town. It took most of the trip.

My workshops with members of the opposition Pakatan Harapan coalition took place at what Dick Cheney would call an undisclosed location. (Though I assume the incumbent regime knew anyway.) I faced representatives of five parties. The first thing I heard was that the five factions didn't get along too well; it would be hard to get them to work together. In all-hands workshop sessions five clumps of people staked out separate zones of the room, resisting interaction.

I told the group the law of averages favors those who collaborate. If the opposition parties could agree on a strategy to share and redirect each other's social media content, they'd have more opportunities to connect with far more voters. Any added connection would give a tiny, incremental boost to their chances of dislodging UMNO.

Together we studied the analytics around social media keywords and trending topics. I got the five factions to cooperate temporarily on prioritizing a few topics each, building memes around them, then cross-posting each other's memes. Over the course of the next 24 hours, we would study the analytics and see what transpired.

The evening of post-those-memes day, a couple went viral fast—perhaps because recipients could not figure out why one party was posting another's material. The next morning there was a whole different energy in the training room. Members of different factions were mixing, laughing, trading high-fives and compliments. We scanned the internet analytics to quantify the compound impact of their collaboration; we discussed how and why certain messages took off, and how to replicate the effect across the digital infosphere, with other messages as the payload.

By the end of the workshop it was positively huggy in there. I was told that if I could get those five stubborn factions to work in concert, IRI had done its job; framing an incentive to cooperate was Pakatan Harapan's biggest goal. But in the next breath I was warned not to get too full of myself. The ruling UMNO had been in power since 1957, I was reminded. The chances of the opposition knocking them out were slim and none.

I said thank you and flew home.

A couple months later, Pakatan Harapan knocked out UMNO and Barisan Nasional, fair and square. Astonishing.

When the digital teams from all those opposition splinter parties learned how to work together for greater impact—and read the performance reports to guide ever-better voter engagement—something changed. A stunned UMNO government ceded power. It had never happened in Malaysia.

Mahathir bin Mohammed became prime minister again at the age of 92.

Shadi Hamid, a senior fellow at the Project on U.S. Relations with the Islamic World at the Brookings Institution, wrote:

"These events were a reminder of a different kind of democratic euphoria, offering a stark contrast to the pessimism that citizens of Western countries have by now grown accustomed to. Elections do, in fact, have consequences . . . citizens—no matter how bad things get and how corrupt their leaders become—theoretically have *recourse*. They are not powerless. They can organize. They can constrain executive action. They can oppose . . .

"Democracy is a long-term solution to the problem of how to manage conflict peacefully. It's about giving citizens at least the option (one they may choose not to take) of replacing their representatives and experimenting with different candidates, parties, and even ideologies. It's also about that feeling that you, as a citizen, can actually alter the course of your own country, and that your nation, at least in theory, believes that you matter enough to have that power. There is a joy in knowing this . . .

"Malaysia offers a reminder that there is no substitute for this most essential of democratic functions: the chance, even if it often resides on a theoretical plane, that political outcomes are not permanent. There is that natural push and pull of democratic competition, with all the messiness that entails. But that messiness and uncertainty can be a good thing."[4]

That is what the new digital democracy, optimized for good, is all about.

When the election results were called, Matthew Hays sent me a note.

Hi Cyrus:

I'm sure you saw the news. A truly historic day for Malaysian democracy. They will see a change in government for the first time in 60 years. You certainly played a part. Syed Saddiq, who came to your training, won his seat for MP against a longtime incumbent, becoming the youngest elected in Malaysia's history.

Syed was among my youngest workshop participants—only 25 in 2017—and the most inquisitive. Charismatic, clear-eyed, and tireless, he also became Malaysia's Minister of Youth and Sports, and turned down scholarships to Oxford to remain involved in domestic politics. Honestly, Syed's done some controversial things, not least of which was supporting a ban on Israeli athletes from competing in the World Para Swimming Championships in order to punish the Netanyahu government for its treatment of Palestinians—a move that led to Malaysia losing the right to host the event.[5] Not great, but in a responsive democracy the public can take a leader to task for unpopular acts. Elsewhere, to my delight, Syed tabled a bill in Parliament to lower the voting age in Malaysia to 18. In July 2019, it passed in the lower house, the Dewan Rakyat, together with measures enabling automatic voter registration and allowing 18-year-olds to run for office.[6]

Now it was fall 2019 and I was back in Kuala Lumpur, disembarking from the KLIA Ekspres and finding my hotel. The Malaysian political system was not totally transformed, exactly, but to me, the streets seemed full of opportunity. On this trip, I remembered to marvel at the spectacular skyline and eat some top-shelf *nasi lemak*. Time permitting, I promised myself I would go see the Kampung Baru night market.

The most promising sign of all—the O. Henry twist ending to this story—was who hosted my trip this time. It was the former ruling party that asked me to return—UMNO and members of the Barisan Nasional coalition.

Matthew Hays had rotated back to New York, so a new IRI handler brokered this encounter. He wanted me to meet with former ruling party dignitaries and digital practitioners to prove IRI doesn't play favorites. After their loss, representatives of the long-standing incumbents, finding themselves on the outs, had taken the measure of the political winds and wanted legitimate routes back in. The forces that had maintained authority in Malaysia from 1957 to 2018, sometimes with, as Freedom House put it, "gerrymandering . . . restrictions in campaigning, in addition to election day fraud"? The guys who intimidated me in that coffee shop two years earlier, calling me the American out to overthrow their government? They had been duly unelected. Now they were looking to IRI for a similar primer on campaigning by the rules.

We met in small, informal groups. We talked about some of the emerging digital capabilities—technological innovations, from geolocation to demographic targeting, they could utilize to frame and deliver their messages. We discussed ways to under-

We talked about where the red lines lie. How to be relevant without becoming invasive or abusive.

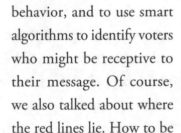

stand human emotion and behavior, and to use smart algorithms to identify voters who might be receptive to their message. Of course, we also talked about where the red lines lie. How to be relevant without becoming invasive or abusive. How to target voters without violating their privacy. How to be persuasive and partisan, but not lie or traffic in fake news—because trust matters most. Even more than power. In an open digital political system that depends on trust, victory through deception cannot endure and, in the long run, degrades everything.

I hope my friends in Malaysia, exploring a new political world where a once-impregnable ruling party can actually lose a fair election, and leveraging the digital infosphere with ethics and a conscience can help you win, found the encounter as inspiring and downright thrilling as I did.

On my way home, I again passed the serene little rain forest within the Kuala Lumpur airport. Like the rain forest, the political progress I witnessed was not huge, exactly. Not yet. But real. Heartening and hopeful. Democracy seemed more than salvageable; it seemed laden with new potential.

Now for America.

ACKNOWLEDGMENTS

I didn't ask permission from Rob Goodling to share my story about laying cable in the OEOB. I thank him now for that assignment, which awakened my interest in digital politics. Of course, my internship in the Dan Quayle office would likely not have happened at all had I not lost a coin toss to my brother Joshua, which led to my bumping into Les Novitsky in the synagogue parking lot that summer afternoon. Thanks to both; they could not have known what they set in motion.

My colleagues from CNN, including co-author Tom Farmer, inspired me then as well as now, particularly those in the show units led by Rick Davis and Daniel Silva. Rick remains at CNN as executive vice president, News Standards and Practices. Dan, of course, became the globally admired author of spy thrillers. He was working on his first, *The Unlikely Spy*, when I departed CNN for *Slate* 25 years ago. It looks like writing might pan out for Dan someday.

Larry King Live executive producer Tammy Haddad interviewed me for my first job at CNN, which makes her responsible for my meeting Michael Kinsley, which changed my life. She remains a postmodern media force in the capital.

In 1995 my friend Brett Dalrymple did most of the driving as we road-tripped from Washington D.C. to Seattle, giving me time to read up on Microsoft before starting what would prove to be a decade at *Slate*. Michael Kinsley, who put together the winning *Slate* team, remains a friend and mentor today. If there was a Cult of Kinsley, I'd join.

When Chuck Defeo called to suggest I relocate from Santa Monica to Washington, D.C., I didn't hesitate and remain thankful he thought of me.

Scott Moore, with whom I worked at *Slate*, MSN, Yahoo, and Cheezburger, is currently CEO of AdLightning. His ongoing impact on my career and personal well-being has been beneficial beyond words, and I'm very grateful.

Karen Jagoda was hosting eVoter Institute events in Washington before campaigning online was cool, and her attendees continue doing important work today. Through the Institute I met Jonah Seiger, a fellow digital political pioneer and to me a particularly wise and professionally generous one, and Bara Vaida, a respected D.C. journalist and my go-to Zoom yoga instructor during the COVID-19 quarantine.

Thank you to Chuck Davis, my brother from another mother and long-time business partner, for agreeing to be interviewed for this book and for reviewing an early draft. Chuck is now focused on population health management, continuing his trailblazing work in analytics.

My friend Chris Widener, the *New York Times* best-selling author, motivational speaker, and onetime U.S. Senate candidate, encouraged me to write this book. Thanks to Chris; to Dan Baum, a Washington D.C. executive and long-time trusted advisor; and to entrepreneur John Dick, whom I have known since 2007. We're still collaborating.

The team at IRI is exceptional to work with, especially the group in Kuala Lumpur. One day I hope to visit my politically astute friend Praba Ganesan's durian farm. Matthew Hays made himself available on a moment's notice in New York, and we had a chance to remember our mutual friend Alo. May he rest in peace.

The founder and president of Democracy Live, Bryan Finney, shared with me his passion for electoral integrity and restoring faith in democracy, and I appreciate his support.

Appreciation also goes to Neville Isdell for permission to quote from an unpublished op-ed, and to Pete Weissman at Thought Leader Communications for making the introduction.

Thanks to the entire Made for Success team and the Heathman family for the production expertise they brought to the *Bombarded* project. Thanks to Scott Wilson for valuable manuscript reviews and editing suggestions, Brendan Farmer for correcting an early draft, and Dawn Farmer for letting *Bombarded* research material bedeck the living room during stay-at-home orders.

I have made treasured, lifelong friends through the Seattle lacrosse community, specifically the Legion of Goon.

Thank you to my immediate and extended family for keeping the Krohn family bond strong.

And last but not least, thank you for reading this far.

ENDNOTES

Introduction

[1]Anna Merlan, "Bleach Ingestion Advocates Are Thrilled By Trump's 'Disinfectant' Comments," Vice.com, 28 April 2020. https://www.vice.com/en_us/article/884wgv/bleach-ingestion-advocates-are-thrilled-by-trumps-disinfectant-comments?utm_source=reddit.com

[2]David Brooks, "The Bernie Sanders Fallacy," *The New York Times,* 16 January 2020. https://www.nytimes.com/2020/01/16/opinion/the-bernie-sanders-fallacy.html?algo=top_conversion&fellback=false&imp_id=364842943&imp_id=496499880&action=click&module=trending&pgtype=Article&region=Footer

[3]Joel Kotkin, "Is America About to Suffer its Weimar Moment?" *The Daily Beast,* December 30, 2019. https://www.thedailybeast.com/is-america-about-to-suffer-its-weimar-moment?ref=home

[4]"How Tech Hijacks Our Brains, Corrupts Culture, and What to Do Now." *A Minute with Sam Sanders,* NPR, May 21, 2019. https://www.npr.org/2019/05/15/723671325/how-tech-hijacks-our-brains-corrupts-culture-and-what-to-do-now

[5]Kevin B. Smith, Matthew V. Hibbing, John R. Hibbing, "Friends, Relatives, Sanity, and Health: The Cost of Politics," University of Nebraska, September 25, 2019. https://journals.plos.org/plosone/article?id=10.1371/journal.pone.0221870

[6]David Brooks, "The Media is Broken—And Not for the Reasons You Think," *The New York Times,* 26 December 2019. https://www

.nytimes.com/2019/12/26/opinion/media-politics.html?smid
=nytcore-ios-share&fbclid=IwAR2K8jWjZ7HwLxF-KzG6gUE58SCx
tUN6t7dWYBthZIOZ2PrqWkApCSGfO9o

[7]From Wearable X. https://www.wearablex.com/

[8]iPropertyManagement.com. https://ipropertymanagement.com
/research/iot-statistics

[9]Jonathan Haidt and Tobias Rose-Stockwell, "The Dark Psychology
of Social Networks," *The Atlantic,* December 2019. https://www
.theatlantic.com/magazine/archive/2019/12/social-media-democracy
/600763/

[10]P.W. Singer and Emerson T. Brooking, *Like War: The Weaponization
of Social Media.* 2018, Eamon Dolan, division of Houghton Mifflin
Harcourt. Pg. 3.

[11]Robin Koerner, *If You Can Keep It: Why We Nearly Lost It and How
We Get It Back.* Stairway Press, 2016. Pg. 24.

[12]George Packer, "We Are Living in a Failed State," *The Atlantic,*
June 2020. https://www.theatlantic.com/magazine/archive/2020/06
/underlying-conditions/610261/

Chapter One: Tuesday, November 2, 2032

[1]Rachel Bade, Mike DeBonis, and Josh Dawsey, "Inside the Decision
to Impeach Trump: How Both Parties Wrestled with a Constitutional
Crisis," *Washington Post,* 18 December 2019.

[2]William Roberts Clark, University of Michigan; Matt Golder and
Sona Golder, Pennsylvania State University; *Power and Politics: Lessons
from an Exit, Voice, and Loyalty Game.* Unpublished paper, 2013.
https://projects.iq.harvard.edu/files/pegroup/files/clark_golder.pdf

[3]Gallup Organization, party affiliation 2004-2019. https://news
.gallup.com/poll/15370/party-affiliation.aspx

[4]Leslie Josephs, "Georgia's lieutenant governor says he will 'kill' Delta
tax break unless airline reinstates relationship with NRA," CNBC.com,
26 February 2018. https://www.cnbc.com/2018/02/26/georgia-lt-gov
-will-kill-delta-tax-break-unless-airline-restores-nra-ties.html

Chapter Two: Portrait of the Digital Strategist as a Young Man

[1] Dana Floberg, "US Students are Being Asked to Work Remotely. But 22% of Homes Don't Have Internet," *The Guardian* (UK), 23 March 2020. https://www.theguardian.com/commentisfree/2020/mar/23/us-students-are-being-asked-to-work-remotely-but-22-of-homes-dont-have-internet

[2] Covid Tracking Project. https://covidtracking.com/data/

[3] Centers for Disease Control and Prevention, "Coronavirus Disease 2019 (COVID-19)," cdc.gov. https://www.cdc.gov/coronavirus/2019-ncov/cases-updates/cases-in-us.html

[4] Jonathan Swan and Sam Baker, "Trump and Some Aides Question Accuracy of Virus Death Toll," Axios.com, 6 May 2020. https://www.axios.com/trump-coronavirus-death-toll-d8ba60a4-316b-4d1e-8595-74970c15fb34.html

[5] Nick Bilton, "Coronavirus is Creating a Fake News Nightmarescape." *Vanity Fair*, 2 March 2020. https://www.vanityfair.com/news/2020/03/coronavirus-is-creating-fake-news-nightmarescape-social-media?itm_content=footer-recirc

[6] @toddstarnes: Todd Starnes Twitter account, 8 May 2020. https://twitter.com/toddstarnes/status/1258870865481121793

[7] Charlie Warzel, "Open States, Lots of Guns. America Is Paying a Heavy Price for Freedom," *The New York Times*, 5 May 2020. https://www.nytimes.com/2020/05/05/opinion/coronavirus-deaths.html

[8] Morning Consult, "Coronavirus Trend Tracker: How the Coronavirus Outbreak is Impacting Public Opinion: 1 in 5 Republicans Say They Would Not Get COVID-19 Vaccine; Support for Leaders' Handling of the Outbreak is Falling Across the Board," 5 May 2020. https://morningconsult.com/form/coronavirus-outbreak-tracker/#section-99

[9] Nick Bryant, "Coronavirus: What This Crisis Reveals About US - and its President," BBC.com, 24 March 2020. https://www.bbc.com/news/world-us-canada-52012049?fbclid=IwAR1IVxbiXjKayiJTeRGhq9ynxa_BbviBHJRJY4lOykcJmU8WGi7UFbOm0Yg

[10]David Gilbert, "A Broadband Engineer Was Spat on by a 5G Conspiracy Theorist. Then He Got Coronavirus," Vice.com, 7 May 2020. https://www.vice.com/en_us/article/4ayg8g/a-broadband -engineer-was-spat-on-by-a-5g-conspiracy-theorist-now-he-has -coronavirus?utm_source=reddit.com

[11]Bloomberg, "5G Virus Conspiracy Theory Fuelled by Coordinated Effort Involving Bot Accounts, Researchers Say," *South China Morning Post,* 10 April 2020. https://www.scmp.com/tech/gear /article/3079328/5g-virus-conspiracy-theory-fuelled-coordinated-effort -involving-bot

[12]Taylor Hatmaker, "Platforms Scramble as 'Plandemic' Conspiracy Video Spreads Information Like Wildfire," TechCrunch.com, 7 May 2020. https://techcrunch.com/2020/05/07/plandemic-video-judy -mikovits/

[13]Brandy Zadrozny and Ben Collins, "Coronavirus Deniers Take Aim at Hospitals as Pandemic Grows," NBC News, 30 March 2020. https://www.nbcnews.com/tech/social-media/coronavirus -deniers-take-aim-hospitals-pandemic-grows-n1172336

[14]Vaughn Hillyard, "Police Say Death of Arizona Man is Not Being Investigated As a Homicide," NBCNews.com, 24 March 2020. https://www.nbcnews.com/politics/politics-news/police-say-death -arizona-man-not-being-investigated-homicide-n1195591

[15]Janelle Irwin Taylor, "Florida Official Recommends Blow Dryer at Your Face to Combat Coronavirus; Don't do That," FloridaPolitics. com, 22 March 2020. https://floridapolitics.com/archives/324644 -okeechobee-official-recommends-pointing-a-blow-dryer-at-your-face -to-combat-coronavirus-dont-do-that

[16]Matthew S. Schwartz, "Missouri Sues Televangelist Jim Bakker For Selling Fake Coronavirus Cure," NPR, 11 March 2020. https://www .npr.org/2020/03/11/814550474/missouri-sues-televangelist-jim -bakker-for-selling-fake-coronavirus-cure

[17]"Coronavirus Outbreak Spurs a Wave of Suspicious Websites." The Coronavirus Outbreak: Latest Updates, *The New York Times* update, 24 March 2020. https://www.nytimes.com/2020/03/24

/business/coronavirus-stock-market-live-tracker.html?action=click&p
gtype=Article&state=default&module=styln-coronavirus-markets
&variant=show&region=MID_MAIN_CONTENT&context=storyline
_updates_business#link-79d9c1c2

[18]Tony Romm, "Fake Cures and Other Coronavirus Conspiracy
Theories are Flooding WhatsApp, Leaving Governments and Users with
a 'Sense of Panic,'" *The Washington Post,* 2 March 2020. https://www
.washingtonpost.com/technology/2020/03/02/whatsapp-coronavirus
-misinformation/

[19]Kyle Daly, "Coronavirus Misinformation Seeds Ground for Digital
Scams," Axios.com, 15 April 2020. https://www.axios.com/coronavirus
-misinformation-seeds-ground-for-digital-scams-d1f5a020-54a9-4e41
-877e-ecf9c2cec081.html

[20]@GovPritzker: J.B. Pritzker Twitter account, 22 March 2020.
https://twitter.com/GovPritzker/status/1241770144545869826

[21]David Choi, "Axl Rose Calls Treasury Secretary Steve Mnuchin
an 'Asshole' After Guns N' Roses Music is Played During Trump's
Visit to a Mask Factory," *Business Insider,* 6 May 2018. https://www
.businessinsider.com/axl-rose-calls-treasury-secretary-steve-mnuchin
-an-asshole-2020-5?utm_source=reddit.com

[22]Garrett Graff, "What Americans are Doing Now is Beautiful,"
The Atlantic, 19 March 2020. https://www.theatlantic.com/ideas
/archive/2020/03/inspiring-galvanizing-beautiful-spirit-2020/608308/

[23]@brianstelter: Brian Stelter Twitter account, 18 April 2020. https://
twitter.com/brianstelter/status/1251532625942130689

[24]Paul Bedard, "Trending: Out-of-Control Teenagers Coughing on
Grocery Store Produce," *Washington Examiner*, 20 March 2020. https://
www.washingtonexaminer.com/washington-secrets/trending-out-of
-control-teens-coughing-on-grocery-store-produce

[25]Elisha Fieldstadt, "Grocery Store Throws Out $35K Worth
of Food that Woman Coughed on in 'twisted prank,'" NBCNews.
com, 26 March 2020. https://www.nbcnews.com/news/us-news
/grocery-store-throws-out-35k-worth-food-woman-coughed-twisted
-n1169401?cid=public-rss_20200326

[26] Jack Nicas, "The Man With 17,000 Bottles of Hand Sanitizer Just Donated Them," *The New York Times,* 15 March 2020. https://www.nytimes.com/2020/03/15/technology/matt-colvin-hand-sanitizer-donation.html

[27] Amber Jayanth, "Milford Grad Goes Viral for Shrugging Off Virus During Spring Break Trip," FOX 19 Cincinnati, 19 March 2020. https://www.fox19.com/2020/03/20/milford-grad-goes-viral-shrugging-off-virus-during-spring-break/

[28] @CT_Bergstrom: Carl T. Bergstrom Twitter account, 26 March 2020. https://twitter.com/CT_Bergstrom/status/1243252341756669953

[29] Dennis Romero, "3 McDonald's Workers Hurt After Customer Attack Over Coronavirus Limits, Oklahoma Police Say," NBCNews.com, 7 May 2020. https://www.nbcnews.com/news/us-news/3-mcdonald-s-workers-hurt-after-customer-attack-over-coronavirus-n1201681

[30] David Aaro, "Alabama Cop Appears to Body-Slam Walmart Shopper for not Wearing Face Mask: Video," FoxNews.com, 7 May 2020. https://www.foxnews.com/us/alabama-cop-appears-to-body-slam-walmart-shopper-for-not-wearing-face-mask-video

[31] Eric Cortellessa, "US Far-Right Extremists are Now Calling Social Distancing a Nazi Policy," *The Times of Israel,* 10 May 2020. https://www.timesofisrael.com/us-far-right-extremists-are-now-calling-social-distancing-a-nazi-policy/

[32] @antoniogutterez, U.N. Secretary General Antonio Guterres Twitter account, 14 April 2020. https://twitter.com/antonioguterres/status/1250095790959267841

[33] Katrin Bennhold, "'Sadness' and Disbelief from a World Missing American Leadership," *The New York Times,* 23 April 2020. https://www.nytimes.com/2020/04/23/world/europe/coronavirus-american-exceptionalism.html?algo=top_conversion&fellback=false&imp_id=460058955&imp_id=424788301&action=click&module=trending&pgtype=Article&region=Footer

[34] Fintan O'Toole, "Donald Trump has Destroyed the Country he Promised to Make Great Again," The Irish Times, 25 April 2020. https://www.irishtimes.com/opinion/fintan-o-toole-donald-trump-has

-destroyed-the-country-he-promised-to-make-great-again-1.4235928? mode=sample&auth-failed=1&pw-origin=https%3A%2F%2Fwww .irishtimes.com%2Fopinion%2Ffintan-o-toole-donald-trump-has -destroyed-the-country-he-promised-to-make-great-again-1.4235928

[35]James McCarten, "Americans Have More Trust in Canadians Than Themselves, Poll Suggests," Canadian Press via Huffpost.ca, 6 May 2020. https://www.huffingtonpost.ca/entry/americans-trusting-canadians -coronavirus_ca_5eb2e9bdc5b613518d494366?ncid=other_trending _qeesnbnu0l8&utm_campaign=trending

[36]Hunter S. Thompson, *Fear and Loathing in Las Vegas: A Savage Journey to the Heart of the American Dream.* Popular Library, 1971. Pg. 180.

[37]Kurt Schlosser, "Israeli President Coming to People's Homes via Unique Hologram Video Tech from Seattle Startup," GeekWire .com, 28 April 2020. https://www.geekwire.com/2020/israeli-president -coming-peoples-homes-via-unique-hologram-video-tech-seattle-startup/

Chapter Three: Coding Issues

[1]Issie Lapowsky, "He Complained About Democrats' Tech 'Morass'—Then Built the Iowa App," *Protocol,* 5 February 2020. https://www.protocol.com/shadow-app-iowa-caucus

[2]McKay Coppins, "The Billion-Dollar Disinformation Campaign to Reelect the President," *The Atlantic,* March 2020. https://www .theatlantic.com/magazine/archive/2020/03/the-2020-disinformation -war/605530/?fbclid=IwAR29Hzpb2KF5w-OKkMIc0ItVpCZY f96ON_nMEzJLR69367zgdBFJxenRS-M

[3]Orion Rummler, Facebook Executive Argues Digital Ads Got Trump Elected," Axios.com, 7 January 2020. https://www.axios .com/facebook-trump-2016-election-bosworth-2ee80dea-b96c-408b -95e9-76f0b7c5ef7f.html?utm_source=newsletter&utm_medium =email&utm_campaign=newsletter_axiospm&stream=top

[4]Thomas B. Edsall, "Trump's Digital Advantage Is Freaking Out Democratic Strategists," *The New York Times,* 29 January 2020. https://

www.nytimes.com/2020/01/29/opinion/trump-digital-campaign
-2020.html

[5]Quint Forgey, "AOC: 'In Any Other Country, Joe Biden and I Would Not Be in the Same Party'," *Politico,* 6 January 2020. https://www.politico.com/news/2020/01/06/alexandria-ocasio-cortez-joe-biden-not-same-party-094642?fbclid=IwAR0h498buoVMTGqRfy7YPnEazQm071A50SuOYIAmuq2St9KhYXqfMUPWgtU

[6]Gerald Chait, Director/CEO, Marketing by Objectives Pty Ltd. B2B Marketing, 18 March 2015. https://www.b2bmarketing.net/en/resources/blog/half-money-i-spend-advertising-wasted-trouble-i-dont-know-which-half

[7]Hal Malchow, *The New Political Targeting.* Campaigns and Elections Magazine, 2003. Pgs. 4-5.

[8]Kathryn Montgomery and Jeff Chester, "The Digital Commercialization of US Politics—2020 and Beyond," Center for Digital Democracy, 16 January 2020. https://www.democraticmedia.org/article/digital-commercialisation-us-politics-2020-and-beyond

[9]Nick Corasaniti and Quoctrung Bui, "Facebook Political Ads: Which States are 2020 Democrats Betting On?" *The New York Times,* 17 January 2020.

[10]Ann Banks, "Dirty Tricks, South Carolina, and John McCain," *The Nation,* 14 January 2008. https://www.thenation.com/article/archive/dirty-tricks-south-carolina-and-john-mccain/

[11]P. W. Singer and Emerson T. Brooking, *LikeWar: The Weaponization of Social Media.* Eamon Dolan, division of Houghton Mifflin Harcourt, 2018. Pg. 119.

[12]Joshua Green and Sasha Issenberg, "Inside the Trump Bunker, With Days to Go," Bloomberg.com, 27 October 2016. https://www.bloomberg.com/news/articles/2016-10-27/inside-the-trump-bunker-with-12-days-to-go

[13]Matthew Rosenberg, Nicholas Confessore, and Carole Cadwalladr, "How Trump Consultants Exploited the Facebook Data of Millions," *The New York Times,* 17 March 2018. https://www.nytimes.com/2018/03/17/us/politics/cambridge-analytica-trump-campaign.html

[14]Brennan Weiss, "A Russian Troll Factory Had a $1.25 Million Monthly Budget to Interfere in the 2016 US Election," *Business Insider,* 16 February 2018. https://www.businessinsider.com/russian-troll-farm -spent-millions-on-election-interference-2018-2

[15]P. W. Singer and Emerson T. Brooking, *LikeWar: The Weaponization of Social Media.* Eamon Dolan, division of Houghton Mifflin Harcourt, 2018. Pgs. 118-120.

[16]Daniel Kreiss: *Prototype Politics: Technology-Intensive Campaigning and the Data of Democracy.* Oxford University Press, 2016. Pgs. 204-207.

[17]Nick Corasaniti and Quoctrung Bui, "Facebook Political Ads: Which States are 2020 Democrats Betting On?" *The New York Times,* 17 January 2020. https://www.nytimes.com/interactive /2020/01/17/us/politics/democrats-political-facebook-ads.html?nl =todaysheadlines&emc=edit_th_200118?campaign_id=2&instance _id=15129&segment_id=20444&user_id=b43261659350c774 56b4aa21a6122ac7&regi_id=413701190118

[18]Nick Fouriezos, "Meet the Democrats' Most Dangerous Digital Strategist," Ozy.com, 5 September 2019. https://www.ozy.com/news -and-politics/meet-the-democrats-most-dangerous-digital-strategist /95569/

[19]Kim Zetter, "How Close Did Russia Really Come to Hacking the 2016 Election?" *Politico,* 26 December 2019. https://www.politico .com/news/magazine/2019/12/26/did-russia-really-hack-2016-election -088171

[20]Andy Kroll, Rolling Stone, "Hackers are Coming for the 2020 Election—And We're Not Ready," *Rolling Stone,* 17 January 2020. https://www.rollingstone.com/politics/politics-features/trump-election -hacking-russia-iran-ransomware-interference-938109/

[21]Ellen Nakashima, "Russian Spies Hacked Ukrainian Gas Company at Heart of Trump Impeachment Trial, Company Says," *The Washington Post,* 13 January 2020. https://www.washingtonpost .com/national-security/russian-spies-hacked-ukrainian-gas-company-at -heart-of-trump-impeachment-trial/2020/01/13/db50b2b0-366c-11ea -bb7b-265f4554af6d_story.html

[22]Andy Kroll, Rolling Stone, "Hackers are Coming for the 2020 Election—And We're Not Ready," *Rolling Stone,* 17 January 2020. https://www.rollingstone.com/politics/politics-features/trump-election -hacking-russia-iran-ransomware-interference-938109/

[23]Andy Kroll, Rolling Stone, "Hackers are Coming for the 2020 Election—And We're Not Ready," *Rolling Stone,* 17 January 2020. https://www.rollingstone.com/politics/politics-features/trump-election -hacking-russia-iran-ransomware-interference-938109/

[24]Ibid.

[25]Matthew Rosenberg, Nicole Perlroth, and David E. Sanger, "'Chaos is the Point': Russian Hackers and Trolls Grow Stealthier in 2020," *The New York Times,* 10 January 2020. https://www.nytimes .com/2020/01/10/us/politics/russia-hacking-disinformation-election .html?fbclid=IwAR08NUKK7jJ1kgTCaPcyhBZHFZIVahzEHjj3kpix kANScxiDYsZJwxDeexw

[26]OpenSecrets.org, 2012 Presidential Race. https://www.opensecrets .org/pres12/index.php

[27]Alex Clark: "Breitbart's Boyle: Our Goal is the Elimination of the Entire Mainstream Media," Breitbart.com, 19 July 2017. https://www .breitbart.com/the-media/2017/07/19/breitbarts-boyle-goal-elimination -entire-mainstream-media/

[28]Mia Jankowicz, "It Looks Like People with No Real Interest in Bloomberg are Signing Up to Be Grassroots Campaigners Because He Pays $2,500 a Month, *Business Insider,* 24 February 2020. https://www .businessinsider.com/bloombergs-2500-month-campaign-fee-is-attracting -lukewarm-workers-2020-2

[29]Scott Bixby, "Mike Bloomberg is Paying 'Influencers' to Make Him Seem Cool," *The Daily Beast,* 7 Febryary 2020. https://www .thedailybeast.com/mike-bloomberg-is-paying-influencers-to-make -him-seem-cool-9

[30]McKay Coppins, "The Billion-Dollar Disinformation Campaign to Reelect the President," *The Atlantic*, March 2020. https://www .theatlantic.com/magazine/archive/2020/03/the-2020-disinformation -war/605530/?fbclid=IwAR29Hzpb2KF5w-OKkMIc0ItVpCZY f96ON_nMEzJLR69367zgdBFJxenRS-M

[31] Ibid.

[32] Lee Fang, "New Details Show How Deeply Iowa Caucus App Was Embedded in Democratic Establishment," The Intercept, 4 February 2020. https://theintercept.com/2020/02/04/iowa-caucus-app-shadow -acronym/

[33] Emily Stewart, "Acronym, the Dark Money Group Behind the Iowa Caucuses App Meltdown, Explained," *Recode*, Vox.com, 8 February 2020. https://www.vox.com/recode/2020/2/5/21123009/acronym -tara-mcgowan-shadow-app-iowa-caucus-results

[34] *For What It's Worth*, "The Future of Progressive Tech," Wonder Media Network, 30 January 2020. https://for-what-its-worth .simplecast.com/episodes/the-future-of-progressive-tech-jJIx7K04

[35] Nick Corasaniti, Sheera Frankel, and Nicole Perlroth, "App Used to Tabulate Votes Is Said to Have Been Inadequately Tested," *The New York Times*, 3 February 2020. https://www.nytimes.com/2020/02/03 /us/politics/iowa-caucus-app.html

[36] Ciara O'Rourke, "What We Know About Shadow, Acronym, and the Iowa Caucuses," PolitiFact.org, 4 February 2020. https://www .politifact.com/article/2020/feb/04/what-we-know-about-shadow -acronym-and-iowa-caucuse/

[37] Suzanne Downing, "'Shadow' App is Part of a Bold Influence Machine for Democrats to Defeat Trump," MustReadAlaska.com, 9 February 2020. https://mustreadalaska.com/shadow-app-is-part-of -a-bold-influence-machine-for-democrats-to-defeat-trump/

[38] Michelle Cottle, *The New York Times* Editorial Board, 6 February 2020. https://www.nytimes.com/2020/02/06/opinion/iowa-caucuses -democrats.html?action=click&module=RelatedLinks&pgtype=Article

[39] Kate Fazzini, "Iowa Caucus Debacle is One of the Most Stunning Tech Failures Ever," CNBC.com, 4 February 2020. https://www.cnbc .com/2020/02/04/iowa-caucus-app-debacle-is-one-of-the-most-stunning -it-failures-ever.html

[40] Associated Press, "Amid Irregularities, AP Unable to Declare a Win- ner," 6 February 2020. https://www.wtnh.com/newhampshireprimary /amid-irregularities-ap-unable-to-declare-winner-in-iowa/

41Reid J. Epstein, Sydney Ember, Trip Gabriel, and Mike Baker, "How the Iowa Caucuses Became an Epic Fiasco for Democrats," *The New York Times,* 9 February 2020. https://www.nytimes.com/2020/02/09 /us/politics/iowa-democratic-caucuses.html?nl=todaysheadlines& emc=edit_th_200210&campaign_id=2&instance_id=15850&segment _id=21129&user_id=b43261659350c77456b4aa21a6122ac7&regi _id=413701190210

42Jack Gillum and Jessica Huseman, "The Iowa Caucuses App Had Another Problem: It Could Have Been Hacked," ProPublica.org, 5 February 2020. https://www.propublica.org/article/the-iowa-caucuses -app-had-another-problem-it-could-have-been-hacked

Chapter Four: Techlash

1Margaret Talev, "Axios-Ipsos Coronavirus Index Week 9: Americans Hate Contact Tracing," Axios.com, 12 May 2020. https://www .axios.com/axios-ipsos-coronavirus-week-9-contact-tracing-bd747eaa -8fa1-4822-89bc-4e214c44a44d.html

2Tony Romm, Elizabeth Dwoskin, and Craig Timberg, "U.S. Government, Tech Industry Discussing ways to Use Smartphone Location Data to Combat Coronavirus," *The Washington Post,* 17 March 2020. https://www.washingtonpost.com/technology/2020/03/17 /white-house-location-data-coronavirus/

3Geoffrey A. Fowler, "Smartphone Data Reveal Which Americans are Social Distancing (And Not)," *The Washington Post,* 24 March 2020. https://www.washingtonpost.com/technology/2020/03/24/social -distancing-maps-cellphone-location/

4CES: https://www.ces.tech/About-CES.aspx

5"The Best Products of CES 2020," CNET.com, 9 January 2020. https://www.cnet.com/pictures/cnets-20-favorite-products-of -ces-2020/

6Brooke Auxier, Lee Rainie, Monica Anderson, Andrew Perrin, Madhu Kumar, and Erica Turner, Pew Research Center, "Americans and Privacy: Concerned, Confused and Feeling Lack of Control

Over Their Personal Information," 15 November 2019. https://www
.pewresearch.org/internet/2019/11/15/americans-and-privacy-concerned
-confused-and-feeling-lack-of-control-over-their-personal-information/

[7]Colin Lecher and Russell Brandon, "Is Huawei a Security Threat?
Seven Experts Weigh In," *The Verge,* 17 March 2019. https://www
.theverge.com/2019/3/17/18264283/huawei-security-threat-experts
-china-spying-5g

[8]Nancy Scola and Cristiano Lima, "Tech's Newest Leaders Shrug
Off D.C.," *Politico,* 10 January 2020. https://www.politico.com
/news/2020/01/10/ces-tech-policy-097403

[9]Ibid.

[10]Stephen Manes and Paul Andrews, "Gates," Simon & Schuster,
1994. Page 132.

[11]Kim Murphy, "The Decline and Fall of Seattle," *Los Angeles Times,*
4 August 2002. https://www.latimes.com/archives/la-xpm-2002-aug
-04-tm-seattle31-story.html

[12]SentinelOne, "The History of Cyber Security - Everything You
Ever Wanted to Know," SentinelOne.com, 10 February 2019. https://
www.sentinelone.com/blog/history-of-cyber-security/

[13]Tessa Lyons, Facebook project manager, "Hard Questions:
How Is Facebook's Fact-Checking Program Working?" Facebook,
14 June 2018. https://about.fb.com/news/2018/06/hard-questions-fact
-checking/

[14]Roger McNamee, *Zucked: Waking Up to the Facebook Catastrophe,*
Penguin Press, 2019. Pg.5.

[15]Ross Lajeunesse, "I Was Google's Head of International Relations.
Here's Why I Left," *Medium,* 2 January 2020. https://medium.com
/@rossformaine/i-was-googles-head-of-international-relations-here-s
-why-i-left-49313d23065

[16]Kate Conger, "Google Removes 'Don't Be Evil" Clause From Its
Code of Conduct," Gizmodo, 18 May 2018. https://gizmodo.com
/google-removes-nearly-all-mentions-of-dont-be-evil-from-1826153393

[17]Brad Smith, *Tools and Weapons: The Peril and Promise of the Digital
Age.* Penguin Press, 2019.

[18]Politics & Prose website. https://www.politics-prose.com /book/9781984877710

[19]Peggy Noonan, "Overthrow the Prince of Facebook," *The Wall Street Journal,* 6 June 2019.

[20]Carroll Doherty and Jocelyn Kiley, "Americans have become much less positive about tech companies' impact on the U.S.," Pew Research Center, 29 July 2019. https://www.pewresearch.org/fact -tank/2019/07/29/americans-have-become-much-less-positive-about -tech-companies-impact-on-the-u-s/

[21]Thomas Friedman, "Trump, Zuckerman & Pals are Breaking America," *The New York Times,* 29 October 2019. https://www .nytimes.com/2019/10/29/opinion/trump-zuckerberg.html

[22]Ibid.

[23]Charles Sykes, "Zuckerberg Won't Save Us," *The Bulwark,* October 25, 2019. https://thebulwark.com/mark-zuckerberg-wont -save-us/

[24]Matt Steib, "Alexandria Ocasio-Cortez Has Some Good Questions for Mark Zuckerberg, *New York* Intelligencer, 23 October 2019. http:// nymag.com/intelligencer/2019/10/aoc-has-some-great-questions-for -mark-zuckerberg.html

[25]Gallup Party Affiliation tracking poll, 2004-2019. https://news .gallup.com/poll/15370/party-affiliation.aspx

[26]Brian Feldman, "The Real Reason Facebook Won't Ban Political Ads," New York, 28 October 2019. http://nymag.com/intelligencer /2019/10/the-consequences-of-facebook-banning-political-ads.html

[27]Jessica Corbett, "Hundreds of Facebook Employees to CEO Zuckerberg: 'Free Speech and Paid Speech Are Not the Same Thing'," Common Dreams, 28 October 2019. https://www.commondreams. org/news/2019/10/28/hundreds-facebook-employees-ceo-zuckerberg -free-speech-and-paid-speech-are-not-same

[28]Monika Bickert, Vice President, Global Policy Management, Facebook: "Enforcing Against Manipulated Media," Facebook online newsroom, 6 January 2020. https://about.fb.com/news/2020/01 /enforcing-against-manipulated-media/

[29]Tony Romm, Drew Harwell, and Issac Stanley-Becker, "Facebook Bans Deepfakes, Sources Say, but New Policy may not Cover Controversial Pelosi Video," *The Washington Post,* 6 January 2020. https://www.washingtonpost.com/technology/2020/01/06/facebook -ban-deepfakes-sources-say-new-policy-may-not-cover-controversial -pelosi-video/

[30]Carlie Porterfield, "Twitter Suspends Account Copying Trump's Tweets For 'Glorifying Violence'," Forbes.com, 3 June 2020. https:// www.forbes.com/sites/carlieporterfield/2020/06/03/twitter-suspends -account-copying-trumps-tweets-for-glorifying-violence/#5dacd- d387e20

[31]Kate Conger and Mike Isaac, "Defying Trump, Twitter Doubles Down on Labeling Tweets," *The New York Times,* 28 May 2020. https://www.nytimes.com/2020/05/28/technology/trump-twitter-fact -check.html

[32]Twitter, Jack Dorsey account, 30 October 2019. https://twitter .com/jack/status/1189634360472829952

[33]Twitter, Brad Parscale account, 30 October 2019. https://twitter .com/parscale/status/1189656652250845184

[34]Email from Microsoft.com, "Welcome to MyAnalytics," 7 January 2020.

[35]Geoffrey A. Fowler, "What Does Your Car Know About You? We Hacked a Chevy to Find Out," *The Washington Post,* 17 December 2019. https://www.washingtonpost.com/technology/2019/12/17/what -does-your-car-know-about-you-we-hacked-chevy-find-out/

[36]Nila Bala, "Why Are You Publicly Sharing Your Child's DNA Information?" *The New York Times*, 2 January 2020. https://www. nytimes.com/2020/01/02/opinion/dna-test-privacy-children.html? searchResultPosition=1

[37]The Market Segmentation Study Guide. https://www.segmentation studyguide.com/

[38]Mark Penn, *Microtrends: The Small Forces Behind Tomorrow's Big Changes.* Twelve division of Grand Centrtal Publishing, 2007. Pgs. Xiv, xvii.

[39]Kara Swisher, "Facebook Loves to Pass the Buck," *The New York Times,* 13 January 2020. https://www.nytimes.com/2020/01/13/opinion/facebook-political-ads-lies.html?nl=todaysheadlines&emc=edit_th_200114?campaign_id=2&instance_id=15084&segment_id=20311&user_id=b43261659350c77456b4aa21a6122ac7&regi_id=413701190114

[40]Kashmir Hill, "The Secretive Company That Might End Privacy as We Know It," *The New York Times,* 18 January 2020. https://www.nytimes.com/2020/01/18/technology/clearview-privacy-facial-recognition.html?searchResultPosition=1

[41]Audra D. S. Burch, "How 17 Outsize Portraits Rattled as Small Southern Town," *The New York Times,* 19 January 2020. https://www.nytimes.com/2020/01/19/us/newnan-art-georgia-race.html?action=click&module=Top%20Stories&pgtype=Homepage

[42]Ibid.

[43]Jonathan Haidt and Tobias Rose-Stockwell, "The Dark Psychology of Social Networks," *The Atlantic*, December 2019. https://www.theatlantic.com/magazine/archive/2019/12/social-media-democracy/600763/

[44]Mark Scott, "In 2020, Global 'Techlash' Will Move from Words to Action," Politico, 31 December 2019. https://www.politico.eu/article/tech-policy-competition-privacy-facebook-europe-techlash/

[45]Ibid.

[46]Emma Goldberg, "'Techlash' Hits College Campuses," *The New York Times,* 11 January 2020. https://www.nytimes.com/2020/01/11/style/college-tech-recruiting.html?smid=nytcore-ios-share&fbclid=IwAR2a69sx6ZcPvrNYN3rLdFTzi9ns1reUUBjt1MIF0c8lcI5pTP20b7FhQng

[47]Jonathan L Fisher and Aaron Mak, "The Evil List," *Slate,* 15 January 2020. https://slate.com/technology/2020/01/evil-list-tech-companies-dangerous-amazon-facebook-google-palantir.html

Chapter Five: Unreliable Narrators

[1]Liz Crokin, "Coronavirus a Cover for Mass Arrests?" YouTube, 12 March 2020. https://www.youtube.com/watch?v=XVcD5VAxmao

[2]Kyle Mantyla, "Liz Crokin Claims Celebrities are Getting Coronavirus from Tainted Adrenochrome Supply," Right Wing Watch, 18 March 2020. https://www.rightwingwatch.org/post/liz-crokin-claims-celebrities-are-getting-coronavirus-from-tainted-adrenochrome-supply/

[3]Kyle Mantyla, "Liz Crokin Predicts that Tom Hanks Will Soon be Arrested for His Supposed Involvement in Satanic Pedophilia," Right Wing Watch, 2 January 2020. https://t.co/n20eejUiHg

[4]Ryan Smith, "Former Chicago Gossip Columnist Liz Crokin is Now a Star Among Far-Right Conspiracy Theorists," ChicagoReader.com, 6 April 2018. https://www.chicagoreader.com/Bleader/archives/2018/04/06/former-chicago-gossip-columnist-liz-crokin-is-now-a-star-among-far-right-conspiracy-theorists

[5]Jackie Mansky, "The Age-Old Problem of Fake News," *Smithsonian,* 7 May 2018. https://www.smithsonianmag.com/history/age-old-problem-fake-news-180968945/

[6]Ibid.

[7]Kevin Fallon, "Fooled by 'The Onion': 9 Most Embarrassing Fails," *The Daily Beast,* 14 July 2017.

[8]Cate Doty, "Tabloid Eaten by Aliens! Fake Columnist Loses His Job!", *The New York Times,* 30 July 2007. https://www.nytimes.com/2007/07/30/business/media/30weekly.html?_r=0

[9]Sasha Baron Cohen, "The 'Silicon Six' Spread Propaganda. It's Time to Regulate Social Media Sites," *The Washington Post,* 25 November 2019. https://www.washingtonpost.com/outlook/2019/11/25/silicon-six-spread-propaganda-its-time-regulate-social-media-sites/

[10]CJR Editors, "Poll: How Does the Public Think Journalism Happens?" *Columbia Journalism Review,* Winter 2019. https://www.cjr.org/special_report/how-does-journalism-happen-poll.php

[11]Joe Pompeo, "'The Times Has Become a Book-Deal Factory': With a Flood of Star Reporters Thinking of Book Leave, Management

Delivers a 'Wrist Slap'", Vanity Fair, 22 May 2019. https://www
.vanityfair.com/news/2019/05/the-new-york-times-book-deals

[12]Mark Penn, *Microtrends: The Small Forces Behind Tomorrow's Big
Changes.* Twelve division of Grand Centrtal Publishing, 2007. Pg. 134.

[13]Tony Maglio, "Sorry, President Trump—'Morning Joe' is Posting
Highest Ever Viewership This Quarter," TheWrap.com, 28 March
2019. https://www.thewrap.com/trump-wrong-morning-joe-ratings
-fact-check/

[14]David Jackson and Gary Marx, "Will the Chicago Tribune Be the
Next Newspaper Picked to the Bone?", *The New York Times,* 19 January
2020. https://www.nytimes.com/2020/01/19/opinion/chicago
-tribune-alden-capital.html

[15]Julie Bosman, "How the Collapse of Local News is Causing a
'National Crisis,'" *The New York Times,* 20 November 2019. https://
www.nytimes.com/2019/11/20/us/local-news-disappear-pen-america
.html

[16]PBS Ombudsman Michael Getler, "Lehrer's Rules," PBS.org,
11 December 2009. http://www.pbs.org/ombudsman/2009/12
/lehrers_rules.html

[17]BBC.co.uk, "Scandalous Scoop Breaks Online," 25 January
1998. http://news.bbc.co.uk/2/hi/special_report/1998/clinton
_scandal/50031.stm?utm_source=newsletter&utm_medium
=email&utm_campaign=&stream=top-stories#_ga=2.189471907.923
164010.1579883175-680065453.1568746218

[18]Liron Hakim Bobrov, "Market Intelligence Blog: US Media
Pujblications Ranking H1 2018," SimilarWeb.com, 11 July 2018. https://
www.similarweb.com/blog/us-media-publications-ranking-h1-2018

[19]Robert W. McChesney, Foreword, *The Stewart/Colbert Effect: Essays
on the Real Impact of Fake News,* edited by Amarnath Amarasingham.
McFarland & Company, 2011.

[20]Ibid.

[21]Patrice Tadonnio, "'A Serial Liar': how Sarah Palin Ushered in the
'Post-Truth' Political Era in Which Trump Has Thrived," *Frontline*,
pbs.org, 10 January 2020. https://www.pbs.org/wgbh/frontline

/article/a-serial-liar-how-sarah-palin-ushered-in-the-post-truth-political
-era-in-which-trump-has-thrived/?utm_source=email&utm_medium
=social&utm_campaign=share_button

[22]Callum Borchers, "'Fake News' Has Now Lost all Meaning," *The Washington Post*, 9 February 2017. https://www.washingtonpost.com/news/the-fix/wp/2017/02/09/fake-news-has-now-lost-all-meaning/

[23]Glenn Kessler, "Planned Parenthood's False Stat: 'Thousands' of Women Died Every Year Before Roe," *The Washington Post*, 29 May 2019. https://www.washingtonpost.com/politics/2019/05/29/planned-parenthoods-false-stat-thousands-women-died-every-year-before-roe/

[24]Ben LeFebvre, "Republicans Brewing Russian Scandal to Target the Greens," Politico.com, 23 July 2017. https://www.politico.com/story/2017/07/23/fracking-russia-republicans-240834

[25]Anna Merian, "Bleach Ingestion Advocates Are Thrilled by Trump's 'Disinfectant' Comments," Vox.com, 28 April 2020. https://www.vice.com/en_us/article/884wgv/bleach-ingestion-advocates-are-thrilled-by-trumps-disinfectant-comments?utm_source=reddit.com

[26]Harriet Sherwood, "Half of Americans Don't Know 6m Jews Were Killed in Holocaust, Survey Says," UK *Guardian*, 22 January 2020. https://www.theguardian.com/world/2020/jan/22/holocaust-survey-americans-pew-research-center

[27]Tom Jensen, "Trump Leads Rubio Even Heads to Head in Florida," *Public Policy Polling*, 25 February 2016. https://www.publicpolicypolling.com/polls/trump-leads-rubio-even-head-to-head-in-florida/

[28]Scott Bixby, "Far-Left Internet Thinks Mayor Pete is a Secret Agent," *Daily Beast*, 8 January 2020. https://www.thedailybeast.com/far-left-internet-thinks-mayor-pete-buttigieg-is-a-secret-agent

[29]Brandy Zadrozny, "On Facebook, Fears of Parasites Push People to Post Pictures of Feces and Pursue Dangerous Remedies," NBCNews.com, 13 November 2019. https://www.nbcnews.com/tech/tech-news/facebook-fears-parasites-push-people-post-pictures-feces-pursue-dangerous-n1081286

[30]Katy Waldman, "How the Internet is Changing Our Reading Habits," *Financial Review*, 4 January 2015. https://www.afr.com/life

-and-luxury/arts-and-culture/how-the-internet-is-changing-our-reading-habits-20150102-12gpv0

[31]Stephen Ansolabehere, Harvard University; Cooperative Congressional Election Study, 2016-18. https://cces.gov.harvard.edu/

[32]James D. Walsh, "The Force of Trump's Lying Has Ruptured the Space-Time Continuum: Steve Schmidt on Impeachment," *New York,* October 26, 2019. http://nymag.com/intelligencer/2019/10/steve-schmidt-on-trump-impeachment-2020-and-howard-schultz.html

[33]WebArchive.org. https://web.archive.org/web/20200102150518/https://ajuanews.com/ocasio-cortez-and-omar-vow-to-remove-seniors-entitlements-social-security-medicare/?fbclid=IwAR09tss-b2CSllOywO79-eT2T4brFMSghSF5puh4PT1BcmzjodbY699N2BGg

[34]Daily World Update, January 2020. https://dailyworldupdate.us/

[35]*Real Time with Bill Maher: Overtime.* HBO, 24 January 2020.

[36]Elie Mystal, "The Republicans Have Revealed Their Impeachment Strategy—Lying," TheNation.com, 22 January 2020. https://www.thenation.com/article/cipollone-impeachment-lies/

[37]Joe Hoft, "Democrats Have 'Adopted the Nazi Version of—the "BIG LIE" As a Way to Impeach the President!'"—Former US Attorney Joe diGenova," TheGatewayPundit.com, 22 January 2020. https://www.thegatewaypundit.com/2020/01/democrats-have-adopted-the-nazi-version-of-the-big-lie-as-a-way-to-impeach-the-president-former-us-attorney-joe-digenova/

[38]Lawrence O'Donnell Twitter account, 24 January 2020. https://twitter.com/Lawrence/status/1220895706522771456

[39]Laura Ingraham Twitter account, 24 January 2020. https://twitter.com/IngrahamAngle/status/1220675232916295681

[40]David Sirota, "BERN NOTICE: What We Cannot Discuss," Sanders campaign digital newsletter, 15 August 2019. https://bernie.substack.com/p/bern-notice-what-we-cannot-discuss

[41]Alex Raskin, "Stephen Curry's Agent Issues Denial After 'ABSOLUTELY' Fake Nude Pics of the Warriors Star Emerge, Sending Twitter Users into Total Meltdown," Daily Mail, 20 December 2019.

https://www.dailymail.co.uk/news/article-7814743/Stephen-Currys
-agent-issues-denial-ABSOLUTELY-fake-nude-pics-Warriors-star
-emerge.html

[42]Christopher Hooton, "Rogue One: Peter Cushing Resurrected as Grand Moff Tarkin via CGI was Impressive, But Was it Ethical?" *Independent* (UK), 19 December 2016. https://www.independent.co.uk /arts-entertainment/films/news/rogue-one-cgi-grand-moff-tarkin-actor -peter-cushing-princess-leia-carrie-fisher-animated-a7483991.html

[43]Maggie Miller, "Senators Urge Social Media Companies to Take Action Against 'Deepfake' Videos," *The Hill*, 2 October 2019. https:// thehill.com/policy/cybersecurity/464043-senators-urge-social-media -companies-to-take-action-against-deepfake

[44]Mark Binelli, "Old Musicians Never Die. They Just Become Holograms," *The New York Times*, 7 January 2020. https://www .nytimes.com/2020/01/07/magazine/hologram-musicians.html? te=1&nl=the-new%20york%20times%20magazine&emc=edit _ma_20200110?campaign_id=52&instance_id=15079&segment _id=20210&user_id=b43261659350c77456b4aa21a6122ac7&regi _id=4137011920200110

[45]Alex Ritman, "James Dean Reborn in CGI for Vietnam War Action-Drama," *Hollywood Reporter*, 6 November 2019. https://www .hollywoodreporter.com/news/afm-james-dean-reborn-cgi-vietnam -war-action-drama-1252703

[46]David Ingram and Jacob Ward, "How Do You Spot a Deepfake? A Clue Hides Within Our Voices, Researchers Say." NBCNews .com, 16 December 2019. https://www.nbcnews.com/tech/tech-news /little-tells-why-battle-against-deepfakes-2020-may-rely-verbal -n1102881?cid=eml_nbn_20191216

[47]Matthew Rosenberg, Nicole Perlroth, and David E. Sanger, "Chaos is the Point: Russian Hackers and Trolls Grow Stealthier in 2020," *The New York Times*, 10 January 2020. https://www.nytimes .com/2020/01/10/us/politics/russia-hacking-disinformation-election .html?fbclid=IwAR08NUKK7jJ1kgTCaPcyhBZHFZIVahzEHjj3kpix kANScxiDYsZJwxDeexw

[48]Farhad Manjoo, "Only You Can Prevent Dystopia," *The New York Times,* 1 January 2020. https://www.nytimes.com/2020/01/01/opinion /social-media-2020.html?nl=todaysheadlines&emc=edit_th_200102? campaign_id=2&instance_id=14867&segment_id=19983&user_id =b43261659350c77456b4aa21a6122ac7&regi_id=413701190102

Chapter Six: Are You Being Served?

[1]Kaiser Health News (KHN), "Over 2,000 Ventilators in National Stockpile Are Unusable Because of Months-Long Contract Lapse," *KHN Morning Briefing,* 2 April 2020. https://khn.org/morning -breakout/over-2000-ventilators-in-national-stockpile-are-unusable -because-of-months-long-contract-lapse/

[2]Adam Clark Estes, "America's Emergency Medical Stockpile is Almost Empty. Nobody Knows What Happens Next," *Recode* via Vox .com, 7 April 2000. https://www.vox.com/recode/2020/4/3/21206170 /us-emergency-stockpile-jared-kushner-almost-empty-coronavirus -medical-supplies-ventilators

[3]Kevin Liptak, "Trump Shrugs Off Responsibility for Any Hospital Equipment Shortages By Saying it's Up To States," CNN.com, 19 March 2020. https://www.cnn.com/2020/03/19/politics/trump-masks -ventilators/index.html

[4]Matthew Karnitschnig, "The Incompetence Pandemic," *Politico,* 16 March 2020. https://www.politico.com/news/2020/03/16 /coronavirus-pandemic-leadership-131540

[5]Neal E. Boudette and Andrew Jacobs, "Inside G.M.'s Race to Build Ventilators, Before Trump's Attack," *The New York Times,* 30 March 2020. https://www.nytimes.com/2020/03/30/business/gm -ventilators-coronavirus-trump.html

[6]Brian Cooley, "How the Seats In an F-150 Helped Ford Make Ventilators and Respirators," CNET.com, 7 April 2020. https://www .cnet.com/news/how-the-seats-in-an-f-150-helped-ford-make-ventilators -and-respirators/

[7] @realDonaldTrump; Donald Trump Twitter account, 27 March 2020. https://twitter.com/realDonaldTrump/status/1243557418556162050

[8] Kenneth I. Chenault and Rachel Romer Carlson, "It's Time for the Business Community to Step Up," *The New York Times,* 18 March 2020. https://www.nytimes.com/2020/03/18/opinion/business-coronavirus.html

[9] Thomas Buckley, "Distilleries and Breweries Pivot to Producing Hand Sanitizer," *Bloomberg BusinessWeek*, 23 March 2020. https://www.bloomberg.com/news/articles/2020-03-24/companies-revamp-to-make-hand-sanitizer-and-coronavirus-products

[10] Maren Larsen and Maura Fox, "How Outdoor Brands Are Pitching in to Stop COVID-19," *Outside*, 8 April 2020. https://www.outsideonline.com/2411472/outdoor-brands-fighting-coronavirus

[11] Nicolette Accardi, "Harbor Freight Stores Donating All Masks and Gloves to Help Fight Coronavirus," NJ.com, 23 March 2020. https://www.nj.com/business/2020/03/harbor-freight-stores-donating-all-masks-and-gloves-to-help-fight-coronavirus.html

[12] Jessica Lee, "Is Trump Admin Seizing COVID-19 Protective Equipment from States?" Snopes.com, 24 April 2020. https://www.snopes.com/fact-check/trump-admin-seizing-ppe/

[13] Peter Wade, "Congressional Witness: 'I'm a Republican. I Voted for President Trump . . . I Am Embarrassed'," Rolling Stone, 15 May 2020. https://www.rollingstone.com/politics/politics-news/congressional-witness-i-voted-for-president-trump-i-am-embarrassed-1000629/

[14] Christopher Weaver, Betsy McKay, and Brianna Abbott, "America Needed Coronavirus Tests. The Government Failed," *The Wall Street Journal*, 19 March 2020. https://www.wsj.com/articles/how-washington-failed-to-build-a-robust-coronavirus-testing-system-11584552147

[15] Jim VandeHei, "CEOs are America's New Politicians," Axios.com, 19 August 2019. https://www.axios.com/ceos-business-roundtable-social-issues-corporate-purpose-7d6c1f35-5d07-4b35-981d-4f9c009bcef4.html

[16]Aaron K. Chatterji and Michael Toffel, "The New CEO Activists," *Harvard Business Review,* January-February 2018. https://hbr.org /2018/01/the-new-ceo-activists

[17]Garrett Graff, *The First Campaign: Globalization, the Web, and the Race for the White House,* Farrer Strauss and Giroux, 2007. Pg. 12.

[18]Weber Shandwick and KRC Research, "CEO Activism in 2017: High Noon in the C-Suite," Research report issued 2017. https://www .webershandwick.com/wp-content/uploads/2018/04/ceo-activism-in -2017-high-noon-in-the-c-suite-1.pdf

[19]Blickwink, "10 Most Controversial United Colors of Benetton Ads," Alistgator.com, 22 March 2012. http://www.alistgator.com /top-ten-controversial-united-colors-of-benetton-ads/

[20]Alexi C. Cardona, "Leaked Emails: Norwegian Pressures Sales Team to Mislead Potential Customers About Coronavirus," *Miami New Times,* 11 March 2020. https://www.miaminewtimes.com/news /coronavirus-norwegian-cruise-line-leaked-emails-show-booking-strategy -11590056

[21]Joe Maniscalco, "'Essential' Frontline Workers In Open Revolt Over Unsafe Conditions," DCReport.org, 27 March 2020. https:// www.dcreport.org/2020/03/27/essential-frontline-workers-in-open -revolt-over-unsafe-conditions/

[22]Jasmine Garsd, "'Delete the Delivery Apps, Say Restaurants Hard Hit by COVID-19," *Marketplace,* 16 April 2020. https://www .marketplace.org/2020/04/16/restaurants-hit-covid19-say-delete -delivery-apps/

[23]Lucy Handley, "Trust in Governments Surges During Pandemic but People are Disappointed with CEO Performance," CNBC.com, 5 May 2020. https://www.cnbc.com/2020/05/05/trust-in-governments -increases-during-pandemic-but-ceos-disappoint.html

[24]Andrew Reid, "Best Practices for Marketing During and After COVID-19," *Entrepreneur,* 10 May 2020. https://www.entrepreneur .com/article/349535

²⁵Aaron K. Chatterji and Michael Toffel, "The New CEO Activists," *Harvard Business Review,* January-February 2018. https://hbr.org/2018/01/the-new-ceo-activists

²⁶Benjamin Butterworth, "What does 'Woke' Mean? The Origins of the Term, and How its Meaning has Changed," iNews.co.uk, 22 January 2020. https://inews.co.uk/news/uk/woke-what-mean-meaning-origins-term-definition-culture-1370797

²⁷Gallup, "Confidence in Institutions Survey," Gallup Organization, 1973-2019. https://news.gallup.com/poll/1597/confidence-institutions.aspx

²⁸"The World's Most Reputable Companies 2019," Forbes.com. https://www.forbes.com/pictures/5c76e402a7ea43100043d1fb/the-worlds-most-reputable/#2d4c0fde7a6b

²⁹"Reelection Rates Over the Years," OpenSecrets.org. https://www.opensecrets.org/overview/reelect.php

³⁰Daniel Bennett, "The End of the Campaign and the Beginning of Elected Office: Correspondence Management and CRM," *Constituent Relationship Management: The New Little Black Book of Politics.* Institute for Politics, Democracy & the Internet, The George Washington University Graduate School of Political Management, March 2007. Pg. 53-54.

³¹Travis Bullard, Senior Director, APCO Worldwide and APCO corporate communications and brand practice leader, message to clients, December 2019.

³²Tara Jones, "How 5 Companies Used Kaizen Effectively," Effex Management Solutions blog, 30 June 2017. http://blog.effexms.com/how-5-companies-used-kaizen-effectively

³³"Intel: The Incredible Profit Machine," University of Washington. http://coin.wne.uw.edu.pl/jhagemejer/io/io_wyklad3.pdf

³⁴Dan Solomon and Paula Forbes, "Inside the Story of How H-E-B Planned for the Pandemic," *Texas Monthly,* 26 March 2020. https://www.texasmonthly.com/food/heb-prepared-coronavirus-pandemic/

³⁵"Anheuser-Busch Sending 150,000 Cans of Emergency Drinking Water to Missouri and Oklahoma to Aid Flood Relief Efforts," press

release, Anheuser-Busch.com, 27 May 2019. https://www.anheuser
-busch.com/newsroom/2019/05/anheuser-busch-sending-150-000
-cans-of-emergency-drinking-water-.html

[36]@steak_umm, Steak-umm Twitter account, 6 April 2020. https://
twitter.com/steak_umm/status/1247343900475490304

[37]LMA, "Most Hated Railway Puts 15-Year-Old In Charge Of Their
Twitter Account, And Things Escalate Quickly," BoredPanda.com,
July 2017. https://www.boredpanda.com/15-year-old-railways-twitter
-spokesman-southernrail-eddie/?utm_source=google&utm_medium
=organic&utm_campaign=organic

[38]Radhika Saghani, "#askeddie: Meet the Work Experience Boy Who
Saved Southern Rail," The Telegraph (UK), 15 July 2017. https://www
.telegraph.co.uk/men/thinking-man/meet-eddie-smith-work-experience
-boy-saved-southern-rail/

[39]Molly Roberts, "Mr. Peanut Had to Die," *The Washington
Post*, 23 January 2020. https://www.washingtonpost.com/opinions
/2020/01/23/mr-peanut-had-die-if-only-be-born-again/?utm_campaign
=wp_week_in_ideas&utm_medium=email&utm_source=newsletter
&wpisrc=nl_ideas

[40]Milton Friedman, "The Social Responsibility of Business is to
Increase its Profits," *The New York Times Magazine*, 13 September
1970. http://umich.edu/~thecore/doc/Friedman.pdf

[41]Business Roundtable, "Business Roundtable Redefines the Purpose
of a Corporation to Promote 'An Economy That Serves All Americans,'"
Businessroundtable.org, 19 August 2019. https://www.business
roundtable.org/business-roundtable-redefines-the-purpose-of-a-corporation
-to-promote-an-economy-that-serves-all-americans

[42]Hrishikesh Athalye, "How Woke Capitalism is Cashing in on
Social Movements," YouthKiAwaaz.com, 7 February 2019. https://
www.youthkiawaaz.com/2019/02/what-is-woke-capitalism/

[43]Tovia Smith, "Backlash Erupts After Gillette Launches A New
#MeToo-Inspired Ad Campaign," NPR.org, 17 January 2019. https://
www.npr.org/2019/01/17/685976624/backlash-erupts-after-gillette
-launches-a-new-metoo-inspired-ad-campaign

[44]Amazon Employees for Climate Justice, "Amazon Employees Share Our Views on Company Business," Medium.com, 26 January 2020. https://medium.com/@amazonemployeesclimatejustice/amazon -employees-share-our-views-on-company-business-f5abcdea849

[45]Theodore Schleifer, "Some Oracle Employees Plan to Walk Off the Job to Protest Larry Ellison's Trump fundraiser," Recode.com, 19 February 2020. https://www.vox.com/recode/2020/2/13/21136577 /larry-ellison-fundraiser-donald-trump-oracle-employees

[46]Matthew Yglesias, "The Raging Controversy Over the NBA, China, and the Hong Kong Protests, Explained," Vox.com, 7 October 2019. https://www.vox.com/2019/10/7/20902700/daryl-morey-tweet-china -nba-hong-kong

[47]Neville Isdell, unpublished op-ed, December 2019.

[48]Dion Rabouin and Amy Harder, "Climate Change Becomes a Top Business Threat," Axios.com, 24 January 2020. https://www .axios.com/climate-change-business-threat-467376e9-99a6-47e8-bffa -954c4a72c098.html

[49]Umair Irfan, "Trump's Fight with California Over Vehicle Emissions Rules has Divided Automakers," Vox.com, 5 November 2019. https://www.vox.com/policy-and-politics/2019/11/5/20942457 /california-trump-fuel-economy-auto-industry

[50]Aaron K. Chatterji and Michael W. Toffel, "The New CEO Activist," *Harvard Business Review,* January-February 2018. https:// hbr.org/2018/01/the-new-ceo-activists

[51]Margaret Talev, "Inside the Effort to Get U.S. Companies to Popularize Early Voting," Axios.com, 11 May 2020. https://www .axios.com/exclusive-business-coronavirus-early-voting-absentee -217f9429-2af8-4f7b-87d9-2e9c1d8f9b3f.html

[52]Umair Haque, *The New Capitalist Manifesto: Building a Disruptively Better Business.* 2011, Harvard Business School Press.

[53]Gene Johnson, "Greyhound to Stop Allowing Immigration Checks on Buses," Associated Press, 21 February 2020. https://apnews.com /dc560c3581783c746aee1544c8ad1c85

[54]Miriam Jordan, "A Migrant Family Takes a Greyhound Across America," *The New York Times*, 26 May 2019. https://www.nytimes.com/interactive/2019/05/26/us/greyhound-immigration.html

[55]American Civil Liberties Union, "The Constitution in the 100-Mile Border Zone," https://www.aclu.org/other/constitution-100-mile-border-zone

[56]Gregg, *Valley News*, 3 August 2017.

[57]Weber Shandwick and KRC Research, "CEO Activism in 2017: High Noon in the C-Suite," Research report issued 2017. https://www.webershandwick.com/wp-content/uploads/2018/04/ceo-activism-in-2017-high-noon-in-the-c-suite-1.pdf

[58]Yael Halon, "Brandon Judd Rips New Greyhound 'Sanctuary Buses' Policy: 'They're Putting Profit Above the Safety of the American People'," FoxNews.com, 23 February 2020. https://www.foxnews.com/media/brandon-judd-greyhound-sanctuary-buses-policy

Chapter Seven: I Can See Chaos from My House

[1]Nadja Sayej, "Aidy Bryant Wants to Change the Way We Talk About Other People's Bodies," Shondaland.com, 22 January 2020. https://www.shondaland.com/inspire/a30609224/aidy-bryant-shrill-interview/

[2]Leia Idliby, "Army Sergeant Getting Death Threats After Conspiracy Theorists Falsely Label Her Coronavirus 'Patient Zero'," Mediaite.com, 27 April 2020. https://www.mediaite.com/news/army-sergeant-getting-death-threats-after-conspiracy-theorists-falsely-label-her-coronavirus-patient-zero/

[3]Therin Alrik, "Why I Stopped Arguing Politics on Social Media," *Gen*, Medium.com, 27 February 2019. https://gen.medium.com/why-i-stopped-arguing-politics-on-social-media-f695344d3e3

[4]Monica Anderson and Dennis Quinn, "46% of Social Media Users Say They Are 'Worn Out' by Political Posts and Discussions," Pew Research Center Factank, 8 August 2019. https://www.pewresearch

.org/fact-tank/2019/08/08/46-of-u-s-social-media-users-say-they-are -worn-out-by-political-posts-and-discussions/

[5]Steven D. Stark, *Glued to the Set: The 60 Television Shows and Events That Made Us Who We Are Today.* 1997, The Free Press, division of Simon & Schuster. Pg. 202.

[6]Jon Katz, "Birth of a Digital Nation," *Wired*, 1 April 1997. https:// www.wired.com/1997/04/netizen-3/

[7]Joseph Bernstein, "Alienated, Alone, and Angry: What the Digital Revolution Really Did to Us," Buzzfeed.com, 17 December 2019. https://www.buzzfeednews.com/article/josephbernstein/in-the-2010s -decade-we-became-alienated-by-technology

[8]German Lopez, "Trump's White House Banner Claims 'America Leads the World in Testing.' That's Wrong," Vox.com, 11 May 2020. https://www.vox.com/2020/5/11/21255128/coronavirus -testing-trump-white-house-briefing

[9]Russell Berman, "When Nancy Pelosi Confronted Donald Trump," *The Atlantic,* 28 September 2017. https://www.theatlantic. com/politics/archive/2017/09/when-nancy-pelosi-confronted-donald -trump/541488/

[10]Carter Sherman and David Uberti, "Google Maps Is Still Directing Women Seeking Abortions to Pro-Life Clinics—and a Memorial for the 'Unborn'," *Vice News*, 6 September 2019. https://www.vice.com /en_us/article/ywap9b/google-maps-is-still-directing-women-seeking -abortions-to-pro-life-clinics-and-a-memorial-for-the-unborn

[11]Adam Gabbatt, "How Local 'Fake News' Websites Spread 'Conservative Propaganda' in the US," *The Guardian*, 19 November 2019. https://www.theguardian.com/us-news/2019/nov/19/locality -labs-fake-news-local-sites-newspapers

[12]L. Gordon Crovitz, "How Amazon, Geico, and Walmart Fund Propaganda," *The New York Times*, 21January 2020. https://www .nytimes.com/2020/01/21/opinion/fake-news-russia-ads.html

[13]YouTube. https://www.youtube.com/watch?v=GD5qDnk2wVw

[14]Chris Dwyer, "Trump Shares 'Deep Fake' GIF of Joe Biden Sticking His Tongue Out in Series of Late-Night Twitter Posts After

his Briefing Was Cut Short - Even Retweeting HIMSELF Three Times," *Daily Mail,* 27 April 2020. https://www.dailymail.co.uk/news /article-8260455/Trump-shares-deep-fake-GIF-Joe-Biden-sticking -tongue-series-late-night-posts.html

[15]YouTube. https://www.youtube.com/watch?v=NkuaEXbrv1k

[16]"You Have No Privacy, Get Over It," Fox Business News column, 31 July 2013. https://www.foxbusiness.com/features/you-have-no -privacy-get-over-it

[17]Henry Mance, "Is Privacy Dead?" Financial Times, 18 July 2019. https://www.ft.com/content/c4288d72-a7d0-11e9-984c-fac8325aaa04

[18]Bill Budington, "Ring Doorbell App Packed with Third-Party Trackers," Electronic Frontier Foundation, 27 January 2020. https:// www.eff.org/deeplinks/2020/01/ring-doorbell-app-packed-third-party -trackers

[19]Michael Kan, "The Cost of Avast's Free Antivirus: Companies Can Spy on Your Clicks," PCMag.com, 27 January 2020.

[20]Joseph Cox, "Leaked Documents Expose the Lucrative Market for Your Web Browsing Data," Vice.com, 27 January 2020. https://www .vice.com/en_us/article/qjdkq7/avast-antivirus-sells-user-browsing -data-investigation

[21]Martin Pollard, "Even Mask-Wearers Can Be ID'd, China Facial Rcognition Firm Says," Reuters, 9 March 2020. https://www.reuters .com/article/us-health-coronavirus-facial-recognition/even-mask-wearers -can-be-idd-china-facial-recognition-firm-says-idUSKBN20W0WL

[22]Allison Duncan, "Mind-Reading Technology is Closer Than You Think," Fast Company, 15 August 2019. https://www.fastcompany .com/90388440/mind-reading-technology-is-closer-than-you-think

[23]Stephen Chen, "'Forget the Facebook Leak': China is Mining Data Directly from Workers' Brains on an Industrial Scale," *South China Morning Post,* 29 April 2018. https://www.scmp.com/news/china /society/article/2143899/forget-facebook-leak-china-mining-data -directly-workers-brains

[24]Nissan Future Technology Brief, Nissan-Global.com. https://www .nissan-global.com/EN/TECHNOLOGY/OVERVIEW/b2v.html

[25]Max Read, "Why We Should Ban Facial Recognition Technology," New York Intelligencer, 30 January 2020. http://nymag.com /intelligencer/2020/01/why-we-should-ban-facial-recognition-technology .html

[26]PRRI, "Fractured Nation: Widening Partisan Polarization and Key Issues in 2020 Presidential Elections," 20 October 2019. https:// www.prri.org/research/fractured-nation-widening-partisan-polarization -and-key-issues-in-2020-presidential-elections/

[27]Mark Murray, "NBC/WSJ Poll: Country Remains Divided Over Trump's Impeachment Trial," NBCNews.com, 2 February 2020. https:// www.nbcnews.com/politics/meet-the-press/nbc-wsj-poll-country -remains-divided-over-trump-s-impeachment-n1128326

[28]Jeffrey M. Jones and Lydia Saad, "U.S. Support for More Government Inches Up, But Not for Socialism," Gallup, 18 November 2019. https://news.gallup.com/poll/268295/support-government -inches-not-socialism.aspx

[29]Joshua Green, "Internal RNC Poll: Complacent Trump Voters May Cost RNC Control of Congress," *Bloomberg BusinessWeek,* 18 September 2018. https://www.bloomberg.com/news/articles /2018-09-18/internal-rnc-poll-complacent-trump-voters-may-cost-gop -control-of-congress

[30]Rebecca Traister, "The Immoderate Susan Collins," *New York,* 18 February 2020. https://nymag.com/article/2020/02/the-immoderate -susan-collins.html

[31]Eli Saslow, "'Nothing on This Page is Real': How Lies Become Truth in Online America," *The Washington Post,* 17 November 2018. https://www.washingtonpost.com/national/nothing-on-this-page-is -real-how-lies-become-truth-in-online-america/2018/11/17/edd44cc8 -e85a-11e8-bbdb-72fdbf9d4fed_story.html

[32]Gallup party affiliation survey, 2-15 January 2020. https://news .gallup.com/poll/15370/party-affiliation.aspx

[33]Molly Osberg, "I Will Personally Be Thrilled if Stephen Miller Dies of Covid-19," Jezebel.com, 8 May 2020. https://jezebel.com/i-will -personally-be-thrilled-if-stephen-miller-dies-of-1843348268

[34]@markknoller: Mark Knoller (CBS News) Twitter account, 28 January 2020.

[35]Robert Tracinski, "Did the New York Times Actually Endorse Amy Klobuchar for VP?", TheBulwark.com, 22 January 2020. https://thebulwark.com/did-the-new-york-times-actually-endorse-amy-klobuchar-for-vp/

[36]Rick Pearson, "Illinois Senate President John Cullerton talks about Blagojevich, bipartisanship and changes brought by social media as his time in Springfield comes to an end," Chicago Tribune, 6 January 2020. https://www.chicagotribune.com/politics/ct-illinois-senate-president-john-cullerton-20200103-27qggmvcb5cohcrlwksi3beczy-story.html

[37]Tim Alberta Twitter account, 30 January 2020. https://twitter.com/TimAlberta/status/1223086332987179009

[38]Dylan Byers Twitter account, 27 January 2020. https://twitter.com/DylanByers/status/1221947525277671426

[39]Gallup, "Confidence in Institutions," Surveys 1973-2019. Gallup.com. https://news.gallup.com/poll/1597/confidence-institutions.aspx

[40]Lee Rainie and Andrew Perrin, "Key Findings About Americans' Declining Trust in Government and Each Other," Pew Research Center, 22 July 2019. https://www.pewresearch.org/fact-tank/2019/07/22/key-findings-about-americans-declining-trust-in-government-and-each-other/

[41]John F. Harris, "He Is Our O.J.," Politico, 9 January 2020. https://www.politico.com/news/magazine/2020/01/09/trump-support-impeachment-096606

[42]Jelani Cobb, "Voter-Suppression Tactics in the Age of Trump," The New Yorker, 21 October 2018. https://www.newyorker.com/magazine/2018/10/29/voter-suppression-tactics-in-the-age-of-trump

[43]John Whitesides, "Polling Places Become Battleground in U.S. Voting Rights Fight," Reuters, 16 September 2018. https://www.reuters.com/article/us-usa-election-vote-precincts-insight/polling-places-become-battleground-in-u-s-voting-rights-fight-idUSKCN11M0WY

[44]John Fund, *Stealing Elections: How Voter Fraud Threatens Our Democracy.* 2008, Encounter Books. Pgs. 131-141.

[45]Cameron Joseph, "The Nightmare Scenario: Trump Loses in 2020 and Refuses to Concede," Vice.com, 16 November 2019. https://www .vice.com/en_us/article/59nv98/the-nightmare-scenario-trump-loses -in-2020-and-refuses-to-concede?utm_source=reddit.com

[46]Richard L. Hasen, "The 2020 Loser May Not Concede. Their Voters Won't, Either." *The Washington Post,* 24 January 2020. https:// www.washingtonpost.com/outlook/the-loser-of-novembers-election -may-not-concede-their-voters-wont-either/2020/01/23/4d81be8c -3d6c-11ea-baca-eb7ace0a3455_story.html

[47]Andy Kroll, "Hackers are Coming for the 2020 Election—And We're Not Ready," *Rolling Stone*, 17 January 2020. https://www .rollingstone.com/politics/politics-features/trump-election-hacking -russia-iran-ransomware-interference-938109/

[48]Umair Haque, "This is How a Society Dies," Eudaimonia, Medium.com, 9 December 2019. https://eand.co/this-is-how-a -society-dies-35bdc3c0b854

[49]Ibid.

[50]Mike Godwin, Electronic Frontier Foundation, 12 January 1005. https://web.archive.org/web/20120829094739/http://w2.eff.org/Net _culture/Folklore/Humor/godwins.law

[51]Josh Jones, "Hannah Arendt Explains How Propaganda Uses Lies to Erode All Truth and Morality: Insights from The Origins of Totalitarianism," OpenCulture.com, 24 January 2017. http://www .openculture.com/2017/01/hannah-arendt-explains-how-propaganda -uses-lies-to-erode-all-truth-morality.html

[52]Kevin Roose, "Online Cesspool Got You Down? You Can Clean It Up, for a Price." *The New York Times Magazine,* 13 November 2019. https://www.nytimes.com/interactive/2019/11/13/magazine /internet-premium.html

[53]Lauren Feiner, "Google CEO Takes a Jab at Apple's Security Pitch: 'Privacy Cannot be a Luxury Good," CNBC.com, 8 May 2019. https://www

.cnbc.com/2019/05/08/google-ceo-says-privacy-cannot-be-a-luxury
-good.html

[54]U.S. Census Bureau via Brookings Institution, "2018 Voter Turnout
Rose Dramatically for Groups Favoring Democrats, Census Confirms,"
2 May 2019. https://www.brookings.edu/research/2018-voter
-turnout-rose-dramatically-for-groups-favoring-democrats-census
-confirms/

[55]*The Economist*/YouGov poll of 1,500 U.S. adult citizens, conducted
28-31 December 2019. https://d25d2506sfb94s.cloudfront.net/cumulus
_uploads/document/2r6hyqtv9p/econTabReport.pdf

[56]Umair Haque, "This is How a Society Dies," *Eudaimonia,* Medium
.com, 9 December 2019. https://eand.co/this-is-how-a-society-dies
-35bdc3c0b854

[57]Rick Shenkman, "The Shocking Paper Predicting the End of
Democracy," *Politico,* 8 September 2019. https://www.politico.com
/magazine/story/2019/09/08/shawn-rosenberg-democracy-228045

Chapter Eight: Try My Amazing Five-Step Program

[1]Janna Anderson and Lee Raine, "Many Tech Experts Say
Digital Disruption Will Hurt Democracy," Pew Research Center,
22 February 2020. https://www.pewresearch.org/internet/2020/02
/21/many-tech-experts-say-digital-disruption-will-hurt-democracy
/?fbclid=IwAR2M9r6XPAh3V6JPosOyv1oOehWn4BlkMY8TPkib
_Wc6nljU78OA8z-raEM

[2]Ibid.

[3]Shoshanna Zuboff website, "About" page. https://shoshanazuboff
.com/book/shoshana/

[4]Shoshanna Zuboff, "You Are Now Remotely Controlled," *The New
York Times,* 24 January 2020. https://www.nytimes.com/2020/01/24
/opinion/sunday/surveillance-capitalism.html?action=click&module
=Opinion&pgtype=Homepage

[5]Ina Fried, "Tech's Moment to Shine (or Not)," Axios.com,
18 March 2020. https://www.axios.com/google-facebook-techs

-moment-to-shine-or-not-94a03e2c-7b2^d-4c34-b20b-68a4d2d21c20
.html?utm_source=newsletter&utm_medium=email&utm_campaign
=newsletter_axiosam&stream=top

[6]Issie Lapowsky, "Kirsten Gillibrand's New Bill Would Establish a US Data Protection Agency," *Protocol,* 13 February 2020. https://www
.protocol.com/federal-privacy-agency-gillibrand

[7]Sean Burch, "Facebook Will Remove Content Organizing Protests Against Stay-at-Home Orders, Zuckerberg Says," TheWrap.com, 20 April 2020. https://www.thewrap.com/facebook-will-remove-posts
-coronavirus-stay-at-home/

[8]Alexander Hall, "Facebook Unleashed AI to Purge Platform of 'Hate Speech'," Newsbusters.org, 13 May 2020. https://www.newsbusters
.org/blogs/techwatch/alexander-hall/2020/05/13/facebook-unleashed
-ai-purge-platform-hate-speech

[9]Donie O'Sullivan, "Facebook Takes Down Trump Ads 'For Violating Our Policy Against Organized Hate'," CNN.com, 18 June 2020. https://www.cnn.com/2020/06/18/tech/facebook-trump-ads
-triangle-takedown/index.html

[10]Donie O'Sullivan, "Twitter Says it Will Label Misleading Coronavirus Tweets—Even if They're from Trump," CNN.com, 11 May 2020. https://www.cnn.com/2020/05/11/tech/twitter
-coronavirus-misinformation/index.html

[11]Annie Palmer, Twitter CEO Jack Dorsey Has an Idealistic Vision for the Future of Social Media and is Funding a Small Team to Chase It," CNBC.com, 11 December 2019. https://www.cnbc.com/2019/12/11
/twitter-ceo-jack-dorsey-announces-bluesky-social-media-standards
-push.html

[12]Gordon Pennycook and David Rand, "The Right Way to Fight Fake News," *The New York Times,* 24 March 2020. https://www
.nytimes.com/2020/03/24/opinion/fake-news-social-media.html

[13]Rishika Dugyala, "'Manipulated Media': Twitter Applies New Label to Edited Video of Biden," *Politico,* 8 March 2020. https://
www.politico.com/news/2020/03/08/manipulated-media-twitter
-biden-video-124116

[14]Justin McCarthy, "In U.S., Most Oppose Micro-Targeting in Online Political Ads," Gallup Organization / Gallup blog, 2 March 2020. https://news.gallup.com/opinion/gallup/286490/oppose-micro-targeting-online-political-ads.aspx

[15]Dave Levinthal, "Death Threats Directed at Elections Regulator," The Center for Public Integrity, 17 May 2016. https://publicintegrity.org/politics/death-threats-directed-at-elections-regulator/https:/publicintegrity.org/politics/death-threats-directed-at-elections-regulator/

[16]Allyson Chiu, "Facebook Wouldn't Delete an Altered Video of Nancy Pelosi. What About One of Mark Zuckerberg?" *The Washington Post,* 12 June, 2019. https://www.washingtonpost.com/nation/2019/06/12/mark-zuckerberg-deepfake-facebook-instagram-nancy-pelosi/?noredirect=on

[17]Travis Bullard, Senior Director, APCO Worldwide and APCO corporate communications and brand practice leader, message to clients, December 2019.

[18]Sonam Sheth, "Trump Accuses Twitter of 'Interfering In the 2020 Presidential Election' After it Fact-Checked His False Tweets About Voting by Mail," *Business Insider,* 26 May 2020. https://www.businessinsider.com/trump-accuses-twitter-interfering-2020-race-voting-ballot-fact-check-2020-5

[19]Nandita Bose and David Shepardson, "Trump's Executive Order Targets Political Bias at Twitter and Facebook: Draft," Reuters, 28 May 2020. https://www.reuters.com/article/us-twitter-trump-executive-order-social/trumps-executive-order-targets-political-bias-at-twitter-and-facebook-draft-idUSKBN2340MW?utm_source=newsletter&utm_medium=email&utm_campaign=newsletter_axiosam&stream=top

[20]Sasha Baron Cohen, "The 'Silicon Six' Spread Propaganda. It's Time to Regulate Social Media Sites," *The Washington Post,* 25 November 2019. https://www.washingtonpost.com/outlook/2019/11/25/silicon-six-spread-propaganda-its-time-regulate-social-media-sites/

[21]Paul Sandle, "Britain to Make Social Media Platforms Responsible for Harmful Content," Reuters Technology News, 12 February 2020.

https://www.reuters.com/article/britain-tech-regulation-statement
/britain-to-make-social-media-platforms-responsible-for-harmful
-content-idUSL9N27J00J

[22]Adam Conner, "The Case for a Progressive Vision on Tech Policy,"
MorningConsult.com, 15 August 2019. https://morningconsult.com
/opinions/the-case-for-a-progressive-vision-on-tech-policy/

[23]Author interview with Chuck Davis, 12 January 2020.

[24]George Gilder, *Life After Google: The Fall of Big Data and the
Rise of the Blockchain Economy.* Regnery Gateway, 2012. Pgs. 5,7,9,
47-48, 108.

[25]Confronting A Data Privacy Crisis, Gillibrand Announces
Landmark Legislation To Create A Data Protection Agency," Press
release from the office of Sen. Kirsten Gillibrand, D-New York,
13 February 2020. https://www.gillibrand.senate.gov/news/press
/release/confronting-a-data-privacy-crisis-gillibrand-announces-landmark
-legislation-to-create-a-data-protection-agency

[26]Russell Brandom, "Sen. Josh Hawley Proposes FTC Overhaul
to Take on Google and Facebook," The Verge, 10 February 2020.
https://www.theverge.com/2020/2/10/21131212/hawley-ftc-proposal
-antitrust-doj-big-tech

[27]Kate Kaye, "How the Tech Industry Coordinated to Squelch
Algorithm Transparency in the New NAFTA Deal," RedTailMedia
.org, 8 November 2018. https://redtailmedia.org/2018/11/08/how
-the-tech-industry-prevented-algorithm-transparency-in-nafta-2-0/amp/

[28]Author interview with Chuck Davis, 12 January 2020.

[29]"Algorithmic Transparency: End Secret Profiling," Electronic
Privacy Information Center, undated, epic.org. https://epic.org
/algorithmic-transparency/

[30]Shoshanna Zuboff, "You Are Now Remotely Controlled," *The New
York Times,* 24 January 2020. https://www.nytimes.com/2020/01/24
/opinion/sunday/surveillance-capitalism.html?action=click&module
=Opinion&pgtype=Homepage

[31]Scott Bauer, "52 People Who Took Part in Wisconsin's Primary
Have Tested Positive for Coronavirus," Associated Press via Time

.com, 29 April 2020. https://time.com/5829264/wisconsin-primary-coronavirus/

[32]Sarah Ferris, Melanie Zanona, and Heather Caygle, "Anxiety Grows in Capital as Lawmakers Weigh Remote Voting," *Politico*, 19 March 2020. https://www.politico.com/news/2020/03/19/congress-coronavirus-pandemic-137414

[33]Bob Fitzrakis and Harvey Wasserman, "We Need Universal Mail-In Ballots for the 2020 Election," Truthout.org, 27 March 2020. https://truthout.org/articles/we-need-universal-mail-in-ballots-for-the-2020-election/

[34]Jerry Lambe, "Local Officials Are Deeply Concerned That Congress Won't Address COVID-19 Threat to Elections," LawandCrime.com, 23 March 2020. https://lawandcrime.com/covid-19-pandemic/local-officials-are-deeply-concerned-that-congress-wont-address-covid-19-threat-to-elections/

[35]Gabriella Novello and Erika Smithson, "No, Voting by Mail is Not 'Ripe for Voter Fraud'," WhoWhatWhy.org, 29 April 2020. https://whowhatwhy.org/2020/04/29/no-voting-by-mail-is-not-ripe-for-voter-fraud/

[36]Kim Zetter, "Why Vote-by-Mail May Not Save our Elections from the Virus' Disruption," *Politico,* 17 March 2020. https://www.politico.com/news/2020/03/17/vote-by-mail-elections-coronavirus-134618

[37]Joe Brotherton, "Coronavirus Will Change the World Permanently. Here's How," *Politico* Magazine, 19 March 2020. https://www.politico.com/news/magazine/2020/03/19/coronavirus-effect-economy-life-society-analysis-covid-135579#elections

[38]Christopher Stern, "Virus Fears Spark Calls for Online Voting," The Information, 12 March 2020. https://www.theinformation.com/articles/virus-fears-spark-calls-for-online-voting

[39]John Bowden, "Turnout Almost Doubles in Seattle Area Election After Mobile Voting Implemented," The Hill, 5 March 2020. https://thehill.com/policy/technology/486161-turnout-almost-doubles-in-seattle-area-election-after-mobile-voting

[40]Ibid.

[41]Emily S. Rueb, "Voting by Phone Gets a Big Test, but There Are Concerns," *The New York Times,* 23 January 2020. https://www.nytimes.com/2020/01/23/us/politics/mobile-voting-washington.html

[42]Tiffany Hsu and Marc Tracy, "Local News Outlets Dealt a Crippling Blow by This Biggest of Stories," *The News York Times,* 23 March 2020. https://www.nytimes.com/2020/03/23/business/media/coronavirus-local-news.html

[43]David Bauder, "News Outlets, Long Resistant to Government Help, Take Loans," Associated Press, 22 April 2020. https://abcnews.go.com/Entertainment/wireStory/news-outlets-long-resistant-government-loans-70295212

[44]Tiffany Hsu and Marc Tracy, "Local News Outlets Dealt a Crippling Blow by This Biggest of Stories," *The News York Times,* 23 March 2020. https://www.nytimes.com/2020/03/23/business/media/coronavirus-local-news.html

[45]John Koblin, "The Evening News is Back," *The New York Times,* 24 March 2020. https://www.nytimes.com/2020/03/24/business/media/coronavirus-evening-news.html

[46]Pew Research Center, "For Local News, Americans Embrace Digital but Still Want Strong Community Connection," 26 March 2019. https://www.journalism.org/2019/03/26/for-local-news-americans-embrace-digital-but-still-want-strong-community-connection/

[47]Joshua P. Darr, Matthew P. Hitt, and Johanna L. Dunaway, "Newspaper Closures Polarize Voting Behavior," *Journal of Communication*, Vol. 68, Issue 6, December 2018, pgs. 1007-1028. https://doi.org/10.1093/joc/jqy051

[48]Alan Greenblatt, "When No News Isn't Good News: What the Decline of Newspapers Means for Government," *Governing,* 24 April 2019. https://www.governing.com/topics/politics/gov-newspapers-government-studies.html

[49]Cecilia Kang, "The Decimation of Local News Has Lawmakers Crossing the Aisle," *The New York Times,* 12 January 2020. https://www.nytimes.com/2020/01/12/technology/google-facebook-newspapers.html?action=click&module=MoreIn&pgtype=Article&region=Footer

&action=click&module=MoreInSection&pgtype=Article&region
=Footer&contentCollection=Business

[50]Craig Silverman, "Last Press Council in U.S. Will Close Next Month," Poynter.org, 10 April 2014. https://www.poynter.org /reporting-editing/2014/last-press-council-in-u-s-will-close-next -month/

[51]Mike Rispoli, "Why the Civic Info Consortium is Such a Huge Deal," FreePress.net, January 16, 2020. https://www.freepress.net /our-response/expert-analysis/insights-opinions/why-civic-info-consortium -such-huge-deal

[52]"Announcing the First Round of Grants Supporting Local Newsrooms' Coronavirus Coverage," Facebook Journalism Project, 26 March 2020. https://www.facebook.com/journalismproject /programs/community-network/coronavirus-grants-news-reporting -recipients-round-1

[53]Federal Election Commission, Status of the Presidential Election Campaign Fund, 31 January 2020. https://www.fec.gov/resources /cms-content/documents/PECF_monthly_report_2020.pdf

[54]Roger McNamee, *Zucked: Waking Up to the Facebook Catastrophe*, Penguin Press, 2019. Pg. 10.

[55]Charlotte Alter, *The Ones We've Been Waiting For: How a New Generation of Leaders Will Transform America*, Viking, 2020.

[56]Rick Shenkman, "The Shocking Paper Predicting the End of Democracy," Politico, 8 September 2019. https://www.politico.com /magazine/story/2019/09/08/shawn-rosenberg-democracy-228045

[57]Adrienne Day, "Can a Nonreligious Church Save Politics?", Nationswell.com, 5 December 2018. https://nationswell.com/eric -liu-civic-saturday-secular-church/

[58]Courtney E. Martin, "Preaching Faith in Democracy," *The New York Times,* 2 July 2019. https://www.nytimes.com/2019/07/02 /opinion/preaching-faith-in-democracy.html

[59]Jamelle Bouie, "Bernie Sanders and the Case of the Missing Youth Vote," *The New York Times,* 13 March 2020. https://www.nytimes .com/2020/03/13/opinion/bernie-sanders-young-voters.html

[60]Eliza Mackintosh, Finland is Winning the War on Fake News. What it's Learned May be Crucial to Western Democracy," CNN .com, May 2019. https://edition.cnn.com/interactive/2019/05/europe /finland-fake-news-intl/

[61]Alan C. Miller, "News Literacy Boosts Trust in Local news," Knight Foundation, 9 January 2020. https://knightfoundation.org/articles /news-literacy-boosts-trust-in-local-news/

[62]Sam Gringlas, "With an Election on the Horizon, Older Adults Get Help Spotting Fake News," NPR.org, 26 February 2020. https:// www.npr.org/2020/02/26/809224742/with-an-election-on-the-horizon -older-adults-get-help-spotting-fake-news

[63]Sarah Kurpiel, "Evaluating Sources: The CRAAP Test," Benedictine University Library. https://researchguides.ben.edu/source-evaluation

[64]Jonathan Haidt and Tobias Rose-Stockwell, "The Dark Psychology of Social Networks," *The Atlantic,* December 2019. https://www .theatlantic.com/magazine/archive/2019/12/social-media-democracy /600763/

[65]Hank Stuever, "Investigating Amazon, PBS's 'Frontline' Opens the Smiling Cardboard Box and Finds George Orwell," *The Washington Post,* 17 February 2020. https://www.washingtonpost .com/entertainment/tv/investigating-amazon-pbs-frontline-opens-the -smiling-cardboard-box-and-finds-george-orwell/2020/02/17/7f00dc88 -4dd2-11ea-bf44-f5043eb3918a_story.html?utm_campaign=wp_post _most&utm_medium=email&utm_source=newsletter&wpisrc=nl_most

[66]Joel Kotkin, *The Next Hundred Million: America in 2050.* The Penguin Press, 2010. pg. 4.

[67]George Gilder, *Life After Google: The Fall of Big Data and the Rise of the Blockchain Economy.* Regnery Gateway, 2012. Pg. 174.

[68]David Brooks, "A Ridiculously Optimistic History of the Next Decade," *The New York Times*, 3 January 2020. https://www .nytimes.com/2020/01/02/opinion/2020s-decade.html?te=1&nl =david-leonhardt&emc=edit_ty_20200103?campaign_id=39& instance_id=14937&segment_id=20020&user_id=b43261659350c 77456b4aa21a6122ac7&regi_id=4137011920200103

[69]Saritha Rai, "400 Million Social Media Users Are Set to Lose Their Anonymity in India," Bloomberg.com, 12 February 2020. https://www .bloomberg.com/news/articles/2020-02-12/400-million-social-media -users-set-to-lose-anonymity-in-india

[70]Ibid.

[71]T.M. Scanlon, *What We Owe to Each Other*. Belknap Press, Harvard University, 2008.

[72]Jan-Werner Müller, "We Must Help One Another or Die," *The New York Times*, 19 March 2020. https://www.nytimes.com/2020/03/19 /opinion/coronavirus-politics.html

[73]Rudy Takala, "Gov. Cuomo: People Who Don't Wear Masks Could 'Literally Kill Someone'," Mediaite.com, 4 May 2020. https:// www.mediaite.com/news/gov-cuomo-people-who-dont-wear-masks -could-literally-kill-someone/?utm

Chapter Nine: Citizen Janey

[1]Janna Anderson and Lee Rainie, "Many Tech Experts Say Digital Disruption Will Hurt Democracy," Pew Research Center, 21 February 2020. https://www.pewresearch.org/internet/2020/02/21/many-tech- experts-say-digital-disruption-will-hurt-democracy/

Epilogue: Malaysia

[1]Freedom House, *Freedom in the World 2019*, Malaysia Profile. https://freedomhouse.org/report/freedom-world/2019/malaysia

[2]Freedom House, *Freedom in the World 2017*, Malaysia Profile. https://freedomhouse.org/report/freedom-world/2017/malaysia

[3]Sheith Khidhir Bin Abu Bakar, "Maria Held Under Sosma: Shocking News for Paulsen," *Free Malaysia Today*, 19 November 2016. https:// www.freemalaysiatoday.com/category/nation/2016/11/19/maria-held -under-sosma-shocking-news-for-paulsen/

[4]Shadi Hamid, "What Democracies Can Learn from Malaysia," *The Atlantic*, 16 May 2018. https://www.theatlantic.com/international /archive/2018/05/malaysia-democracy-najib/560534/

[5]Reuters, "Malaysia Stripped of World Para Swimming Championships After Banning Israeli Athletes," ESPN.com, 27 January 2019. https://www.espn.com/olympics/story/_/id/25862160/malaysia -stripped-world-para-swimming-championships-banning-israeli-athletes

[6]Martin Carvalho et al, "Dewan Rakyat Passes Bill to Amend Federal Constitution to Lower Voting Age to 18," *The Star,* thestar.com.my, 16 July 2019. https://www.thestar.com.my/news/nation/2019/07/16 /federal-constitution-amended-to-lower-voting-age-to-18/

INDEX

ABOUT THE AUTHORS

 Since the dawn of the digital era Cyrus Krohn has been recognized as a front-line digital innovator— a publisher, political strategist, entrepreneur, and commentator focused on the fate of our fragile American democracy amid unprecedented technological upheaval.

From his early days launching *Slate*, where he helped frame the digital information culture in ways that still reverberate today, to his current role advising Democracy Live, the largest US provider of cloud and tablet-based voting technologies, Krohn has labored to make our exploding tech toolset propel better outcomes for society. *Business Insider* named Krohn one of the Top 50 US digital political strategists, and he has advised organizations internationally including in Malaysia, Costa Rica, and France.

Krohn launched his career at an intern in the first Bush White House in the office of Vice President Dan Quayle. He worked in the CNN Washington bureau producing programs including

Larry King Live and *Crossfire*. He led digital political projects for Microsoft and Yahoo and managed digital campaigns at federal, state and local levels, including during the 2008 presidential election between John McCain and Barack Obama.

Krohn edited *The Slate Diaries*, published by PublicAffairs Books, with best-selling authors Michael Kinsley and Jodi Kantor.

Krohn has lectured on the Internet's impact on democratic systems at the Personal Democracy Forum, Georgetown University, The Aspen Institute, Harvard, and MIT. He served on the Board of Advisors of the George Washington University Institute for Politics, Democracy and the Internet and the E-Voter Institute. Krohn graduated from the University of Lynchburg.

Veteran writer and strategist Tom Farmer is a former CNN executive producer and winner of Peabody, Telly, Cicero Speechwriting, and CableACE awards. He produces thought leadership initiatives with eminent figures in technology, cybersecurity, finance, higher education, and philanthropy.

At CNN Farmer was a senior Washington editorial supervisor and executive producer of *Larry King Live*, where he produced the infamous 1993 NAFTA debate between Ross Perot and Vice President Al Gore and interviews with Mikhail Gorbachev, Yasir Arafat, and Margaret Thatcher.

As the Internet reshaped information culture, Farmer worked in the Seattle agency world as a strategy or creative director, solving digital challenges for Converse, Tommy Bahama, National Geographic, and AT&T. He directed *Face the Facts USA*, a digital voter engagement initiative for The George Washington University. His consultancy, Brick Duck Communications, is based in Chicago.